24.95

# AMERICAN SCENARIOS

# AMERICAN SCENARIOS

## The Uses of Film Genre

# Joseph W. Reed

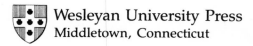 Wesleyan University Press
Middletown, Connecticut

"Faust and His Disease" first appeared, in a somewhat different form, in *Planks of Reason*, edited by Barry Keith Grant, Metuchen, N.J., and London: The Scarecrow Press, 1984.

Grateful acknowledgment is made to the following for permission to reprint various song titles: "The Best Things in Life Are Free," "Did You Ever Have the Feeling that You Wanted to Go and Still Have the Feeling that You Wanted to Stay?" "Moses Supposes," and "Pass that Peace Pipe" are used by permission of F.B.K. Entertainment World. "Buckle Down Winsockie" and "The Varsity Drag" are used by permission of Warner/Chappell Music, Inc. "Never Gonna Dance," "Pick Yourself Up" (music by Jerome Kern and Dorothy Fields, Copyright © 1936 T. B. Harms Company, c/o The Welk Music Group, Santa Monica, CA 90401 and Chappell & Co.), and "Carioca" (music by Vincent Youmans, lyrics by Gus Kahn and Edward Eliscu, Copyright © 1933 Max Dreyfus and Vincent Youmans, copyright renewed and assigned to T. B. Harms Company), international copyright secured, all rights reserved, are used by permission of The Welk Music Group and Chappell & Co. "Cuanto la Gusto" (music by Gabriel Ruiz, English lyrics by Ray Gilbert), Copyright © 1940 by Promstora Hispano Americana de Musica, S.A., Copyright © 1948 by Peer International Corp., copyrights renewed. "Dear Mr. Gable" Copyright Roger Eden. "It Might as Well Be Spring," Copyright © 1945 by Williamson Music Co., used by permission, all rights reserved. "Rock Around the Clock" Copyright MCMLIII by Myers Music, Philadelphia, Penn. U.S.A., copyright renewed and assigned to Capano Music, 237 Chestnut Street, Westville, New Jersey 08093. "Tangerine," Copyright © 1942 by Famous Music Corporation, copyright renewed 1969 by Famous Music Corporation.

All inquiries and permissions requests should be addressed to the Publisher, Wesleyan University Press, 110 Mt. Vernon Street, Middletown, Connecticut 06457

## Library of Congress Cataloging-in-Publication Data

Reed, Joseph W., 1932–
American scenarios : the uses of film genre / Joseph W. Reed.—
1st ed.
p.     cm.
Includes index.
ISBN 0-8195-5215-1
1. Film genres—United States.   2. Motion pictures—United States.
I. Title.
PN1993.5.U6R44   1989
791.43'09'093—dc19                                      88-27930
                                                              CIP

Manufactured in the United States of America

FIRST EDITION

To Terry Halladay and Bill Reese

*"Always, Sir, set a high value on spontaneous kindness. He whose inclination prompts him to cultivate your friendship of his own accord, will love you more than one whom you have been at pains to attach to you."*

—Samuel Johnson, *Life*, May 1781

## Also by Joseph W. Reed

*English Biography in the Early
Nineteenth Century (1800–1838)*

*Faulkner's Narrative*

*Three American Originals:
John Ford, William Faulkner, & Charles Ives*

## Editor

*Barbara Bodichon's American Diary, 1857–1858*

*The Business of Motion Pictures*

*The Sesquicentennial Papers,*
Wesleyan University

With G. R. Creeger,
*Selected Prose and Poetry of the Romantic Era*

With Wilmarth S. Lewis,
*Walpole's Castle of Otranto*

With Jeanine Basinger and John Frazer,
*Working with Kazan*

With Wilmarth S. Lewis,
*Walpole's Family Correspondence*
The Yale Edition of
Horace Walpole's Correspondence, Vol. 36

With Frederick A. Pottle,
*Boswell, Laird of Auchinleck*
The Yale Edition of the
Private Papers of James Boswell, Vol. XI

# ACKNOWLEDGMENTS

This book began in a faculty seminar with two colleagues, Jeanine D. Basinger and Richard S. Slotkin. I am grateful to them for insights and for hours of delight as we watched and talked. In this and much else they are superb intellectual companions. We were twice supported by Wesleyan Faculty Project Grants, and I was supported for a dozen years by Wesleyan Faculty Research Grants.

My students in courses called Prisons, High School, Werewolves, and Costume, American Family, and Images of America have shared much of this study, and I have learned from them; I thank particularly Adam Usdan, Adam Leff, Adam Levy, Anna McCarthy, Dan Edelman, Jim Fairbrother, Raphael Worrick, Joss Whedon, Michael Mosedale, and Jonathan Sahula. Kit Reed, Richard Slotkin, Jeanine Basinger, Terry Halladay, Mack Reed, and Ian Harvey read drafts and have offered valuable suggestions. Joan Jurale, Ed Rubacha, and Steve Ross have answered particular queries. Matthew Tyrnauer and Janet Morgan were very helpful on the index.

This is the second book of mine to be edited by Jeannette Hopkins; in the first I did not know how to thank her properly. For this book, to say enough would be to suggest how much of its shape is hers or to suggest that its errors are hers. Much of it is, they are not; they are surely mine. I will only add I cannot imagine a better editor.

*Middletown, Connecticut*
*June 1988*

# CONTENTS

# LIST OF ILLUSTRATIONS

All illustrations in this book are used by courtesy of the Stills Collection, the Museum of Modern Art, New York.

*They reached the picture show. It was like a miniature
fairyland with its lighted lobby and colored lithographs of
life caught in its terrible and beautiful mutations. . . .
The lights flicked away; the screen glowed silver, and soon
life began to unfold, beautiful and passionate and sad,
while still the young men and girls entered, scented and
sibilant in the half dark, their paired backs in silhouette
delicate and sleek, their slim, quick bodies awkward,
divinely young, while beyond them the silver dream accu-
mulated, on and on.*

—William Faulkner, "Dry September"

*"Who are you? Just another American who saw too many
movies as a child?"*

—Alan Rickman in *Die Hard*

# AMERICAN SCENARIOS

# INTRODUCTION

A friend who was dying began to suspect that she was disappointing her daughter as she talked to her. The daughter seemed to expect more of her in the way of answers. She finally said to her, "This isn't a movie."

In a way, of course, it is all a movie: we continually live one movie or another, or a scene, or a genre fragment as we move through anything from mundane encounter to major transition, from a chance meeting to those moments in which we enter a room to discover that all the parts have been handed out before we arrived and we must take the one that's left.

As my friend said, things never work out according to the script and the course of human events is seldom as neat as movies are. Yet I believe we all lead lives that take their cue from film genre, and that we lead generic lives because we're Americans. Of course American lives came before the movies. But even at the beginning there was a sense of script. How else could the Puritans so surely have persuaded their fellow inhabitants of this wild new land that the imaginary landscape they saw was what mattered—and not the real one. Without a sense that an American script was possible Jefferson would have lacked a framework on which to form *his* version of the American scenario (starting with *Notes on the State of Virginia*), the story of a people arrived from far away, now themselves clearly in need (as the land had been at first) of clearing and cultivation and new standards drawn on the European model *but.* . . . Jefferson's *but* was that it should be as cultured as Europe but without the baleful influence of monarchy. Improved.

3

Edward Taylor, Phillis Wheatley, Michael Wigglesworth followed these leads and spelled out in poems each a scripted plan. Survivors of Indian captivity would return to white society and write up their experiences with an idea of identity and a sense of role, part written by individual, part by national identity, roles hovering between personal and national destiny.[1] Each of us is obsessed with the idea that personal *is* national and vice versa, somehow. These people had been captured because they were white, but they wrote their accounts because now they found their experience had made each of them more than just another white. It should be clear from my examples that I do not think American scenarios are by any means all to the good, hooray for the red-white-and-blue. Without some kind of scenario copycat crimes would not take place. American character, American triumph, American greed, and American racialism are all founded in such scenarios. But always with that peculiar mix they hover between individuality and nationality. Without nationality the individual lacks definition, without individual tale (however closely it might fit in with what captives before had written) the nationality lacks instance.

Crèvecoeur and Franklin and James Fenimore Cooper saw the new need demanded a new script and each supplied his own. (D. H. Lawrence is getting at something like a sense of an American scenario in *The Classic American Literature*, as were Van Wyck Brooks and F. O. Matthiessen.) Early on Americans lived Westerns or Empire Pictures, Boys' Book Adventures or Americana; later they moved on to Immigrant and Cavalry Pictures, to Costume (the Civil War regiments and their strange need to dress up as Zouaves, the Spanish-American War with Teddy Roosevelt's Churchillian need to indulge in cavalry charges out of the past), Women's Pictures, and War. Americans found some of this in Horatio Alger's stories of earnest youth, or in dime novels and penny dreadfuls, in Davy Crocketts and Daniel Boones and other well-thumbed paperbound tales, passed from hand to hand, traced over and spelled out, and then in some measure lived. Poe had some new bits of script we couldn't at first tell was ours, Dreiser some more and Emily Dickinson. Thoreau, Emerson, and Margaret Fuller recast the shape of scenario. Escaping slaves made narratives that brought a script to the unscripted, an experience formerly without scenario or author. Twain made of his life a new script for the lives of others. Without sense of script Whitman would never have writ, and without American life his script could never have been made to fit so well the readers who found there a responsive chord. Lincoln devised (as Edmund Wilson attests[2]) his script for the Union. And then came Buffalo Bill's Wild West Show with its little scenes of America's just-then-current international adventures. And dog and pony shows. My parents were of an age that their offhand reference contained arcane stuff drawn from road-show versions of *Uncle Tom's Cabin* and Barnum's Museum (I think neither of them had seen JoJo the Dog-Faced Boy, but they knew him well enough in the "scenario" sense, and called me "JoJo the Dog-Faced Boy." If that's not popular culture, I don't know what is. *And* script). And Mailer and Barthelme and Faulkner and Ellison. And ever since 1903 or 1893 (or whenever one wants to date the dawn of the movie) most everyone's been living a movie. Of course which movie depends on our circumstances, what movie is called forth by what happens to us.

This book is about what we know from these movies and how they work on our imaginations. In Faulkner's *Light in August* Joe Christmas in emulation of Max and Mame begins to wear his hat in a new way, to smoke in a different way. He doesn't know what to be, so he looks to others for this and tries what they do. Movies in just such an offhanded way tell us how to behave in matters more serious than hats and smokes: we do it that way because we saw it in a movie. Where did you get that? From some movie.

In a more serious way, how we see ourselves, what we think of us, what we think our world is like, how we think it works, all come from the movies (and now from television as well). This runs all the way from seemingly unimportant but revealing fashion notes, to something like what Henry James calls our "imagination of disaster." It is as if our sense of the force of gravity has been formed not by a jump from a high place, but from watching a movie about it, because so much of our experience has been vicarious—known, heard, seen, felt, and smelled in a movie. The quietness of a peaceful street (*Young Tom Edison, Halloween*), the waters of a placid bay (*The Way We Were, The Birds*), a breeze moving over a field (*Sea of Grass, Badlands, North by Northwest*) give us in context images of peace or threat, calm or chaos. In Comedy or Western or Musical (*The General, Wagonmaster, Top Hat*) we see ideals of freedom, ease, and wealth; or in the same genres we see the opposite (*The Gold Rush, Ulzana's Raid, Oliver!*)—entrapment, distress, and penury. From movies comes our surest sense of how things move (I don't mean trains or planes or cars because probably our living experience dominates what we know from movies in these familiar things—muscle memory is stronger —but certainly for most of us the sense of horses depends on movies). From movies we know how processes edge toward completion: this is less Oh this is just like what happened to me, than If this happens and then this, then this is inevitable. The snapping shut of a door (*Godfather, Part II, Gone With the Wind*), the awful realization (*Intolerance, Dressed to Kill*) that all the parts have come together, that this is the clincher, that all things do and will work toward their end.

And what the System is about. Who is Miss Right, who is Mr. Big. Where the buck stops. Where the rainbow (or the hope) ends. What freedom might be like. Or prison. How to move through a closed door into a familiar but darkened room. What to think about in the shower. How to pull a heist. Never to divide our forces. Never to say die unless we can take a lot of them with us. How to be a child, or a woman, or a man, or a werewolf or a mixed-up genetic accident.

This leaves out the dream function of the movies, the cliché that in them we can find our wildest sexual fantasy, the fulfillment of our fondest wish, our dream of wealth, our personal Arabian Nights tale or, conversely, our fear of flying, our snake pit or rat cage or personal pit or pendulum. I would stress that every genre participates in the making of scenario: the girl's dream in *National Velvet* is mine even if I am a man; we may hate to run, but girl or boy, we love to win the race in *Gallipoli* (see chapter 10). In a Science-Fiction Picture we are, I suppose, at our most profoundly American in our response to the threat of this or that postatomic Blood Rust (chapter 11); but Marie Curie, Polish, works in her lab as *us*, as *me* (chapter 2). In a Horror Picture we are at the mercy of our most subjective empathetic identification when Larry Talbot sees the muddy footprint on the rug (chapter 4), but even an offhand objective moment in the most abstract Western can bring us to similar subjectivity (chapter 12).

---

Any movie in genre study is as important as any other. Some are more interesting, certainly some produce better results when studied than others, but there is democracy in genre. Stanley Cavell writes,

The movie seems naturally to exist in a state in which its highest and its most ordinary instances attract the same audience. . . . You do not really like the highest instances unless you also like typical ones. You don't even know what the highest are instances of unless you know the typical as well. *(The World Viewed, 5–6)*

The same is true genre to genre: some are more interesting, but none is "better" than the other: there are Westerns and Teen Slashers and Space Operas and High School Pictures. It is no more possible to say a given genre or subgenre is just trash than it was to say the Western was worthless. Some of the best days of film study I have had were the result of watching obscure or out-of-the-way movies from so-called trash genres—titles involving generic mixtures: *A Lady Without Pass-*

*port, Tripoli, Torchy Blane in Chinatown, Tender Comrade, House of Women, The Immortal Sergeant, Woman Obsessed, The Pink Jungle, The Naked Jungle.*[3] Here are wonderful mutants. Watching *Stagecoach, Casablanca,* and *Dracula* over and over would never have yielded what these pictures did. Repetition is probably the chief tool for genre criticism, but applying insights again and again to the same material will never give us a sense of what genre does. Movies come from movies, and any given movie repeats things from hundreds of others. The several ways repetition functions in genre give a hint of its blind force and mercurial flexibility. Sometimes in genre the repetition continues without sense. Like a headless chicken *A Lady Without Passport* (chapter 5) goes on touching generic bases as if we hadn't already found out the movie isn't *about* anything.

It is less interesting that every genre produces a sense of new scenarios than that each genre describes, devises its scenarios so they differ from those of the other genres. This in turn relates to the way each genre works, resembling but differing from all other genres; and *this* is determined in part by the genre's source, its heritage, its individual evolution. In providing a scenario slightly different from that last genre each new genre reveals behavior.

---

Everyone is an expert on movies; even more people claim to be experts on movie genre. Genre is one of those things that goes without saying: you know, like they did in the old movies. To let anything go without saying is a mistake if you are attempting to make study serious. Such a sentence as *"Star Wars* is a Western" is not a serious statement for discussion with grown-ups. Such silly, if familiar, assumptions must be questioned and home truths challenged if we are to get on to anything new.

A movie's genre is its chief label. We can then refine that label by more labels: subgenres, sub-subgenres, ramifications of place and profession, conventions of character and story line (as Hawks says, boy meets boy, boy loses boy). If we do this we may arrive at a Western/Range Wars/on the Border point of view: Farmer. A movie that starred Gene Autry would be different from one that starred Gary Cooper (at the very least it would have singing) and this would be indicated by another kind of label. Then if the movie had a lynching, a chase, if the lead woman in it played a schoolmarm, if the movie had a dance, we could make a checklist of types, situations, and elements included.

I suppose following this out would ultimately give us something like taxonomy in biology: special functions and parts classed under more common functions and parts until a system emerges which looks like an inverted tree. But what would it profit us? It might make a system, but the system wouldn't tell us much about the way film genre *works*. Taxonomy gives ever-thinner slices, more and more precise subsets, without giving us a handle on difficulties: *A Lady Without Passport*, to say nothing of complex masterpieces, *Stagecoach* and *El Cid*.

Any movie is formed by generic language, with exchanges, transfers, transformations, exceptions. Genre is not stereotype or cliché; genre is a dynamic flow of interchangeable parts involved in combinations which resemble organic growth, not a set of laws or a paint-by-the-numbers picture. Because of exchanges and combinations genre is less like biology than like language. Every movie is the product of its historical context, but it is less significant to know that *The Great Train Robbery* had the first Whatever than to realize that *White Heat* imitated it. The exchange between movies of whatever period is paramount in genre study; this is how movies talk to each other, and to us. *American Scenarios* uses some less-discussed genres and some Biggies as examples, to try to get at how that language is spoken.

---

What are the genres? I choose to name them this way: the three great families of genre are Western (chapter 12), Women's, and War (chapter 10). Some British critics call Women's Pictures Melodrama; I prefer to call them Women's: I think melodrama a useful term in dramaturgy, but Women's better suggests how this powerful genre affects all the other genres. I think Women's is central, which is why the reader will find it in every chapter.

War Film is (as Jeanine Basinger so clearly defines it[4]) Combat Films of World War II. Movies about other wars don't belong in this genre because they are not defined, do not work the same way—a categorical difference. An early lesson of genre is that it is not ruled by subject matter but rather by how a movie inherits traits from other movies and how it evolves these traits into new forms.

Melodrama is also used sometimes to describe Film Noir (chapter 11). This is powerful, the best defined and most carefully described genre, the most stylistically distinguished of them all, more so even than the Western. It is perhaps the only genre with no bad movies, because the measure of style necessary to identify a Film Noir excludes bummers.

The next three major genres are translations from drama or fiction: Comedy, Musical (chapter 9), and Costume (1). Four more are simply great subjects—Crime, Spy/Thriller, Action/ Adventure (11), and Horror (4). Science Fiction (11) and Epic (12) complete an even dozen major genres.

There are many more genres: there are the great movie places—City, Desert, Jungle/Swamp, Outer Space; great movie conveyances (also great subjects): the stagecoach, the car, the train; there are motifs that move from genre to genre: birth and death and marriage and theft; there are events—dream, chase—so intrinsically filmic that when they appear in a movie, sometimes only for a moment, the movie tilts in their direction. There are Star Vehicles, the Joan Crawford, the Roy Rogers, the John Wayne Movie (chapter 13); there are freak genres (the Midget Film, Kung Fu) and fright genres (Red Baiting, the Yellow Peril, see chapter 11), and profession genres

(Composer and Man in the Gray Flannel Suit, chapter 5). There are Harem and Pirate Pictures (9) and Prison (6) and Empire (12), Animal and Sports Pictures (9). There are Family Pictures (7, 10) and Americana (10). And High School (7) and Inventor (2). Finally there are *auteur* genres (chapters 5, 9, 13). The Ford Western is not just a Western, nor is the Hitchcock Picture just a Crime Picture or a Thriller. Masters make genres, not the other way around. An *auteur*'s mastery overwhelms whatever genre he finds to work in. The Western didn't make John Ford a great director, Ford helped make the Western a great genre.

What more there is to genre, what is left out when we say all genre is divided into so many parts is really what this book is about. The spaces that lie between any two or three of these genres, borderlands where genres mix, the way in which genre explains *parts* of movies, how movies trade parts, the evolution of one genre into something different, the dwindling of an old genre and the emergence of a new, the interpenetration of star vehicle and genre, all these lie beyond the agreed-upon Big Genres.

This book doesn't cover everything—far from it; the archaeology of genre has barely begun. There is not any reliable enough survey of movies that were made and genres they might fall into. And to know the output does not, of course, solve all genre problems. The making of programmers: was Gene Autry a star or a function in the B-movie industry? If he was a star then by its definition he never made a B-movie.[5] We need to know much more about the silents, as much perhaps about those movies lost to us as about those we still have; when we recognize how many *are* lost forever, this need-to-know may turn out to be more than we can ever know.

Chapter 1 starts with Costume; chapter 2 deals with a related genre (or perhaps a subgenre), the Inventor Picture; 3 is a subgenre of Costume, Film-Bios or lives on film. Chapter 4 deals with Horror, a mainline genre, and a problem of definitive subgenre. Chapter 5 identifies some movie parts, portable genre units; 6, a puzzle of genre, Prison and Escape questions the relationship between subgenres and genre units; 7, the High School Picture, a new genre, brings up problems of origin. Chapter 8 is a speculation on one prevalent genre unit, the Cockroach Race. Chapters 9–12 take up in brief compass the rest of the major genres and some minor ones, and 13 poses some problems which have appeared regularly throughout the book.

I think genre is important because only by getting genre taken seriously can we get movies taken seriously. And movies must be taken seriously. These days we can use all the liberal arts we can scrape together: they will make us free—or at least they'll try their best.

The genre of this book is Costume: it is about the past and all too often it has to resort to telling instead of showing. I wish the book could just show the movies. Or better, I wish the book were a Western so it could just *be*.

# GENRE

# 1. WRITING WITH A FEATHER
## The Costume Picture

---

*"Do you think I was right then, Monsieur Liszt?"*
*"It's magnificent. Tell me his name again. . . . Pleyel will publish this, I promise."*

—The Phantom of the Opera

In *The Picture of Dorian Gray* Dorian visits a low district called Bluegate Fields. He is ushered into a staired hall by an Igor-like dwarf out of *Frankenstein*. Dorian is there for his depraved pleasure—either to do something vile to someone or for someone to do something vile to him. On this side of a door, playing a Chopin prelude on a square piano, is a man done up to look like Liszt. What has brought this man in this particular getup to this place in this picture? Why Liszt?

---

Aficionados of the Costume Picture are odd. They giggle when they admit that Costume is the kind of movie they like; maybe they are too apologetic about the overwrought objects of their love. They would command more respect were they more straightforward, less apologetic in their admiration. And they are right, it is not respectable to like Costume Pictures. To say one likes *The Fall of the Roman Empire*, *El Cid*, or *War and Peace* is barely respectable, but to admit one likes *Marie Antoinette* or *Suez*, much less *Tripoli*, is almost to confess a secret vice. Enthusiasts of Costume Pictures who lack the courage of their convictions will appeal to "reasons"—anything to keep from saying that they *like* movies where guys write with feathers. On the other hand, just try suggesting to one of these folks that a Costume Picture is nothing more than a movie with actors dressing up in a lot of costumes, that Costume is nothing more than grist for Hollywood's mill, worthy of our interest as representative products of the studio perhaps but little else—or that the Costume genre is nothing more than a throwback to theater, and watch the fur fly. As they argue, fans will point out that a Yellow Peril Movie is not a Costume Movie, nor is a Science Fiction Movie, nor are most Musicals, yet all have lots of costumes. Then they will add that Westerns can be Costume Pictures, that Horror Pictures frequently are, but that Costume Picture defines more than what people on the screen are wearing: Costume is more together as a genre, more unified, more independent than that.

To focus on the "pastness" of the Costume Picture, or to identify it as a "slice" of history, describes but does not define it. Description can suggest origins too: these movies came from historical theatrical pageant, novel, and spectacle. Description is crude compared to definition. If we are interested in what these movies are for, where they are headed, if we want to get at the essence of this genre, then where they came from is of little help. We must try to see what happens in many Costume Pictures, what any one of them has in common with any other, try to get at the boundaries the genre has staked out for itself.

We *know* Hollywood indulged in conspicuous consumption in a lot of big Costume Pictures, spent all that money in an attempt to make zibbledy million dollars—spent zibbledy millions to make zibbledy more millions. What these big movies turned out to be once the money was spent is more interesting. Why are they *for us* a kind of indulgence? Is it because they offer us the chance to be (even more than most movies do) innocent bystanders, offer a way of watching life-and-death moral and social actions, while remaining innocent of involvement, even when the movies parallel our present (as they were

COSTUME: Gary Cooper in the company of Messrs. Mason, Dixon, and Washington, *et al*.: Cecil B. DeMille's *Unconquered*, 1947

so often made to) in the distant events of those wonderful rich pasts. Costume Pictures remain quite wonderfully out of reach, even when we are fans or when we get involved—free of the camera's insistence on the literal (that characteristic of Costume that Siegfried Kracauer so distrusts).[1] They allow us to move abroad in time and space, to twitch a cape and thump a riding crop without responsibility for the great matters at hand on the screen. This is a strong appeal.

Another is famous people like Liszt and the odd way they get dropped into these movies. Some are just that: dropped names (Robert W. Service in *The Spoilers* with John Wayne); others nothing much more than a name-in-a-costume (Messrs.

Mason and Dixon in *Unconquered*, Alfred de Musset in *A Song to Remember*). But others, not as thoroughly developed as the heroes of Film-Bios (see chapter 3), are significant participants. Thomas Gainsborough enters *Kitty* as a fully engaged character. He paints the heroine's portrait and by introducing her about, gives her her start. Monsieur Delacroix (as they say in the movie) comes into *A Song to Remember* as a mimetic image. In the same picture Alfred de Musset is just hanging around in the Restaurant des Bohèmes. The dropped-name character is to the fully engaged historical impersonation (de Musset is to Gainsborough) as a flapper dress is to the Storming of the Bastille, as "flavor" or "detail" is to fully developed atmosphere. So the true Costume fan likes to see historical folks he knows clumping on and off screen: the more outrageous the celebrity's appearance the better the fan likes it. The entrance of Castor and Pollux and Aesculapius in one of the Steve Reeves *Hercules* epics is a Costume Picture fan's treasure.

Portability is all in such faces and functions. One would expect Benjamin Franklin to be a portable face *and* function, but he doesn't show up in movies as much as one might expect. Queen Victoria is the Lincoln of England and is all over the place. Queen Elizabeth is a close second. And Disraeli and Byron. George IV (*Beau Brummell*, *The Scarlet Pimpernel*, *Lady Caroline Lamb*, *Kitty*) comes on remarkably strong, but is generally *not* shown as fat as he really was. Whether a portable personage or costume unit can turn up in movies of other genres (what would a Musketeer movie be without a Richelieu?) is one measure of its generic power. Grant and Custer and Sheridan, Buffalo Bill and Calamity Jane and Annie Oakley get into all sorts of Westerns; Franz Joseph is in several Musicals and a Women's Picture, Elizabeth takes part in Swashbuckler and Boys' Book Films. Henry the Eighth is a problem, a troublesome icon without a generic home base.

But Costume fans specialize. Beyond such crude measures as these, I've been making an odd collection of the several screen appearances of Doctor Samuel Johnson. It's likely that Doctor Benjamin Franklin outstrips Johnson in raw number of appearances (and in one memorable collector's dream, *Lloyds of London*, they are introduced to each other *with* Boswell). Johnson proves the point: he can do nothing for a plot, short of a Film-Bio of the *Life of Johnson* (a prospect too awful to contemplate), so there's no excuse to introduce him in a picture. Bum excuse is, though, Costume Film's hallmark. Lame excuses to talk about home runs or printing presses or to summon up a crowd, compose famously at the piano, bleed on its keys, write with a feather.

The point of such walk-ons is that they accomplish a generic function: they signal us we are there at that point in the past almost as well as fully functioning Gainsboroughs do. Such V.I.P.s don't have to add dramatic development or "flavor," or even atmosphere: all they have to do is fulfill the Costume Picture's continuing obligation to prove that it's doing its job—it *is* showing us another time and involving us in it in very odd ways.

The question of this chapter's opening (the puzzle of Dorian Gray's Franz Liszt look-alike) goes, I think, deeper. Part of the answer is product recognition: Napoleon and Lincoln and Jesus are the champs. Byron is a contender for the title of useful human placemark, but seems to lack that common touch the champs have mastered so well. Why? a *People* magazine principle: they are easy to spot. Why do Napoleon, Lincoln, and Jesus seem to be of a different order from all the others? They stand in relation to Doctor Johnson, I suppose, as the death of John Kennedy stands to the death of the Emperor Maximilian: everybody knows the death of Kennedy. Everyone not only *knows* the figures of Lincoln and Napoleon, but can almost do an impression: a hand inside the topcoat for Napoleon, a drawling story for Lincoln.[2] With a hat as handprop. Jesus is a different problem. There are props and settings everyone knows—manger, cross, open tomb, water-walking—but there is no recognized visual image of Jesus as an adult. The Sermon on the Mount (single figure on a rise seen from behind, suffused in light) is unaccountably featured in the Rita Hayworth *Salome*. This perhaps accounts for the fact that Jesus is "person-dropped" into movies less successfully than Napoleon or Lincoln. And that the nineteenth century is really the Costume Film's home base.

---

The recent rash of docudramas on television about the lives of the great Hollywood stars and writers of the Thirties and Forties trades on a variation of the Abraham Lincoln/Liszt principle. Shepperd Strudwick wouldn't work as well as Clark Gable, nor Elmer Rice as well as Ernest Hemingway—not only less interesting but less readily identifiable, not as easy to make into currency.

I cannot answer the Franz Liszt question but I do know what it must mean: it has something to do with how identifiable that mane of white hair, that priest-collar, that black suit are; and how recognizably efficient this makes him as a unit. Partly it turns on usefulness: Liszt has longevity—he is useful for more years than Chopin, for he lived on and on. In spite of its reputation Hollywood tended to get this kind of thing right even when everything else was wrong. Liszt is also useful in more places than Beethoven because of the tours he made, like a rock star. And he is thought to have been a bravura player. These factors, plus the curious unconnected fact that the stereotypical depiction of male music teachers in America (and sometimes of male intellectuals in general) long took its fashion note from Liszt's hair style and costume.

The prevalence of Liszt is a cue to Romantic bravura and something like Romantic corruption. In *Song Without End* Liszt steals other people's music; *The Phantom of the Opera* hints at this but stresses his public-spirited selflessness, a celebrity willing to pitch in. *A Song to Remember* makes him out to be Chopin's first runner-up, more famous but less to be remembered.

COSTUME: Cornel Wilde (Chopin) greets Merle Oberon (George Sand) while Franz Liszt looks on: *A Song to Remember*, 1945

Liszt is willing to give the lad a boost (a bit odd considering that Liszt was a year younger than Chopin). So it is only a short jump from the mad lover of *Song of Love, Lola Montes,* and *Royal Flash* to the Liszt-garbed Chopin-player in *Dorian Gray.* Another clue to this mystery is that it is perfectly possible to remember Liszt in Costume Pictures he never shows up in. Once we expect to see Liszt we see him. This is in the category of significant false sightings, very powerful in our understanding of the way film imagery works. This kind of *must have been,* sworn to by the people who thought they saw it, is a profound film truth.[3]

More important is part of the nature of Liszt's character: he is a calculator, a manipulator, a string-puller. He gets what he wants. He is, in short, just the sort of person we would like to be: a winner, an insider of slightly dubious morality, a facilitator. Someone who stands in for us on the screen. As do Lincoln and Napoleon, cutters of red tape. The Costume Picture's constant study has been to maneuver us as these figures manipulate their own worlds. Costume remains somewhat distant, Liszt gratifyingly pulls the strings. And do not these pictures most frequently turn on such states of smugness and self-satisfied knowing as Liszt, Lincoln, and Napoleon are so frequently to be found in? One of the strongest powers of movies is to make us *of* them, of their world, so that we can in the midst of what we see on the screen see ourselves as insiders, know more than the others on the screen, work from within. A perfect instance of what the computer programmers call interactive fiction. But in the case of Costume *distantly* interactive. Not Jesus. That's a different matter.

V.I.P. appearances are part of a broad general characteristic of self-consciousness in the Costume Picture; it has an apparently endemic fear of mass amnesia. It continually produces more and more to keep us from forgetting what we are watching (or worse, devices to keep the Costume Picture from forgetting what *it* is). These can become Costume's chief characteristic and its self-perpetuating *raison d'être*.

The genre's fear we may forget something is well grounded. Aside from the arcane pleasure I and other fans are willing to admit, the Costume Picture offers few powerful movies. Worse, the genre seems to provide its movies little freedom to develop or evolve. It's rather static. The sweep of history it sets out to provide seems beyond its reach; it can seldom let go of the moment it is constructing so laboriously and step back, take a good look at what it has just done, and figure out what it might mean. Broad scope (not CinemaScope, which enhances) or depth seems to baffle the Costume Picture: its determination (as in *Waterloo*) to give us everything unselectively, whether we need it or not, all too frequently proves that seldom have so many worked so hard for so little.

And the Costume Picture talks too much. It runs off at the mouth. It is so word-dominated that if we turn off the sound the movie usually becomes impossible to make out; we can no longer follow it. Some of the things Costume Pictures do can still work without sound—battles, parades, some street scenes, that characteristic (and apparently inevitable) panning across ranks of expectant faces—all these we can understand without words. Even silent Costume Films pile up title card after title card, *telling* us. Later in the sound era when the historical novel (certainly no ground-breaker among novels) becomes the dominant source of Costume Film, nothing much changes.

There is good reason for this: all these visual clues, all this telling, is an attempt to get us to comprehend the alien past the movie sets us down in. So the movies come to depend on words, so the words produce more and more photoplay. Some wordiness comes from Costume Film's source in historical drama, melodrama, pageant, the nineteenth-century theatre. Plays already mossbacked, the trailing edge, loss leaders of dramaturgy, square and wordy, like school. A friend wrote, "The Costume Movie is the film industry discovering it can make money off of school."[4] I suppose this is another defect of the genre; adaptation is the Costume Picture's accustomed mode, so it is filmically disadvantaged. We routinely condescend to any adaptation: it is bound to differ from its original and is therefore never "up to it."

We are in general so accustomed to preferring the book to the movie (You've seen the movie, now read the *book*; pretty good, but it's not up to the book) we don't give the matter a second thought. What does it mean to declare that Preminger's *Forever Amber* is not "up to" Kathleen Winsor's original? Of course it is, and then some. Preminger makes visual sense out of verbal fuzzballs. Moviemakers felt they had to appeal to a well-known original in order to legitimize for us the fun we were going to have watching the movie. This was just salve for their consciences and, again, something like school. Somebody acquired the property for a movie in the first place because it looked like it might swash or buckle or follow a trend or make an epic. It would be (or would be able to be made) commercial. (Someone even bought Winston Churchill's history of the English-speaking people for a film.) But moviemakers would never admit this. They had to use a didactic argument: if we moviemakers need the guidance of dignified originals, how much more might you in the audience need them? *Memo from David O. Selznick* details his attitude toward *David Copperfield*, *Rebecca*, *Gone With the Wind*, the pious appeal to the Sacrosanct Property in his bullying arguments with people who worked for him. This material has been researched, it's authentic, it's been pre-tested for popularity by being a best-seller: follow *vox populi* and don't go off on your own; depend on the property. This vaunted authority of the original property and the shared task of preserving the original through its passage to the screen takes on a kind of necessity like the "program" of program music—something to guide us as strangers through the movie's strange land. Selznick didn't trust the power of his movies: we could recognize what he didn't give us (or them) credit for.

In the sense in which modernists regard program music as "debased," the Costume Picture is similarly debased. It's tethered to its premises, its exposition, its explication: it will never know that fine careless rapture, that running free, of a great Western (see chapter 12). It becomes plodding, by comparison. And some moviemakers would argue it plods for good reason. What teaches must go slow. With the false god of instructive authenticity to back it up, no professor ever lectured as portentously as the Costume Picture.

But now for the good news: Costume Pictures also do something besides talk and plod: paradoxically they also delight. If this is school, then Costume Picture is more like a field trip than a test. And it's not just because they "bring to life" what they treat, or that they are fun to talk about to other Costume fans—they have more than anecdotal power. What they have is elemental: icons, hints, generic signatures, hallmarks, recognizability, elements which, taken together with elements from other Costume Pictures, make for, as I have said, powerful depiction of moral and social actions. This is an important principle. With Costume it looks as though what makes a genre elemental also makes it elementary: Costume's simplest ingredients are also its firmest foundations. DeMille knew this. Elements we ridicule or regret may also be essential to process because they make clear the outline of essentials. In numbering the stones of the about-to-be-transplanted castle (as Hearst was supposed to have done) we find that this silly system underpins powerful recognitions.

Costume Pictures are, in other words, better than the history they represent. To ask *A Song to Remember* to tell us something profound about Chopin's Nocturnes is not fair when it can give us elemental delight of the sort we get when George Sand enters the darkened room with a candelabrum to reveal Chopin, her new superstar. This isn't history; it's revelation.

---

There is some distance between the delight in this kind of revelation and Costume Picture's schoolmarmish habits, a puzzle of film didacticism. All movies are didactic: any movie attempts to sell us some particular load of clams. But once clams become the movie's aim and end, didacticism takes over and the movie changes. Similarly, once the Sixties or Seventies or Eighties allegory overcomes the rendering of the past, then the name of the game is changed. So authentic detail can become didactic. Once we see that this is happening in a Costume Picture I think we see three levels: representation, the fact of the thing itself; rendering, the "authentic" or invented level the Costume Picture chooses to give us as its resemblance to that fact; and, third, our sense of how close the movie has come to its mark, the distance between fact and resemblance which persuades us the picture matches, or fails, or goes beyond it—the self-conscious tension between past and rendering. So we have the worst of two worlds: Costume Movies have both an obsessive need to say how different this particular past is, and an aggressive desire to say it as self-consciously as possible.

But Costume is even more didactic than this: it goes with the territory. When literature becomes didactic it is because teaching, lecturing, haranguing, pamphleteering, preaching have become more important to it than anything else (representing, enacting, narrating, making myth). So with film, but the least didactic Costume is always debased compared to the best Western or best Women's. Finger-pointing of any kind in the freewheeling world of film narrative is something to be regretted; repetitive finger-pointing is worse. This comes in part of Costume's being the Classic Comics of movies, the sort of movie parents thought it was O.K. to take kids to. This is what gives them the tone of perpetual instruction. Costume Movies are didactic by birthright.

Part of it is that we have to be persuaded of what we take to be authentic: authentic is not fact but what we may be persuaded is fact, what someone can get away with *and* persuade us is fact. A group of examples from *A Song to Remember*: *Fact*: all these literary figures are in Paris; *Authentic*: the restaurant is called "des Bohèmes" and everybody—Sand, Balzac, Chopin, de Musset—is there at one time. It's like walking into Sardi's and finding everyone—from Al Jolson to Marilyn Monroe—there at one time and sitting close enough to their pictures so we can tell which is which. *Fact*: Sand wore pants; *Authentic*: she looked good in them. Photographs suggest she did not. Falsehood can be authentic as long as it is *presentable*, that is, as long as it can seem to us more palatable than what is factual. Authenticity is not Costume Movies' chief aim: they aim to please, and we are the ones they aim to be pleasing.

Fact, short of Documentary, is a false god. Adaptation from fiction, when slavish, cramps film style; the spirit of Documentary gets in the way of the Costume Picture. The Costume Movie is any fun because (perhaps the Costume Movie is worth criticizing at all because) fact can, with such regular and at times manic abandon, be gotten around, or ignored—in so many amusing ways. Authenticity may be factually true up to a point; beyond that, elegant independence, invention, or embroidery rules. Style of authenticity—individuality in the way authenticity is used—is subject to fashion.

Compare the attitude toward the past in any three of the several movie versions of *The Three Musketeers*. The Douglas Fairbanks silent gives us no more than is necessary to set up what he wants to show off, his extraordinary stunts. The MGM/Gene Kelly *Musketeers* gives us more perhaps in terms of a unified and concentrated approach to period costume and decor, but is no truer to the factual world of Louis XIII. The Richard Lester version (*The Three Musketeers* and *The Four Musketeers*) is very much interested (as is his *A Funny Thing Happened on the Way to the Forum*) in the noise, dirt, discomfort, and comic delight of the seventeenth century, something we see in the MGM version only to establish Kelly's comic character or in connection with some of the duels. Or look at any three presentations of Napoleon. Or take knighthood in the versions offered in *Ivanhoe*, *The Court Jester*, *Robin and Marian*. Or take barbarian pearls: just because an ancient culture had pearls does not mean that its women went about covered with them. But *Intolerance*, the silent *Salome*, the Lana Turner *Prodigal* show us the ladies bedizened. To post a wrong advertising bill or get a dress wrong matters only if the movie feels we know something about these things. In movies set in the recent past (as in *Yanks*), the screen will be loaded up with more and more objects—posters, bottles, clothes—the movies think we must remember. But movies will fudge and skimp on the fact of manner or word or deed about which it feels we know little and care less. The moviemakers figure we know King Charles II is a fop because we know what his clothes look like, they may even figure we know he has a dog named after him because in the movie the King is provided with so many King Charles Spaniels to tag about his heels. But *Forever Amber* can ignore the King's factual appeal to women and the force of his address and capitalize instead on George Sanders's brilliantly epicene performance. A lesser director would have fallen back on the expected authenticity. Preminger knew when he had something better than a factual dead king.

*A Song to Remember* lets Chopin drip blood on the keys of his piano because it thinks we must already know he was tubercular. Surely a fortuitous unlikelihood, but just as surely the one thing everyone remembers of that movie. Maybe we know Sand wore pants, even that Chopin wrote Polonaises, but needed schooling on just about everything else: we get the schooling from the film. To have Oberon's George Sand say she is sick to death of Chopin's "Polonaise jumble," while it is the kind of thing Costume Picture fiends live for, is hardly a likely saying from such intellectual lips.

Our delight in such alternate devotion to and abandonment of fact is probably different from that a member of the intended 1943 audience would have had. For us now there is a double delight. Simply to watch this movie being beautiful in that lost-forever, full-production, glorious-Technicolor way is paradise enow, but to see it and love this pretense and remember the presumption in which we believed so firmly when first we saw it is another kind of pleasure. The studio's and the director's protection of Cornel Wilde, showing off what he can do while still keeping him from tipping us off to what he cannot do, is a part of our sense of this glorious artifice. For Wilde to look so good in those clothes, for him to fall so heedlessly and helplessly (and ineloquently) in love, to give us so presentable a decay toward death, is part of both pleasures: our jaded second viewer is for once inseparable from the innocent first.[5]

The Costume Movie takes up fact less as fundamental essence than as a necessary and frequently regrettable nuisance, and substitutes authenticity for it as frequently as possible. The course of any one Costume Picture is a contest between the opposing forces of history, biography, and fact against authenticity and the freethinking, freehanded, movie-to-movie exchange of generic modes. And for us who see it, a contest between when it was made and when we watch it. This is Costume Picture squared, to watch *A Song to Remember* while we imagine we are a part of its Forties audience. It was probably so popular because, except for side glances at Polish freedom, it so surely escaped any allusion to the wartime in which it was released.

---

I want to discuss some of these delights under several headings: the quill pen, the vagrant mob, DiMaggio's home run, the printing press.

That producer who first observed that Costume Pictures are movies where guys write with feathers only recognized an elemental unit, an essential hallmark, but its persistency can make one begin to suspect that some dumb moviemakers must have made a pact to start the tradition of "signing" a Costume Picture by including in it somewhere a quill pen. Svengali writes music with a feather, as do Chopin and Robert Schumann (*Song of Love*). When DeMille's *Cleopatra* introduces feathers for writing we suspect that generic necessity has outstripped Egyptology. *Clive of India* sharpens a feather, then cuts off the extra length as if to prove to us it really *is* a feather. The Claude Rains *Phantom of the Opera* and *A Song to Remember* have in common quills of the most brilliant scarlet that Technicolor can produce, and Merle Oberon not only writes novels with hers, but makes her points in argument by thrusting it at Paul Muni.

Gary Cooper, in DeMille's *The Plainsman*, throws one at the wall map and it sticks there like a dart.

Dorian Gray's smart new fountain pen, which he uses with such an elegant flourish, is the spiritual heir of those quills and further defines their generic function: they are signals to us, a shorthand. By them we know how far along we are in technology. Technology is a ladder up which Dorian's new pen is a couple of rungs beyond parchment and the sand caster. By Cleopatra's or George Sand's feather we measure everyday life in far-off times, feathers the intermediate lower technology between smoke signal and fountain pen. Dorian's fountain pen is a measuring stick for twentieth-century advance. The reasoning of the quill pen is elementary and inescapable: Step 1: This is what they did before they had everything that we now have; it is what we have now that constitutes our advantage over them; Step 2: Look—they had this even way back then. The writing feather, stagecoach, sedan chair are all instances of Step 1.

Step 2 would cover the trepanning in *The Egyptian* and the pneumatic-power-by-sand of *Land of the Pharaohs*, but—even though the technology of it may seem obscure—the paramount example of Step 2 in my experience is the Fifties-style cookout at which Jean Simmons whips up a meal for Edmund Purdom in *The Egyptian*, complete with backyard barbecue fashioned of adobe, a salad bowl with big salad servers, a spatula-substitute, everything except the apron reading "Nobody's Chef." Thus do we cozy up to such distant times, thus admire the reach of ancient civilizations (who knows from Pyramids?), by showing they were not all *that* different from us. They can make us feel down-home in alien surroundings. And the barbecue is at least as authentic as the bath in asses' milk DeMille arranges for Claudette Colbert in *The Sign of the Cross*.

This attempt to give the past a back-home touch is not limited to baths and barbecue pits. If inhabiting a time not our own is one aim of the Costume Picture, another is (once there) to stress our kinship as humans with those other humans long dead, a cinematic Family of Man. We never constructed the Pyramids, fought at Waterloo, or played a duet with Liszt; but we *have* been disappointed, a child, in debt; we have eaten barbecue. Once they are like us, they cannot again be so lost to us. So we stress both ends: familiar cookout, strange quill and parchment and sand caster.

It doesn't end with hand props. The Costume Picture feels a pressing obligation to let us know that the past was mobbed, uncomfortable, and barbaric (see DeMille's gladiators or the Christians, the multiple crucifixions of *Spartacus*, the plague of *Forever Amber*, the torture of *The Sign of the Cross* or *The Adventures of Robin Hood*, or *Murders in the Rue Morgue*). This is Costume's desire to consign us to an alien world of the past. The corresponding search for empathetic kinship in the midst of alien surroundings accounts for one familiar hallmark of DeMille's Costume Pictures. Asides and exchanges pepper the soundtrack in his crowd scenes—the wife berates the husband for getting lousy seats for the Christians vs. Lions tilt in the Colosseum (*The Sign of the Cross*); "Naomi, where's Nathan?" is heard on the soundtrack as thirty thousand extras surge toward us out of Egypt Land (*The Ten Commandments*). An anonymous voice out of the army in *El Cid* tells us "The Cid is wounded; he returns to the city." The focus on banal individual exchange humanizes the faceless mob even as the cookout cozies us up to pagan Egypt. Banal speeches on the one hand trivialize the spectacle that contains them, compromise scope with magnified individual cliché (but what could be more comfortable and familiarizing than cliché?). DeMille's need to insert such stuff shows the great moviemaker's respect for a genre he loved and his knowledge of what he was doing. He knew audience and he knew how to make this kind of thing work. For DeMille it's always school. It never stops. Again the absurd *demonstration* of familiarity doesn't have an entirely ironic result. Something in us is pleased we are being dealt with so directly. DeMille knew this too.

---

Spectacle is of course the ruling passion, the chief reason to make a Costume Picture: to fight a battle, build a monument, surge through the street with revolutionary zeal. And this is one reason Costume Pictures are so hard to take seriously in a conventional way. One reason literary criticism is so inept when applied to film is that critics may be indisputably correct for literature and at the same time completely wrong for movies. Look at Aristotle. By his rules almost everything that would weaken tragedy is good for movies. Spectacle (or, in the terms of the *Poetics, mere* spectacle) is the chief of these. What a pleasure to watch, without the danger of being trampled, the flooded human anthill of *The Rains Came*, the fighting on the battlements of *Intolerance* or *Unconquered*, the entry of the infant emperor in *The Last Emperor*, the ball in *War and Peace*. We launch flights of arrows with *El Cid* and *Henry V*, storm the Bastille in *A Tale of Two Cities*, eat at DeMille's banquet in *The Sign of the Cross* and *Samson and Delilah*. Mere spectacle, indeed. Good movie.

This brings us to another kind of alliance Costume makes with each of us in the audience. When in either version of *The Hunchback of Notre Dame* (1923 or 1939) we take Quasimodo's point of view and suddenly see that thrilling view of the square below and the people rushing back and forth like so many ants, we respond directly to the Costume Picture's primal pull. The slave army on the hill in *Spartacus*, the crashing chariots of *The Fall of the Roman Empire*, the pursuit into the Red Sea in *The Ten Commandments*, all acknowledge this generic essence of spectacle and our inevitable response to it. None makes a more stunning use of this than Griffith does on the steps of his mile-long set in *Intolerance*. First he turns the Denishawn dance into a rout and then into a panic. People are reduced to abstract waves rushing back and forth: thus do extras become ancient societies, thus whole armies of foreign lands come to be employed by Hollywood's new emperors to simulate the mass of ancient battles.

These clouds of witness make Costume's spectacle more than just sweep. In Anthony Mann's *Fall of the Roman Empire* we return to Rome in the middle of a pagan dance and suddenly sense it is totally out of control. Not content with showing it to us, Mann's camera puts us in its midst, and rather more at risk than we are accustomed to be, even in this picture (remember its chariot fight). In *Empire of the Sun* we are more surely caught in the surging panic of Shanghai than is Jim, its hero. "We live in a time of social unrest," the soldier announces in the midst of the panic in *Oil for the Lamps of China* and we know we are in a Costume Picture. Its claim to historic distance is then denied by that movie's insufficient space.[6] But again the double standard: this limited soundstage speaks profoundly of the Costume Picture's potential of expansion: sweep, and time. In *Henry V* Olivier seems a better film director than he is because film and Technicolor make it possible for him to outdo Shakespeare's words in moving us from the cramped Globe to the vasty fields of France.

Remember that choric mob in *The Story of Louis Pasteur*, that runs from sheep pen to sheep pen, our stand-ins on the screen busily representing us. And the choric responses to Georgie Minafer in *The Magnificent Ambersons* (we tend to forget this is a Costume Picture). These are a more formal, more artificial version of that lone voice seeking Nathan among thirty thousand in DeMille's Exodus, and that of the Spanish soldier in *El Cid*. This chorus is the Costume Picture's recognition, as clearly as is the quill pen, that the trip it makes into the past is formal, artificial, and distanced.

Riot, army, auto-da-fé, chariot race, anthill, are what big Costume Movies share with history-painting. This is one side of the coin, the other side is finger-pointing detail that works to bring the mob down to its constituent individuals. DeMille works all this at once—spectacle supported by sweep, and plenty of title cards. DeMille worked his life long to get at the one among the many, even as he tried to keep us from thinking the past was stuck-up or remote or unreachable. He put us in the picture. These times *are* out of reach because they are not our times, but we are continually brought to participate in them somehow by DeMille's skill. DeMille really believes crowds out of the past were like us and that we are like his crowds, so he has us stand about making merry, has us scan the worried faces as the Temple and the idol of Dagon begin to crumble in *Samson and Delilah*, hear those individual conversations at the beginning of the Exodus in *The Ten Commandments*, argue about the guns being shipped to the Indians at the beginning of *The Plainsman*. DeMille feels great issues demand plain truths; great debates demand elemental presentation. He makes the metaphor tangible. In *The Ten Commandments* we have a scene all about Pharaoh's force and Moses's balance; this is given operatic point and climax as Pharaoh throws the weight into the scale with a clank. In another scene costume samples for Nefretiri are balanced against an old rag out of the past as Judith Anderson produces the blanket of the baby Moses. "Oh Moses, you adorable fool!'" "I want plenty of birds' nests in the soup!" (*The Ten Commandments*, *The Adventures of Marco Polo*). We laugh at DeMille's directness, the crudity of his appeal. Yes we are being given the Exodus as if it were our high school prom, but afterwards we remember it as if it happened to us.

Something about this pull of Costume Pictures and DeMille's skill at manipulating it is very like one of our most primal responses to movies. We in the audience are part of a massed subjectivity: we watch them a bit as if it were our lives on the screen. But as I have said, at distance: these are not our lives, they are very big movies. Our relationship to them, distanced by the distances of their times, is fastened by that individual in the mob's midst. As we watch her or him, DeMille's careful attention to us in the audience is evident in a formal acknowledgment, the reaction shot: We see an individual face reacting in horror as the dam breaks or the building tumbles. This becomes an extreme metaphor for my reaction. This is a profound emblem for movie-watching, as central to film aesthetics as the flatness of a picture on the wall used to be to that of painting. Such a reading of it defines "reaction shot" in a profound way. The glance upward at the toppling building in *San Francisco* and the toppling idol in *Samson and Delilah* is connected directly to the way we watch movies. Some of the most unforgettable reactions in film (Robert Walker watching Farley Granger's tennis game in *Strangers on a Train* or Sylvia Sidney weeping as she watches the Cock Robin cartoon in *Sabotage*) are based in our guilt (and pleasure) in eavesdropping. When a movie can show us one such stare and make us conscious of it, as surely as when it shows us an eavesdropper's eye at the spy hole (*Psycho, Baby Doll*) it is presenting the power of pure movie in allegorical outline. So do these rest on the force of that horrible gasp of recognition: the building *will* topple, the car *will* crash. Looking at the screaming worshipper of Dagon in *Samson and Delilah* is, by transference, us looking at our own toppling doom. This is a primal force of film. The Costume Picture excels in it because it recognizes its elements and takes them at face value.

Not our lives, but something like them. This is the Costume Picture's stance: distance and self-consciousness, and it could stand as a general heading for a corresponding human mannerism. A Costume crowd is like the torch-bearing mob in a Horror Picture, or the screaming victims who flee Godzilla. We're there, but Costume's self-conscious distance (or Horror's or Science Fiction's) can preserve our safety in the midst of the mob. We are in the midst, but we are safely apart. Our delight (and the artifice which causes it) is self-conscious and self-referential: our delight that even as we scream with the other individuals in the mob we do not have to share their world. The distance here becomes an anxiety of distancing (something like Harold Bloom's *Anxiety of Influence*), for it can make Poland *then* into Poland *now*, Poland of World War II, and put its concerns up there on the screen for our recognition. Costume also makes the past into an arena for our present concerns.

The Costume Picture mediates between us now and them then: it measures the safety and comfort of our ladder of technology or, in another mode, takes kinship of similar issues as paramount—we are up against just what *they* were. Advantages and disadvantages—for this loss of our modern comforts, our more advanced technology, we have this gain of thrill or color or romance or adventure. This issue will not die; we still see it more or less the way the people on-screen are arguing it. This two-edged sword cuts, of course, only one way, the way the movie wants it to. Exploitation of both kinship and alienation makes the Costume Picture an unstable mixture, and this plays havoc with empathy. Tony Richardson's *Charge of the Light Brigade* (1968) is content to transfer to Victorian warfare a great many attitudes alien to it but comfy in the mid-Sixties with the antiwar movement. Richardson is even willing in this cause to do certain violence to coherence in his depiction of the rather straightforward military movements of the famous Charge itself and make of battlefield confusion our own filmic confusion. Richardson thinks he undertakes this in good cause, to prove a point: war is hell, and as confused as a battlefield is. Confused, though, ought not to be illegible.

John Schlesinger's *Yanks* takes on a number of contemporary attitudes, and eventually shows he doesn't really know what Costume is all about: is the movie to be Then or is it to be Now? If it is to be Then, obsession with male impotence has no place in the 1940s world of *Yanks*. The race riot at the English dance is similar. Surely there was impotence then, and violent race riots in the States, but Schlesinger's white servicemen *believe in* racial unrest and male impotence as white males of the Eighties would. If there had been a race riot at a British base (and surely there was racial conflict in the United States forces in the Forties), we still would not have had the brace of good guys this movie shows us, ready to battle alongside their black brothers for racial justice. The movie is content to be false to the times it shows us. This falsifies the Costume Picture's complete world.

In the words of the old Jimmy Durante song, Did you ever have the feeling you wanted to go and still have the feeling you wanted to stay? If one aim of the Costume Picture is to take us back, why must it always try so hard to keep us abreast of attitudes of our own time? The integrity of the movie is at stake on the one hand and its generic essence on the other. Richardson's *Charge of the Light Brigade* would not think of giving us an out-of-place or out-of-time and even out-of-regiment uniform from the costume storage, or to make Vanessa Redgrave wear a pregnant outfit not properly in period. But Richardson seems to think attention to the little things earns him the right to play fast-and-loose in larger matters, such as warfare in the Crimea. Richardson seems to think that this is too important morally, too significant for him to trust it to historical scrutiny: he rests the outcome of the Charge on David Hemmings's success in carrying a message. It is also too important for him to give the battle the coherence of conventional and workaday left-right editing, so we can't quite follow what happened at Balaklava but see instead a pacifist battle of confusion and mayhem of the kind fashionable in Sixties movies about war.

John Schlesinger and Tony Richardson are content to throw out the period baby for the sake of the very Now bathwater, to abandon periodicity (and, in the act, coherence) for the cause of the present anxiety. Some facts (what Typhoo ads look like in World War II) are evidently more important than the manners of Schlesinger's contemporary characters. The movie's sense of authenticity is subject to the times in which the movie is produced. Authenticity evidently is as authenticity does right now.

In *The Adventures of Robin Hood* Errol Flynn expresses to Olivia de Havilland enlightened feelings about torture as he shows her the refugees John's forces have driven into Sherwood Forest and tells her how difficult it is to feed them all. A stone's throw away from the splendid Technicolor feast and merrymaking (over there beyond the clearing) these poor folks seem to be eating a rather thin stew. "I'm sorry I had to show you that," says Robin. Such secular charity—Robin as United Way—would certainly have been as alien to churchly medieval England as it would have to Robin himself (if he existed). But in this instance it is coherent: the movie's root belief in Robin's hale kindness and in his desire to show Marian *all* his forest —and as long as he is about it, how much more benevolent he is than John or the Sheriff—is paramount. The coherence of the film is more important to Curtiz than trying to keep us abreast of attitudes of our own time. The integrity of the movie is at stake, its generic essence is more important than fact.

---

An invention or scientific advance might be termed the New Thing (the semaphore signal of *Lloyds of London*, the movable-type printing press of *The Hunchback of Notre Dame*); it may begin as an obligatory gesture toward authenticity and shorthand of intermediate technology, but the careful tracing of its invention, development, or expanding use carries the authentic absurdity even farther. At first it might salve the movie's conscience for the freedom it has taken with history. But soon, as in the Egyptian cookout, the very introduction of such New Things in Old Worlds becomes shorthand for the larger attempt at time travel and the Costume Picture's headlong determination to assay its task. It assumes we have arrived here in this time: just see the milestone, it says. As a later audience we can have a satisfaction of the sort proper to those who know the solution this whodunit is going to have. Knowing what that printing press is going to become, we can feel superior to the people in the movie: we know that the ones who approve of the printing press are wise and prophetic, and that those who disapprove of it or scoff at it are unwise and blind.

Beyond the printing press is a key to a potent genre unit. Movies love to invent things. In *Robin and Marian* Robin invents the toothbrush with a stray twig; any number of Costume Pictures during World War II invent Judo. The reason the invention is so potent is that the movie blesses us with hindsight: we know how, in the long run, all this is going to come out. So when a stock fool makes a wrong turn and fails to invent something we are flattered because the movie covers its obvious pandering to us by converting this into another form of surrogacy: I could have told you it would come out this way. Sometimes movies (*The Great Race*) will provide us with a villain who makes more and more gratifying failures of device or invention or New Way.

---

If the quill pen is the Costume Picture's hallmark or signature, its *shlagwort* is the announcement that Joe DiMaggio hit a home run today (*Farewell, My Lovely*) or that Blériot has just flown the channel (*Madame Curie*) or that our Parisian waterfront hoodlums are known as Apaches, just as the sideshow Indians are (*Murders in the Rue Morgue*). This is the oddly unmotivated announcement of contemporary fact or current event we can call the DiMaggio home run. No plot rests on it, the characters don't need it, and the movie doesn't need to remind *itself* that it is a period piece, the announcement is just for us. *He* or *she* just did *that*, so we must be in the past. As if the movie finds it necessary to whisper to us that it knows what it is and where it's at and we should know it too.[7]

To introduce M. Delacroix in *A Song to Remember* is similar but not quite the same thing. He is shown painting a picture, which gives him the power of a mimetic image. This is greater than just a dropped name. Balzac is shown greedily eating (under a fat portrait drawing in the Restaurant des Bohèmes), little better than a dropped name. He has lines but he never functions. Alfred de Musset is a suit of clothes and a dropped name; he is introduced and does nothing (and too bad, for he's played by George Macready). But Joe DiMaggio's alluded-to, dragged-in-from-left-field home run is a time cue, not a living image.

One might argue that in DiMaggio home runs Costume seeks instant nostalgia. But this would be wrong. I appeal to personal experience. I grew up where the Yankees held Spring Training and so I once saw Joe DiMaggio hit a home run. I then knew, I recollect, that these games were contacts with something of more than local importance (any such contact in St. Petersburg, Florida, was rare). Yet this was only Spring Training and surely that particular home run had as little ultimate importance to DiMaggio's career as my presence did to DiMaggio. When my father recalled to me that I had seen this, it was nostalgia for him and for me because we had been there together. Someone I had told recalling to me that I had been there could trigger nostalgia in me, but it would not be nostalgia for them. Just so, it is not nostalgia to be told about DiMaggio by someone in a movie. If the home run were to be re-created dramatically on the screen it would be re-creative waxwork: everybody knows DiMaggio hit home runs, so the actor would have to wear the right uniform and hit the ball right and look sort of like him. The offhand verbal allusion of the Costume Picture is nothing like this. Someone on the screen says to someone else not remotely involved in baseball, "Joe DiMaggio hit a home run today." The purpose is not even to trigger nostalgia for me (and me but distantly): few others in the audience of *Farewell, My Lovely* could have been present when Joltin' Joe really hit one. It's not nostalgia, it's another instance of the Costume Picture doing its job too well. In mid-and late-Sixties movies the almost obligatory reference to the Kennedy assassination or a television droning on in the background covering the funeral is like, I think, the Pearl Harbor announcement for a great many movies made between 1941 and 1945 set in America (and even for some, like *Casablanca*, which were not). This is cue with a greater function, calling up a common participatory event, near-nostalgia, but with the power not only to historicize and unite but also to propagandize.

The DiMaggio home run is like some of the historical allusions in DeMille's *Unconquered* or Vidor's *Northwest Passage*. In a backwoods tavern our hero meets General Washington out surveying, and our American Castor and Pollux, Mr. Mason and Mr. Dixon. It is something like synthetic memory, a wall chart for school, an *aide-mémoire* for the time-traveler. It calls up for us what we may or may not know and puts it in its place as if it *could* be something we *could* have remembered. It puts it in a world the movie would have us believe we now inhabit. True nostalgia cannot stretch beyond the beginning of our lives (or perhaps even beyond our second or third birthdays—not beyond our imprinting period, I suppose). Augmented or induced nostalgia goes farther—we can be made to believe that we recall much we cannot and could not have. Synthetic memory, manufactured to order, is more expansive still. The Costume Picture—like a good parent—seems always to fear we are all slipping into mass amnesia. Back to school again.

---

Costume Pictures that are Something Else—mixed Costume —may be an appropriate final argument. Sometimes Costume overwhelms another genre and sometimes it's just swallowed up. Any picture that tells us of DiMaggio's home run or brandishes a quill pen is in a sense Costume, but whether Costume can dominate the other genres in a mixed film is a question of the force and essence of the other genres in the mix.[8]

Costume/Musicals are commonplace, but Costume tends to yield to the Musical's format and generic essence (*The Dolly Sisters, Singin' in the Rain*—and the huge microphone is surely its quill pen), except for odd mixtures of Costume with Musical and Women's, such as *For Me and My Gal*, in which Women's dominates both Costume and Musical. See, for instance, *The Shocking Miss Pilgrim*'s suffragette rally. In most Costume/Musicals it can fairly be said that the significance of Costume is costumes, or rather, that the Costume genre makes it more interesting to do a musical of the past than a modern-dress (see *My Fair Lady*'s Ascot Gavotte).

Costume/Comedy is a curious aberration. Keaton's *The General* is a noble exception, but some more recent examples have shown the instability of re-creative Comedy. The best are the Richard Lester *Musketeers* movies; the worst is Ken Russell's *Lisztomania* (if it can, in any sense, be termed comic), with Woody Allen's *Love and Death* and Gene Wilder's *Start the Revolution Without Me* falling in between. Costume/Comedy seems to have little sense that Costume is a genre because it sees no reason to take seriously an obligation to the quill pen and the DiMaggio home run: a crowd scene or an anthill shot seems intrusive and out-of-place. But seriousness is a premise of Costume. *The General* knows this and its large scenes are both satisfyingly large and coherent to the rest of the film. So do *El Cid* and *The Fall of the Roman Empire*. Costume/War Picture wipes out characteristics of the Combat Film so they remain Costume Pictures, unless one becomes perverse and assesses the Pearl Harbor announcement as a DiMaggio and a jeep as a quill pen.[9] Costume Picture is an almost constant tributary to the Horror Picture before 1960 (*Murders in the Rue Morgue, The Picture of Dorian Gray*). Even when horror becomes modern-dress, trappings of the Costume Picture remain: capes, sticks, opera clothes (*Dr. Jekyll and Mr. Hyde, Werewolf of London, Blacula*).

When Women's Picture becomes Costume it thrives: or

rather, the Women's Pictures thrive, for no matter how well it defines and identifies itself, the Costume Picture is less carefully demarcated, less self-fulfilling than the Women's Picture: Women's takes its aim more carefully. This would tend to support a thesis that the Women's Picture is a generic super-umbrella to other genres, and that elements of it are more likely than elements of any other genre to creep into other kinds of movies, both generic and nongeneric. I'll get to this argument later on (see chapter 10). But the Western suggests a serious problem of Super Genre. When Westerns became Costume Pictures they are no longer Westerns (*Salome, Where She Danced, Butch and Sundance: The Early Days, The Plainsman*). The problem is not directorial ineptness or failure to know the ground rules: it is that Costume elements, in particular the Costume genre's self-consciousness and constant need to assure itself of its own identity, sap the freedom and confidence and self-reliance of the Western. When one tries to state one's dissatisfaction with one of these mixed bags, the burden of proof falls on just those things that best define a Costume Picture. If a Costume Picture exists to depict the past then it must be up and doing all the time. How different from the Western! All Costume's best devices intrude upon the Western's self-starting quality. A single stroke of an errant quill pen is the card of identity for Costume and destroys the Western. In *The Plainsman* talkiness, wordiness, and telling us over and over again what we must already know replaces that lovely mystery, the graceful interaction of the known and unknown at the heart of a great Western (*The Searchers* or *Rio Lobo*)—how little we know there, but how great is that knowing.

Costume Pictures have their music too, as Keats was wont to say: the choric mobs, the aside overheard in the midst of thirty thousand people, no-excuse asides, the sense that this, finally, is the *most* anyone—even Hollywood—can come up with. And diseases—first and foremost the plague, then (in Romantic Movies) TB. I suppose Acquired Immune Deficiency

Syndrome will be the Costume disease of films to come. And furnishings—the iron-ring chandelier, the high-backed flame-stitched settee in the casement-windowed alcove, poison rings, satin ball dresses. And commencements at West Point. And pouches: pouches with money, with messages, with tools, with hardtack, with a skull, pouches of any kind. And duels, and dueling-masters' training gyms. And meetings behind the cathedral, hurried partings, concealed ladies in hooded capes waiting in the carriage, runaway horses, escapes through the swamp or underwater or through the sewer or the sally port. Sextants, sand casters. Mute, mad, or beaten servant girls, masked women, gypsy dancers. One-eyed, one-handed, one-armed, one-legged men. Blind men who can see. Rats. Racks. All this is excess, but a fine excess nonetheless.

With all its didactic finger-pointing, Lincolns and Napoleons, home runs and printing presses, Costume is still a wonder. It is a genre that makes us a child again, willing to put up with the boring guide because the tour it will take us on is so outlandish, so freeing, so filled with delight. We condescend to it when we talk about it, but while we are watching, for instance, the Richard Lester or the MGM *Three Musketeers* or *El Cid* or even *Queen Christina* or *Lawrence of Arabia*, it is a little bit of heaven.

# 2. A BETTER MOUSETRAP
## The Inventor Movie

*Einstein: E equals m c, E equals m c, but what can come*
*next? Oh dear, oh dear, what can it be?*
*Mrs. Einstein: Oh Albert, could you try m c squared?*
*Einstein: E equals m c squared; why, that's it. E equals*
*m c squared. Thank you, my dear.*

—television play for marionettes put on
by New York schoolchildren, ca. 1963

In the Thirties and Forties Hollywood made a
group of films, based in fact, that recounted the lives of medical researchers, inventors, and men of science. These Inventor
Pictures are synthetic, probably arising from no remote cause
more significant than the need of their producers to turn out a
successful product. Inventor, then, is an invented genre. They
show, of course, ample evidence of ancillary needs and causes
—certainly *The Story of Louis Pasteur* and *Madame Curie* demonstrate the studios' pretension to high seriousness and to educational uplift, as well as their need for a star vehicle for Muni
or for the even more successful Garson/Pidgeon team. These
are movies parents might take a child to, parents who might
give a child Paul De Kruif's *Microbe Hunters* to read, parents
who might ordinarily feel moviegoing lacks respectability: parents (like mine) who wouldn't themselves have gone to the
movies on Sunday, who would limit a child's allowance so as
to limit the movies he saw, the isn't-there-something-better-to-

do-with-your-time parent. This pretension to uplift probably also kept the Inventor genre from free and open development in competition with the Biggies. Of course, had it not been for the necessary strategies, calculations, and pussyfootings of the studios and producers in designing and forming Inventor Movies the format would never have had even enough shape to be repeated often enough to become this well defined. This appeal to what parents think respectable, educational, uplifting, is a significant trace element of genre, one which we'll return to later (see chapter 10).

The first strategy of making Inventor Movies is packaging: how to sell this scientist/inventor/medical researcher—inventor we'll call them all—how can we make the inventor appealing? That the subject matter is factual is no advantage but rather an impediment: if it's a fact, the movies know it needs enlivening. That this is hard stuff, difficult to master, is the next: science is no picnic. And its hero is cold (the white coat, the lab, the test tube). The inventor's adversary may not even be human (anthrax? the villain? are you kidding?). Finally, the raw material must need fixing, because although discovery, invention, or cure can be dramatic, each has a bum rhythm: each is instantaneous, accidental, or tedious: 98 percent perspiration makes Jack a dull boy. Two percent inspiration, even, would drop dead at the box office.

At the center of the problem is the nature of the inventor. What if Hollywood could have discovered what Donald Crick later knew so well in *The Double Helix*[1]: that successful scientists are disagreeable, jealous, hostile, combative, sexually complex? The heroes would have been far more interesting (to say nothing of Madame Curie), but such heroes would not have been appropriate for their audiences of the Thirties and Forties because of the Production Code, the contemporary attitude toward the family (at whom, after all, this movie was being aimed).

I suggest that Inventor Movies have a generic complexity, an odd parallel these movies use with great skill: the Mad Doctor. Why else do these labs all try to appear to be underground labs, even when they aren't under ground? The inventor shares with that unforgettable icon of Horror Films (see chapter 4) not only quirks and fits and starts, but some of his distraction and most of his maddening isolation. Both Mad Doctor and hero Inventor are workaholics. But a *good* Mad Doctor would be as doomed to failure as the good werewolf or the good gunfighter. Television and the comics can manage the good werewolf in the person of the Hulk, but perhaps this is not a character for film. The good gunfighter can be brought off, but only with considerable tidying up. Apparently a given of it is that ultimately he will once more have to take down those guns he thought he had hung up for good and (unless he's rubbed out) hit the fugitive trail once again (*Shane*).

So, facing the thankless task of humanizing inventors (in the narrowest sense of that term), of making inventors softer, more vulnerable, less starchy-white and forbidding machines, the moviemakers come up with handicaps so inventors will be more like us: inventors become dumber, more forgetful, more eccentric. An odd path to humanization, but how much more will we be able to love the inventor, the studios reason, if the thought process (and the scientific process) slows to our speed, or rather slows to the speed of an even lower common denominator's snailtrack. Hollywood inventors are dolts, early and late, young and old, woman and girl, man and boy. The extreme in this regard is Alexander Graham Bell—dumber, more forgetful, and more eccentric than most anyone else in the movies. He is so "humanized" as to be beyond understanding most anything (except perhaps the dawning knowledge that he can't screw Loretta Young until he invents the telephone). The softening up of that starchy-white, forbidding exterior has affected his brain. Pasteur is not far removed from the garden variety absentminded-professor cliché (certainly, in part, the product of a host of movies about professors and klutz scientists in the mass adding up to an academia of fools and an intelligentsia of eggheads of a dangerously fragile sort).[2] The studio apparently feels Madame Curie is sufficiently humanized by her beauty, her motherhood, and the vulnerability brought on by radiation illness and childbed (or perhaps just that she's a woman), so it's not necessary to humanize her by making her extremely dumb. In *Madame Curie* (partly because it's a star—or rather, stars—vehicle) the Women's Picture often dominates Inventor.

Tom Edison is subject to the most articulate humanizing format. Boys will be boys, so to humanize Tom the movie seeks a generic transfusion from boys' books: *Penrod*, and Thomas Bailey Aldrich's *Story of a Bad Boy*, and especially *Tom Sawyer*. The scheme sidesteps *Young Tom Edison*'s biggest problem of structure: this is to be the story of a hero before he has earned the right to be called one, the apprenticeship of an inventor before he has invented anything. But in the boys' books his failings come ready-made: they are those of the Typical American Boy. His father says he's addled, that he'll never amount to anything, and continually tells him to take his hands out of his pockets (is it possible that invention is a lot like what they used to call self-abuse?). Tom's stinkbombs and gas-potions and nitroglycerin, though (by dint of the borrowed *Tom Sawyer*), can be dignified and justified by our expectation that he will become Spencer Tracy later on (in *Edison, the Man*). He's late for the train he works on (selling food, printing the news) so the conductor (Eugene Pallette) snatches him aboard by the ears, deafening him—another of those things the movie expects us to know so it *has* to show it to us. The prototype is something like a Horatio Alger hero. He now and again backslides. Alger heroes' slippages are not as spectacular as Tom's: by doing all the wrong things this lad, it is clear, will go far. Young Tom can still get away with swinging a dead cat on a string because Tom will be Tom (or Tom Sawyer).

Even though Young Tom never invents a single thing, this

INVENTOR: Mother as the necessity of invention: Fay Bainter and Mickey Rooney in Norman Taurog's *Young Tom Edison*, 1940

movie is still the best of the Inventor Pictures. Part of this must be the force of Edison himself (although *Edison, the Man* doesn't convey this force). Edison was still a media figure, famous throughout his lifetime: schoolchildren were still celebrating his birthday through the Forties. Humanization doesn't dilute this character. In this movie character, the portrayal of hero and depiction of a suitable world become one, by virtue of screenplay, direction, production, and Mickey Rooney's performance. It's a good movie. Tom's not dumb like Bell. And he has a firmer hold on our empathy. So he was just an average kid, eh? is a stronger tie than So he was just another dumb guy like me, huh?

Behind any inventor humanized by his handicaps stands, of course, a good woman, the helpmeet represented by Mrs. Einstein in this chapter's epigraph: behind the man the little woman who keeps the meal warm in the oven and inadvertently facilitates science by keeping his precious slides, as well, warm on the stove (what is an invention but a good recipe after all?). *And* when he loses his grant she knows a rich widow nearby (*Dr. Ehrlich's Magic Bullet*). Behind the boy, his mother (Fay Bainter), who keeps coming to the basement to ease her son's long hours at the lab table with milk and apple pie even though eventually she seems to suffer an attack of cellar stairs, bringing on the near-fatal crisis that provides the film with its denouement. Pasteur has wife and daughter. The Curies have each other, for this is an Inventor Movie with a curious sort of feminism at its heart. Pierre gives up his chosen research once it becomes apparent that Marie is on to something more important than he is (possibly because she appears more excited about hers than he is about his), and then stands by her in the hours always darkest just before the telltale glow. But, as if by studio habit, she still measures her life (and the movie measures its passage of time) by her babies and their relative and sequential size. Feminism knows its place at MGM.

Impulse and rhythm are tougher problems of strategy: tougher to understand and tougher for the makers to solve. These movies were perhaps more ridiculed for silly sudden invention (Eureka!) by contemporary parody and comment[3] than for anything else, because here they most distorted credibility and verisimilitude. Bell takes loans from Loretta Young's father while he works away at his invention. Her family seems to be comfortable. So there's a goal (invent the telephone, marry the girl) and a progress toward it, but there's something badly wrong in cause and effect. The difficulty is humanization again, but now it is a *process* that wants humanizing, far more difficult than humanizing humans. Some of the steps of the scientific process (in *Ehrlich*, for instance) can be neatly abstracted in montage without serious distortion, but here the depiction of the experimental process and scientific method is so overwhelmed by human interest that it doesn't make much sense. Controls (in *Ehrlich*) are cast aside when sick infants call: go ahead and cure the babies, science can wait. Accident outstrips scientific design and overcomes a systematic process of elimination (Ehrlich's warmed-over slide and the Curies' ignored but glowing dish). Hard work (especially teamwork) is less significant to scientific progress than the goadings of jealous colleagues or anxious Academy (*Ehrlich, Curie, Pasteur*).

The movie inventor's place in society turns on the matter of "recognition." Scientific or medical achievement is recognized by appropriate reward or ironic lack of it by industry or Academy. The Academy appears in light shafting down (in glorious glass shots) on lofty halls with beautiful chandeliers (*Curie, Pasteur*), but it is given rather short shrift: it bestows a medal, an award, she or he gives a speech of acceptance. *Ehrlich* takes the Academy seriously, using some of these same trappings for the good doctor's tough questioning of the establishment. It rewards him with support for his lab. Dr. Ehrlich seems more aggressive, on the make, than any of these inventors except Young Tom.

The scientific method, the progress of rational intellectual process, matters in these pictures little more than the historical quotations do in Costume. But, as with Costume generally, when one of those movies assumes we already know something about its material it becomes attentive to fact—that is, it then wants to seem responsible. We know before we see *The Story of Alexander Graham Bell* that the inventor had an accident which led him to call his assistant from the next room and, in so doing, inadvertently make the first telephone call. So instead of assuming, as we might expect, that we need to be told less about all this because we already know it, the movie assumes we must be told even more about what we already know, because that's why we came. We probably know even as soon as he appears on the screen that Henry Fonda will be that assistant, fated to receive that first desperate telephone call. So also our faithful Inventor Movie religiously weaves together this fact with details we already know in such a way that we'll be sure to recognize it. Fonda is made doubting, skeptical, and inept (but anyone can tell by looking at him that Henry Fonda would be able to invent the telephone at least twice as fast as Don Ameche, if he had the chance) in order to build up Bell's foresight and his scientific genius. Again it is generic necessity. Griffith would here have given us a title card: "This scene is an actual re-creation of the invention of the telephone."

Loretta Young's deafness in the same picture is similar fact. Bell's wife was really deaf. The movie treats it (like Edison's) as something we already know. Something must be made of it *because* the picture figures we already know it, and it's a performance opportunity for Loretta Young.

---

Industry's reward is more tangible and, of course (the moviemakers believe), more important to the audience because it's money, right in line with the American Way. Industry will make this idea into hard cash, recognizes (as only it can) that what this oddball has been doing is *practical*—and this further humanizes her or his difficult ways. In *Ehrlich* industrial application comes too soon, but a libel suit brings him to his senses in time for a climactic reconciliation with Otto Kruger. We see no patent, royalty, or profit, but rather arsenals of medicine boxes on montaged assembly lines emphasizing worldwide cure —this box will cure Nepal. *Alexander Graham Bell* attempts, unsuccessfully, to make industrial application (and the telephone's inexorable spread) as significant for the second half of the film as the invention of it was for the first half. A businessman turns to Bell and says, "I shall urge all my friends to have nothing to do with it." This doesn't produce much tension *or* a fit adversary: even anthrax might make a better villain than this turkey. Both devices—Academy and industry—are attempts to solve a problem common to the Inventor Movies. The drama of EUREKA! is annoyingly instantaneous; the movie's effort is to spread it over a span of years.

The adversely inclined businessman in *Bell* brings up another problem: the societal matrix of these films. When the adversary is not the spirochete or anthrax or invincible ignorance—and sometimes even when it is—the Academy/Establishment format presents a problem that requires fine-tuning of our allegiances. Americans are so accustomed to an anti-egghead orientation (this is one reason humanization in these movies tends to mean dumbness) that Inventor Movies have to seek out curious devices to get us to root for an egghead or a team of eggheads. Domestic humanization is some help: anyone who eats apple pie so frequently or takes meals at irregular hours must be a lot like us.

A more curious device is to pit bad eggheads against good eggheads, but this confuses our traditional American allegiance: our empathy for the good eggheads is not always clear. We don't like either kind. Bad eggheads want to cut budgets; good ones are willing to change their research project in midstream because they just found a most extraordinary snakebite story in Egypt. Bad eggheads have thicker accents, starchier morning coats, don't like Chinese people; good eggheads have pity on the control group. Bad eggheads come in committees or boards, good eggheads in teams. Bad eggheads have vanity, good eggheads none (as in Otto Kruger vs. Edward G. Robinson).

A surer allegiance strategy is the chorus of dumb but acclamatory stand-ins for us in the audience, a chorus which runs from sheep pen to sheep pen in *Pasteur*, rushing from inoculated to uninoculated sheep and saying totally unlikely but appropriately choruslike things. With such a dumb chorus we ride Tom Edison's train as he saves another madly onrushing train headed for the bridge that's out, with it we stand and suffer mutely outside the diphtheria ward in *Ehrlich*. I think Cecil B. DeMille was responsible for this kind of chorus, and for the isolated individual cry we often hear in the midst of the mob.

But the chorus and the bad eggheads give these movies their strangely abstracted quality of oddly methodical dream. This accounts for much of their appeal. The chorus is as unbelievable and sometimes as delightful as the torchbearing townspeople in a Frankenstein movie, the eggheads as motivelessly malignant as the Blue Meanies of a Japanese space opera. Here is a problem of aesthetics: What do we as audience, now, want this Inventor Movie to be like? What we watch frequently runs counter to good filmmaking, to strong empathy, and often to any sort of credibility. So is this the way we want them to be? Fay Bainter faints on the cellar stairs and we are delighted; Ehrlich's slides get left on the stove and we love it. We aren't watching these movies to learn facts, after all, to be uplifted, or to emulate their heroes. Remember Loretta Young's deafness, something the movie thought we knew already. Even if we don't know it the movie wants us to pretend to know it already. And we dutifully do so, and so we learn. This is how we adopt scenarios. We suspend belief, resist uplift, and revel in these movies, in their defiant, anarchic, and sometimes absurd excess. And made to be excessive, because this is an identity tag for Inventor Pictures. Why? These movies might be nothing more than an amusing subgenre of Costume, a sideline in our professions of the past, except that movies love inventions, New Things (see chapter 1). Instead they resemble each other like Composer Pictures, and seem to be becoming an independent genre.

Are these a subgenre of Costume, or a curious, somewhat attenuated, independent genre? If they are a subgenre, how are they different from Film-Bios (see chapter 3)? If independent, what freestanding characteristics differentiate it from Costume? One of these is easy to answer, the other hard. Inventor Pictures take place in the past, people in them write with feathers, invent the printing press, form themselves into vagrant mobs. So they are Costume, and are a subgenre. But are they like other Film-Bios? I think not, because they are so concocted. Hollywood made them as surely as God made little green apples.

I have named Hollywood as maker of the Inventor Picture. Such commercial needs merely reinforce the view that the movies and the genre they form are concocted. A Western is primarily responsible to its genre and to other individual Westerns; every instance of Western responds to so many tugs and pulls, traditions and developments, that it is difficult to say for certain that any particular part of it has been made to order. In the Inventor Movie the moviemakers work for a commercial end.

Inventor Movies are supposedly fact-based films, responding to the lives of the real inventors. Alexander Graham Bell's awkward assistant (Henry Fonda) corresponds to the less important bumbling and bustling assistant (Robert Walker) in the first Curie lab. But were there really two such fools? No, this is generic necessity. It is by synthetic generic decision that love must take second place for Bell and for Ehrlich, not because their biographies were parallel. Some of the format is similar to Film-Bios, but some is unique to the Inventor Picture. Inventor Movies, like Westerns, are both partly made by concoction and partly by generic necessity, but the proportion is reversed: Westerns have little concoction in a wide expanse of archetype, Inventor Movies little archetype in a sea of concoction. The ruling passion of an Inventor Picture in pursuit of commercial ends is to be as much like its predecessors as possible without breaking the law and without the audience's smelling a rat. The ruling passion of quality Westerns, on the other hand, frequently seems to be to avoid—even in a remake—any suspicion that they are like *any* other Western. An exception: B-Westerns seem to share the love of the rut. Inventor Pictures cherish. But in strong Westerns elaboration of format and event lead to a very complex evolution (see chapter 12).

The first principle—that the Inventor Movie is itself an invention—is joined by a second: now and again an Inventor Picture can shape itself. A corollary: just because a genre movie responds to a commercial need is no reason to think its rules are any harder and faster than those of a mainline genre.

---

*Ehrlich* and *Young Tom Edison* are very good movies, absorbing, participatory, quality stuff: but we tend not to talk about the measured performances of Edward G. Robinson (as Ehrlich) and of Otto Kruger and Ruth Gordon, or the inspired and abandoned excess of Mickey Rooney as much as we do the ways in which these movies represent Hollywood's absurd distortions of process—distorting even film's chief lure—elastic believability. We value this attenuated genre's aberrations, mad inventors bent on their Hollywood processes, deep in loony debates.

It wasn't generic necessity that led to these aberrations and excesses but the filmmakers' and studios' essential distrust of the material and discomfort with its root subject matter: excellence, human ingenuity, thought. On the whole even Hollywood's composers are more intelligent than Hollywood's inventors. Cornel Wilde's Chopin in *A Song to Remember* or even Laird Cregar's mad inhabitant of *Hangover Square* are better reflections of the human kind than Bell or Curie. The composers never had to be humanized. They're artists, not eggheads. It's not every fact-piece, every Film-Bio that must mind its humanization. "Humanization" removes humanity. It goes with just this territory. Think again of Walsh's *Gentleman Jim* or Hawks's *Sergeant York* or Ford's *Wings of Eagles*, or Curtiz's *Yankee Doodle Dandy* (and see the following chapter). Even (to cite a less brilliant, less auteurist example) think of *To Hell and Back*. No. The Inventor Movie became distinct on its winning ways, the silly ease with which it invents for us the telephone, radium, the Magic Bullet, not on the disabilities of fact for making fiction. Genres are (and should be) born, not made. Set out some time to design a new format as forceful and rich and flexible as the Western or the Women's Picture. Not to be concocted.

# 3. AS GOOD AS REAL LIFE
## Film-Bios

*Olsen: What's that?*
*Johnson: King Charles's skull.*
*Olsen: What's that little one then?*
*Johnson: King Charles when he was a little boy.*

—*Hellzapoppin'*, 1942, quoted from memory[1]

Our hearts sink when the title card reads, "This is a true story." Why shouldn't our pulse quicken at the idea that what we are going to see *really happened*? One reason, alas, is our experience with lives on film, Film-Bios. Inventor Movies are in many ways the liveliest biographical films, at least the most relaxed, unbuttoned (one might say, unhinged) about the license with which they concoct.

A major question about Film-Bio (even beyond whether it is a genre or not): When is a movie properly that and when does it join the genre its subject might attach it to? Western/Bios bring up a question about the generic integrity of Film-Bio, using one individual's history or myth to act as signpost in the midst of the mystical West. Most of these are not Biographical Pictures any more than Westerns with stagecoaches are Costume Pictures: they remain Westerns (see *Buffalo Bill, The True Story of Jesse James, The Return of Frank James, The Left-Handed Gun, My Darling Clementine*). As I have said, Westerns are beyond historical particularizing. Old fact can be the starting point or feature or flavor but cannot be allowed to take over. If it starts showing us specific inventions (the Gatling gun of *Salome, Where She Danced*) a Western can disappear without a trace and at once become a Costume Picture (but probably not a Film-Bio). Latin American near-Westerns (*Juarez, Viva Zapata, The Story of Pancho Villa, Villa Rides!, Viva Villa!, Burn, Walker*)—perhaps because of their focus on empire and politics—seem to become Film-Bios.

---

When Edison first started to think about movies he showed about as much imagination as when he first started to think about the future of his talking machine (never mind *combining* these two whiz-bangs). He seemed obsessed with better biography, and thought these machines might enable people to escape imprisonment in their own time, enable them to hear the voices of the dead, see and hear what only men and women long ago could have seen and heard.

Because he never gave fiction film much credit, Edison never realized the revolutionary force of his inventions. Edison was a practical man; fiction film was no more useful than song or dance. Mind, when it came to his patents he was pretty careful about the money fiction films could make. Of course the machines and the art they enabled made possible an escape better than his projected communication beyond the grave, a flight into totally new imaginative and supportive worlds. Edison's ideal movie—that time capsule he envisioned—would have been no better as history than the Costume Pictures were, because they would have recorded for posterity whoever was famous just then: the project would have mired itself in contemporaneous prejudice and fame, the image of that time distorted by its prejudice. I suppose if he had been able to foresee the future of his inventions (picture Edison contemplating the Watergate tapes) he would have turned from his workbench (and his nap-cot) in disgust, never to lavish his tinkerer's persistence on the doodads. Inventors are poor prophets because they dream utopias suitable to their present; so solving and imagining are cut from different cloth.

Fiction films, as if following the inventor's cue, though, developed a taste for rendering the past: movies pretended us into fully realized worlds of the past, visions of knights and ladies, great battles, days of yore. Costume Pictures were one root of the Film-Bio. Silent Costume Pictures started out with lives, much as late Romantic spectacles on the stage did, but thanks to masters such as Griffith, they quickly developed a format and shape which gave to Film-Bios a prominent place as a subgenre of the Costume Picture. And of course they were peppered with familiar faces. Lincoln, Liszt, Sheridan, Custer, Victoria, even George IV wander in and out of Costume Pictures as elemental features of them. With the concentration of a great director some of these biographical short subjects became something more. The Lincoln of John Ford's *The Prisoner of Shark Island* becomes a short Lincoln Movie. It looms so large because of what Lincoln means to Ford: the director makes him mean a little bit of this *more* to us. Lincoln is in this movie not just because he participates in the story of Doctor Mudd (Warner Baxter) or because the mob's feeling about Lincoln's assassination explains the cruelty the mob then wreaks upon Doctor Mudd. And he's not there just to appeal to his power as a champion icon. This Lincoln Movie joins several others (besides, of course, *Young Mr. Lincoln*) as a generic benchmark, something to judge other Lincoln Movies by. Such movies —even short "movies" contained within bigger ones as this one is—have more than biographical import. They are elements of our belief in what we see or have seen, pieces of the history we may know, genre elements by which the movie induces recognition and then attachment.

Together the structures (subgenre of Costume and developed icon) suggest some first principles for Film-Bios:

1) Film is popular and seeks what is simple—sometimes excessively simple; it popularizes popular materials even more.

2) Film is inherently fictional because it is cut up and put back together to form its narrative.

3) Our understanding of a character on film must be more superficial than of that in a written narrative.

4) Movies work by pictures and dialogue, voiceover and title cards; by its nature film must *show*.

5) A film can contain less than a book can; it may transmit more *information* than a book can (according to the thousand-words-per-picture principle), but only so many scenes, so much dialogue, so a Film-Bio must inevitably be more like a brief life than like a definitive biography: film can do Robert Southey's *Nelson*, but not Leon Edel's life of Henry James. Biography at the psychological depth of John Gibson Lockhart's *Scott* or Boswell's *Johnson* (the most cinematic of all biographies), or Longford's *Wellington* is too complex for film. Film can't get there and shouldn't try.

Biographical Pictures, then, will be more successful when they avoid rivalry with printed books, and choose subjects that can be *shown*, lives of action or performance or externals rather than of letters or ideas or virtue. Even when it has chosen its subject well, if a movie life comes on hard parts, it must resolve them with a movie solution. Film-Bio should capitalize on its advantage in getting at what a book cannot: it always will serve a movie to be more *like* a movie, and it doesn't always serve a book to be more like a book. One more route to successful Film-Bio then would be to become more *movie*, for it to mind its movie essence, to eschew words, explanations, explications, attempts at philosophical depth or completeness. Character is Film-Bio's proper subject. Where this can be rendered without resorting to the devices of modern fictional consciousness, movies do the job well: it's their stock in trade.

---

The worst Biographical Films I know (and on an informal survey, the worst by general critical acclamation) are *Wilson*, *Plymouth Adventure*, and *The Story of Christopher Columbus*. Most critics find a little redeeming liveliness in *The Adventures of Mark Twain* and *Alexander the Great*.

*Wilson* may stand for all. It was a major studio effort and Darryl F. Zanuck, its producer, a thorough man; Henry King, its director, was an artist of diverse generic accomplishment. But *Wilson* is a disaster.

Why? Not I think, for any of the reasons most frequently alleged:

1) its star, Alexander Knox was lacking in charisma, presence, energy, and competence;

2) Woodrow Wilson was not readily imaged or (in the French sense) *realized*;

3) *Wilson*'s events are chiefly political;

4) the chosen treatment is reverent.

It is a problem rather much more general than these and more familiar to those who think about movies: the cost of words and piety together. *Wilson* is in trouble because it's dull and it is certainly dull because it's in trouble.

The trouble is narrative engagement. We realize soon after the movie starts that it expects us to have read the book: it's like Selznick's *David Copperfield*. The movie as a whole does not make sense because it never bothers to give us a context for what we see: it just figures we know Dickens's Great Book. *Wilson* assumes we know the context—the Great President from Princeton. When *Wilson* was first released in the Forties, most of its audience held Woodrow Wilson in memory. Fine. But we know less about Wilson now, and it was a dull movie even back then.

But there's something worse. *Wilson* feels if it just lets us know its subject is important we will want to learn more: "Sometimes the life of a man mirrors a nation. The destiny of our country was crystallized in the life and times of Washington and Lincoln . . . and perhaps, too, in the life of another president. This is the story of America, and the story of a man." This kind of thing ought (the movie seems to think) to get us involved. Of course we will want to root for the national aspirations of a President of Princeton, and to recognize his qualifications for the Presidency of the U.S.—after all, he has just led a campaign to stamp out the Princeton Social Clubs: "Mother, stop worrying," says one daughter, "they'll love him."

There's no generic help for it—or rather the movie seldom accepts the generic help available. The newsreels are the movie's liveliest segments, but they only suggest that *Wilson* would have been better if it had been *all* newsreel. For one of the campaigns there's a travel montage—train stations whipping by—and we welcome it as we might a good Mickey Mouse in a long, dull, hard double bill. But even this lively sequence leads nowhere. Other borrowings from assorted genres offer little more. The death of the first Mrs. Wilson brings us a touch of the Southern Movie (Halloween lighting, as in *Gone With the Wind* for the death of Mrs. O'Hara; blacks singing spirituals by lamplight as she succumbs in a fourposter). There's some attempt at pep in the sprightly party conventions. But both are cut short. And we are given more words. And more words.

Wilson's first wife's death and the public criticism of his second wife's machinations are both obvious setups for Women's Picture. But *Wilson* is so completely sure it's on to something more important than genre or liveliness or engagement that it won't (I expect it would say) "compromise its authenticity to Hollywood." Authenticity, as we have seen, is a relative thing. Real speeches are recited in full in the situations (and sometimes in the locations) in which they were first uttered (see also *Gandhi*, another Film-Bio piety). Political and governmental principles are expounded and explicated without narrative excuse or context; national issues are reduced to family speechmaking. *Wilson* compromises nothing to entertainment.

The movie is simply too proud to stoop—as Woodrow Wilson surely was. It reflects, but never illuminates Wilson, so we have no stake in the protagonist. And nothing in the picture is anywhere near crude enough to be American—even with all that bunting. Movie politics tend to be dirty (*The Last Hurrah*, *State of the Union*, *Mr. Smith Goes to Washington*, *The Candidate*, *The Best Man*, *Advise and Consent*), to say nothing of politics on television. This is all too well scrubbed. *Wilson* manages to make political conventions dull.

*Wilson* shares its troubles and its dullness with *Plymouth Adventure* and *The Story of Christopher Columbus*: all are self-important, want to uplift us. There is a direct conventional appeal. And that's all. There's the same failure to engage.

---

Three first-rate Film-Bios share some odd characteristics: *Gentleman Jim*, *Yankee Doodle Dandy*, and *Wings of Eagles*. All are Costume Pictures, each with a different attendant subgenre: Sports (Boxing), Musical (Backstage), War respectively. So there is generic plenty. All avoid *Wilson*'s difficulties, in part by embracing this plenty. But no one would have any trouble calling them Film-Bios first and foremost.

Raoul Walsh's *Gentleman Jim* is the life of Jim Corbett (Errol Flynn), the heavyweight boxer who defeated John L. Sullivan (Ward Bond). It is a generic mix: Sports (Boxing), Costume (Gay Nineties), and Americana (Immigrant). Boxing Pictures have been around almost from the beginning of movies (*Broken Blossoms*, *Battling Butler*, *The Champ*, *The Set-Up*, *Golden Boy*, *Humoresque*, *Champion*, *Raging Bull*) and seem as well to mix it up in their parent genres—Comedy, Women's, Crime, perhaps Immigrant. But as in the College Picture and the Sports Picture, the center of the Boxing subgenre remained subject matter rather than becoming the seed of new genre elements. The difference is profound. The Gay Nineties Film (Keystone Cops movies, *Lillian Russell*, *For Me and My Gal*, *Take Me Out to the Ball Game*) is primitive, although the subject was portable through many different genres. The Nineties had a tremendous appeal for its audiences as false nostalgia, but the Nineties Pictures never managed to get it together generically, unlike, say, Roaring Twenties Pictures (*The Roaring Twenties*, *Love Among the Millionaires, Pete Kelly's Blues*). In the Nineties Picture the Immigrant (especially the Irish) Family is frequent (*In Old Chicago, Strawberry Blonde, The Public Enemy, Scarface, Godfather, Part II, America, America*) and it has a shape of its own. Immigrant is a significant part of the American Scenario—every Immigrant Picture doesn't touch every base, but each uses some part of that great narrative arc, beginning with hardship in the Old Country, struggle to break free, escape, passage, arrival, fight to begin in the States, bringing the others over, escaping ethnic bounds, ending up established in America. *Gentleman Jim* surely represents a sophisticated instance of the Irish Immigrant Picture, with an almost Hitchcockian comment on class.

*Gentleman Jim* triumphs by character: the character of an insufferably egotistical unself-conscious Irish braggart of immense charm. Walsh's footwork (and Flynn's) in keeping this character from becoming a monster nearly matches Corbett's footwork in the ring. In part the character is sure because of generic background (the family that stands behind him), and conflict (antagonistic aristocrats try to thwart him). In a way *Gentleman Jim* devises a narrative strategy similar to that of Welles's *Magnificent Ambersons*. In *Gentleman Jim* there is none of the bittersweet decline inherent in Welles's "Will Georgie get his comeuppance?," but "Will Jim get his comeuppance?" is a similar empathy game. Jim's involves shifting allegiances. The conflict finally ends up comic, and like good comedy, is resolved in a marriage.

The movie opens with a Costume Picture touch: a freeze-frame postcard brought to life, from which we move forward. The hook is nostalgia: an illegal, open-air boxing match, and a helter-skelter Keystone Cops chase end in jail. The Immigrant Family is next (the whole neighborhood knows to shout, "The Corbetts are at it again" when the brothers start fighting—a version of the vagrant mob), the one-for-all, all-for-one of the family-on-the-make.

Corbett starts off with a pushy proposition to an upper-class

A visit to her father's club: Errol Flynn and Alexis Smith in Raoul Walsh's *Gentleman Jim*, 1942

girl (Alexis Smith) who comes to the bank at which he is assistant teller; he gets inside her father's club, promotes this into lunch, a good cigar, and a free ride in his father's cab. In a typically economical sequence Walsh gives us Corbett's way of dealing (because he's Irish) with a hostile and exclusionist world; and this motivates his love/hate for the girl. Jim is an outrageous social climber, and this turns out to be exactly parallel to his overreaching boxing ambition, challenging "the Great John L. Himself." Corbett's victory in the club match undercuts our earlier regrets of his bad manners, the gaffes of his friend (Jack Carson) at the party afterwards. Even the bender which lands them in Salt Lake City becomes a tale not just of Corbett's vulgarity but also of his fallibility: he bears the stuffed shirts no grudge—not even the pretty one.

Once Corbett meets the Great John L. Himself, his Irish braggadacio takes second place: upstart becomes underdog. As we watch the big champion, riding through town like a one-man parade, performing on stage, and eating that Paul Bunyan meal we have read about (too many eggs, too many steaks), we know we are in the presence of an icon. The central conflict is now between upstart underdog and man-become-myth. John L. has become a public event: his performance in a woodchopping marathon, a theatrical "vehicle" arranged for him, finally converts all this into a pageant-allegory.

Corbett has to meet Sullivan before their match, for this is now mythic. The Big Fight is almost an anticlimax because we now know how to root for an impossible (but eminently American) guy. But the party after the fight is not anticlimax at all. When Alexis Smith gives Corbett an enormous hat to fit his swelled head we know this only anticipates the eventual clinch which will end the film. Even if he can cover pretty well that he knows he's earned the hat, he can't cover how much it hurts. The humbling of John L. *is* necessary to conclude John L.'s rise-and-fall myth: his decline must mark Corbett's rise. Corbett gets the jeweled belt. John L. takes large strides, starts new myths. Corbett has to be brought up to his speed. How important John L. is to this picture's structure is a measure of the force in Walsh's building of this generic icon, and, as with Ford's Lincoln, a measure of the director's attachment to the subject. It is also one of Ward Bond's finest performances.

*Gentleman Jim* moves from beginning to end in a single fluid movement. It knows its subject, never loses sight of it, traces a few years of a life (squeezed down to a few months in apparent time elapsed) sufficient to stand for the whole because of its energy, vitality, and characteristic significance. It also contrives for us to adopt a radically perverse empathy with what's going on. This is inherent in Jim Corbett: he is not the conventional Irish swaggerer by any means, but a very original and rather gentle Irish-American blowhard. We are brought to cheer for someone we never expected to like.

*The Wings of Eagles* is the most complex of these three Bios; it too turns on undercutting. There is particular point here to the distance between this movie's events and what ordinarily happens in a Film-Bio. The marriage of Spig Wead (a major screenwriter and John Ford's friend, played by John Wayne) is at the center—or rather, not quite at the center of his life, which is the problem. The marriage breaks down about the same time Wead, in a freak household accident, breaks his back. He recuperates from the fall, but not from the busted marriage, and the movie becomes a profound statement about domesticity. The scene shifts to a spookily uninhabited Veterans' Hospital where Dan Dailey, a CPO crony, carries on a relentless routine with a ukulele ("Gonna move that toe"). Wead cannot bring himself to accept his wife (Maureen O'Hara) even as a visitor to this lonely room. Wead makes a complete professional and moral reformation in the course of an amazing recuperation, but the only possibility the movie offers for saving the marriage seems to be some rosy-hued recollections from a falsely happy past in the service we have seen early in the picture.

Wead changes professions, becomes a screenwriter, only to return to another version of service at the time of Pearl Harbor. Then Ford sketches in for us suggestions of duty, the War, heart attack, and (presumably) death shortly to come. The traditional expectations this film sets up as norm to undercut is the man-woman structure of the service picture—she in love with him, he in love with his Big Job, she sacrifices everything to keep him and keep it together. Very quickly we find that the male ego provides this distortion of the service picture. The Big Job gives Wead the excuse to ignore the family. The false nostalgia of the fuzzy-edged rosy-hued flashback supplies a simpler version of *Gentleman Jim*'s photo-album opening, but this is a past that cannot possibly be recaptured because it never really was. This is contrasted to a complex and certainly miserable present which cannot be understood, at least by Spig Wead. But it can be by us.

John Wayne *acts*, sometimes under the disadvantage of getting everything into a mirror image of his face, the rest of him strapped to a hospital gurney. When Wead walks in to meet John Dodge (meant to be John Ford with Ward Bond enacting the part with particular relish in Ford's real office) we see the man being judged by his crutches when all he wants is a chance to prove himself with, of all things, his typewriter, he who used to race flying boats and wreck officers' clubs. The false nostalgia and happy answers of usual generic outcome are nothing alongside this.

---

*Yankee Doodle Dandy* is superficially similar to *Gentleman Jim*, and as perverse as *The Wings of Eagles*. The parent genre is Backstage Musical—a Musical about show business people. Cagney's skill as an actor and hoofer, and Michael Curtiz's skill in exploiting Cagney[2] make it something more—an inextricable combination, a seamless character much like that made by Walsh and Flynn in *Gentleman Jim*, Ford and Wayne in *Wings*. Cagney gives George M. Cohan (and the film) just the nervous energy, the slight edge of irritation to catch us up. It repeatedly keeps the material and this movie from slipping into just another Backstage Musical, and that conventional structure sets up something much more difficult. It *roughens* the movie. There's an edge to these show people. Cagney sets Cohan counter to the All-American Boy the script keeps telling us he is (and the action keeps showing us he is not). This only suggests that if this is an All-American Boy then the All-American Boy is a thornier matter than Jack Armstrong might suggest.

A montage of stage performances by the Four Cohans is interrupted by the child-star sequence in which Georgie's brash machismo makes the whole family lose its Big Chance with the Keith Orpheum Circuit. Then we have a grown-up version of this as Young Georgie (now Cagney playing him — the movie in a way has been marking time waiting for this entrance) uses his performance as an old codger (using some stage routines) to get the girl to like him: Peck's Bad Boy Backstage. The force of this (as in *Gentleman Jim*) is mostly felt in character: bragging and lying must out, we feel certain. But we're surprised: this Georgie never gets his comeuppance.

The And Then We Wrote sequence for the song *Mary* is the oddest moment in the movie. That it can seem conventional is an amazing example of how easy *Yankee Doodle Dandy* makes its radical restructuring of our expectations seem. Cohan writes the song as a surprise for his wife, gets an audition with Faye Templeton, a superstar, and gives her the song for a show, takes flowers to the wife. Joan Leslie apparently sees this coming; we even get the impression this isn't the first time. She knows, she says, before her husband does, that the song has better uses: it's just too good for a birthday present (*of course*: that's what makes it such a good birthday present). George's career comes first. The script tells us this is professional practicality; the movie shows us Cohan's domestic perfidy. Later Cohan breaks up his partnership with Sam Harris and the script tells us that this just signals a new stage in his career. We see it is something more.

The span is from Cohan's birth (on the Fourth of July) to the Congressional Medal awarded by (that World War II icon) F.D.R. And this final incident (a framing device for the whole film) is an interesting case in point. Cohan is so certain he is being called on the carpet by the President for his satiric portrayal of Roosevelt in *I'd Rather Be Right* that he forgets how big an American he is himself: in becoming a myth Cohan has also drummed up a number of Congressionally citable foursquare American tunes. That's what F.D.R. wants to honor. It's a bit steep to expect us to believe Cohan hasn't heard anything about this honor earlier: something like all those movie fathers who faint and gasp when they discover their little women are pregnant. But Cagney makes us believe it: *his* Cohan is like this. Complete self-absorption in him makes for a kind of zany amnesia. Cagney's hoofer-performer-singer-salesman-trickster is at this movie's center, which makes all this not only believable but attractive. We find ourselves in the middle of a puzzle: How did this movie get us to ally ourselves with so repugnant and corrupt a protagonist? And how oddly human is this combination Cohan/Cagney Curtiz has come up with. By the end of the movie he is still much the same, an oddly human rat, and it's all packed up in a rollicking musical, one of the most thoroughly empathetic musicals ever made. It never becomes a series of *numbers*: rather Cagney somehow makes dramatic scenes into numbers. Music becomes character events (as in the best musicals), but character events are choreographed by this performance and Curtiz's rapid-fire rhythm into rhythmic structures themselves, close to the center of this movie's odd force. This ugly American can sing and dance better than anybody we've ever seen, but in spite of being caught up in the numbers' and the picture's rhythms, we never forget he is a rat—the man we love to hate as hoofer. This is film at its best, and good Film-Bio.

---

I do not mean to suggest that a successful life on film must be as overtly American as these three are, or as perverse, or even as possessed of duality, but rather that perversity and duality seem essential to our empathetic engagement and these seem to be lacking in *Wilson*'s bland nonengagement. The irreverence that results from such engaged perversity may not always work as well as it does in these three films, but the reverence evident in *Wilson* will never work. And surely engagement and disruptive tone have more than a little to do with the factually irresponsible, suspiciously partisan way we engage with the best lives on film. The best Film-Bios anticipate our skepticism about lives on film and outsmart us by finding a way to undercut their own pretense to truth. In the act they make possible the kind of belief we can only see in movies. Corbett, Cohan, and Wead live in an extraordinary way.

The issue of scenarios, though, requires that we ask how they act on us. Nineteenth-century biography was, its critics felt, meant to be a high mark to emulate, to egg us on to the rewards of virtue. At worst (in lives of the Unworthy) biography would provide a Warning Beacon for Vice, earnest of the Shoals of Evil. There is something of this in the fictional biographies of Horatio Alger (more high mark than warning beacon), but I think Film-Bios are badly adapted for this sort of direct didacticism. The best ones hide their still, small light under a bushel of indirection, so that we must play through their complex empathy game before finding that the monster the movie has made us love does indeed have something worth remembering. Surely we want to have a potent line of guff like Flynn's *Gentleman Jim*, to be able to dance up the side of the proscenium like Cagney's *Yankee Doodle Dandy*. But these movies take us a long, hard way to that realization. This, I think, is another way American scenarios work: obscurely.

# 4. FAUST AND HIS DISEASE
## The Horror Picture

"*I'm being turned into Brundle-Fly. Don't you think that's worth a Nobel Prize or two?*"

—Jeff Goldblum in *The Fly*

"*I could do it to a lot of people if I wanted to. I know what people do. I watch them. That's another thing about those movies. Vampires always have ladies, lots of ladies.*
*In real life you can't get people to do what you want them to do.*"

—John Amplas in *Martin*

In *Doctor X* the protagonist is in trouble with the Academy (this tends to happen to Mad Doctors), but the movie never gives us the scene in which he explains, in the patient manner of Doctor Frankenstein, just what he's up to. Instead we see him more or less up to his elbows in goop: he looks up and says, exulting, "*Synthetic Flesh!*" There's a similar moment in *I Was a Teenage Werewolf* when that movie's Mad Doctor, apparently doubling in problems of adolescent adjustment, turns to his assistant and, without any other explanation, revels in the name of his mad product, "*Scopolomene!*" These two passages focus on one absolutely bald-faced thing about Horror—its delight in itself. Horror has a gratifyingly open, if unhinged, delight in what it is about.

But this said, I have to admit Horror is not a very likable or a very flexible genre. It is very strong, durable over the years, powerful, consistent in form and sequencing and icon. This leads to Horror's power as portable short-term genre—the ease with which it can suddenly turn up as an alien genre in the midst of a movie properly belonging to another genre, and take over. Horror Pictures can do this in Western, Women's, War, Comedy, Musical, even as moments of real horror can abruptly enter our lives. For a moment it is what we see in *Sunset Boulevard* (Norma sits with a cigarette clamped symbolically to her finger, poised like a spider as Joe reads her script; the chimpanzee's funeral; von Stroheim's organ recitals); in *Wagonmaster* (the lighting in the shotgun killing before the titles, the Squaw Dance interrupted by a scream); in *Drums Along the Mohawk* (as the Indian Blue Back appears in the cabin window illuminated by a flash of lightning); in *Escape from Alcatraz* (as Clint Eastwood, naked, enters his cell to a similar flash of lightning and a peal of Horror Thunder). Such manifestations are generally produced by accidentals—pose or angle or lighting or costume, the cloud scudding across the moon (*The Onion Field*), rather than by Horror touchstones such as the Wolfman's pentagram, or Baron Frankenstein's lightning-harnessing machine. Even in John Ford's *The Searchers*, a powerful Western sure of its generic identity, Horror takes over just before the Indian attack near the beginning as we feel the awful silence and see the oddly uncharacteristic highly colored Halloween lighting. The passage is punctuated by the abandoned doll and the shadow of the Indian falling upon the little girl hiding outside the cabin.

---

I think the power of Horror Pictures is in the strong psychology (or pathology) of its subgenres, so I'm going to detail a number of them one at a time. The distinctions between one film and the next are less important (and far less distinct) than those between one subgenre and the next because Horror has firm ground rules that produce discipline and force. They also, of course, produce rigidity, as they do in Costume, where similar guidelines (establish the period, stay within it, don't blow it) lead to similar inflexibilities (see, I write with a feather).[1] For both Horror and Costume the rules run counter to what in a great Western makes for freedom. If you've *got* to write with a feather it leaves less time for other things. But if you're in a wagon headed West, anything can happen and frequently does. A poor Western can, of course, be as hidebound as a good Costume, but inflexibility does not so surely go with the territory as it does with a Costume. These ground rules are shared with the people onscreen: they are known not just to us who watch these peculiarly fated and helpless actions unfold on the screen, but also to von Helsing, to Larry Talbot, to Doctor Praetorius, and even to Frankenstein (although he would prefer to ignore any rules that get in the way of his work). What we see is always in the process of fulfilling a pattern we know and they know, so we build in collaboration. The "Don't go in there!" heard in every theater where a Horror Picture is showing is extended into less suspenseful actions as well: we want to caution participants because we feel like participants ourselves. The characters point out to us the missing pieces; we help them along by telling them not to forget the wolfbane. They announce steps that must be taken now or later, and we take the steps together. They deliberately and consciously (sometimes self-consciously) anticipate what is yet to come. In Horror these expectations are so necessary and so definitive that it seems right to call them ground rules.

The variable is time: how quickly any of these steps is taken or the crisis is reached or the point of no return is passed (how soon must we capture Frankenstein's Monster? how much time do we have to drive the stake into Dracula's sleeping form before he wakes?) are matters which vary not just from subgenre to subgenre, but from movie to movie. We must do this and this before we drive in the stake: any movie can adopt variant order and timing to bring us to that point, but it never loses sight of its rules.

A subgenre, as I suggested for Inventor (see chapter 2), is a recognizably discrete category within the larger genre. It shares characteristics of the genre with its fellow subgenres, but just as clearly differentiates itself from the distinct subgeneric elements. Horror Pictures have two kinds of unity, then: the unity of Horror as a whole and the unity of movies of a single subgenre—Wolfman, for example—that make them distinct from movies of any other subgenre—Frankenstein, Invisible Man, Dracula, Mad Doctor, Possession, Jekyll and Hyde. I omit genetic and atomic mutations (*Swamp Thing, It*) which seem to me properly to be subgenres of Science Fiction Film.

This is consonant with the idea that Horror is, in effect, several different diseases: each kind of movie embodies, enacts, comes to confront something like a disease in that each refers back to (or sometimes narrates) a time of "health" or normalcy before this disease struck, an ideal time before horror struck. Each subgenre has fantastic trappings and results and an intensely empathetic outline and form, so we are alienated and attracted, somewhat as we are by someone who is ill.

Fantasy lends distance but there is still fear. Of course we laugh at Horror Pictures, and giggle and poke each other and feel superior. But beneath that, and never far from the surface, Horror Pictures carry a psychological truth all too surely ours.

The Wolfman and Dracula and Mad Doctors (like Doctor Jekyll) are most readily identifiable with our lives because they parallel neurotic behavior we see in our friends and associates; Frankenstein, the Invisible Man, other Mad Doctors, are more fantastic. Most share the power we experience when we read any carefully detailed case history, from the sexual writings of Havelock Ellis to "Can This Marriage Be Saved?" All these things really happened, so *they might happen* to us. The people on screen treat lycanthropy like a disease (they look it up in a medical book or medieval history or a dictionary, and the movie

HORROR: "Stop me before I change again!" Claude Rains and Lon
Chaney, Jr., in George Waggner's *The Wolf Man*, 1941

gives us a close-up of its words, or the characters read them aloud), and it has a disease's name. Part of the confidence of Horror Pictures, the sureness with which they can set such silly things before us, is our fascination with Horror's step-by-step tracing of steps we must take, steps we must not take: Don't go in there!

The Wolfman Picture (*Bigger Than Life*, *Hamlet*, *Hangover Square*, *An American Werewolf in London*, *Werewolf of London*, *The Lost Weekend*, *I Was a Teenage Werewolf*) is strong because its story is so specific. It has a clear idea of the high problem it has to solve. Even for Horror it is an especially task-oriented subgenre —and all Horror is hung up on tasks. The task for the Werewolf is to avoid the inevitable change; for others, not knowing who he is in human form, it is to eliminate him. Our identification is immediate: we watch the Wolfman with such rapt engagement because we have known wolfmen, have seen the hair grow on the backs of their hands—rivals, best friends, politicians, adulterers, prom queens—have seen the muddy footprints from time to time (dare we say it?) on our fine oriental rugs leading up to our own fourposter beds. Wolfman is an account of an Act of God. He is us in a more profound sense than any other figure of Horror.

Lycanthropy seems to be an upper-class disease. Larry Talbot's father in *The Wolf Man* is Claude Rains, clearly British (although Lon Chaney, Jr., seems to have returned from his Yank education a bit old to be his son; at the best, they are ill-matched altogether).[2] Larry picks up the wolf-headed silver walking stick in the shop and we sense he's a toff: he has a way with fine things. The loneliness of the aristo who has to go down to the valley to check it out are part and parcel to this case history. In other words, superiority, what used to be known as a tragic flaw. It's not the cause of the disease (as it is in simplistic explanations of tragic flaw). It may just be that the elitism and snobbery attendant upon horror diseases ("That can't happen to me") make it seem that fashionable

MIXED: A boy and his dad doing homework together: James
Mason and Christopher Olsen in Nicholas Ray's *Bigger Than Life*,
1956

people are more susceptible than common folk. Or maybe it's
the insatiable need Wolfmen have for low-life victims that
aligns them with the aristocracy. Then there's the availability
of silver for curing lycanthropy, the castle hill with the gypsy
camp located at its foot, the oriental rug on which to find the
paw print, the elegant furnishings in the castle (a telescope to
see the full moon, a bookstep to reach that rare volume on the
disease). So, too, slumming at the "little bandbox in the slums"
owned by the society lady (Spring Byington in *Werewolf of London*) and the somewhat phony "roughing it" of the collegiate
Grand Tour hikers in *American Werewolf*, both upper-class. If

instead of Larry Talbot's story *The Wolf Man* were a movie about that first-bitten gypsy character played by Bela Lugosi it would be no fun at all because in Lugosi's story gradual revelation would not be interesting. Who cares about him anyhow? But Larry Talbot lives high on the hill, almost as if in a tragedy: the high situation serves as tower to the gods' lightning, as Baron Frankenstein can tell us.

All this is too easy for tragedy, yes, but that's one good reason we have such things as Werewolf Movies: they're easier than tragedy. More people can experience Horror Pictures than ever felt a thrill of pity or terror or *anything* at a tragedy. Horror is more fun, more empathetic, more immediate and energetic and powerful. Europe (especially England) turns up a lot (even in the travel posters of *Bigger Than Life*). The pentagram (I see it in James Mason's broken mirror of the same film, but this is a bit ingenious); a bit of silver; sometimes a full moon partly covered by the clouds; the hair on the hands; the change, his crossover from human to whatever Wolfman state he may be headed for. (Ibsen's *Ghosts* is even so far as this a Werewolf Movie.) There is a suggestion that the monster commits sexual violence (the bestial suggestion of those back-bending ankles, the lack of "normal" sex—Larry's difficulty with the girls is impotence) and the strong suggestion of rape (unlike Dracula, who seduces). Accidentals of the subgenre (that is, not essential to the case history) are ground fog, stunted and barren tree trunks, and other such trappings, placeless settings for the Wolfman's depredations. There are few happy Wolfmen, although the female werewolf in *Cat People* (I and II), *Curse of the Cat People*, and *The Howling* seems to like her depredations. There are other significant differences: she shows feline tendencies when in human state. And once she goes, there is no change into half-a-human: she's all cat, as far as we can tell. Like Dracula, who goes all bat. Not Larry Talbot.

The Frankenstein Movie (*Murders in the Rue Morgue, Svengali, Deception, The Picture of Dorian Gray, Halloween, Visiting*

*Hours, The Candidate, Westworld, Electric Horseman, Sunset Boulevard, Friday the 13th*) has a monster who suffers from, as Alexander Pope says, this long disease his life—life as a monster that he never asked for. The Doctor, his technological father, is only slightly short of mad; probably only because of his conscience does he fail to measure up as a fully committed Mad Doctor. He lacks something of the delighted abandon and the looniness of truly Mad Doctors. Because Frankenstein's research has exiled him from science's sober communities, he now keeps company with such fringe practitioners as Doctor Praetorius (*Bride of Frankenstein*), an abandoned loony if ever there was one. The Monster's heritage contrasts with that of his upper-class Maker: the Monster is kin to all those common folk from the cemetery that his amalgamation has assembled, clearly not aristos but the commonalty of the dead we all must ultimately share. It may well be that his father's stitching and juicing have given him a heritage surer than the sutured hand or foot or ear. Ultimately in the Frankenstein Movie the prole fights aristos, plebes, and other proles. But we're talking origins now, not results. The Good Doctor Frankenstein, at any rate, is clearly ennobled—he's a Baron.

He's also foreign. We have had some red-white-and-blue Frankensteins and Monsters, but foreign locations seem more frequent than they could be were they accidental. The touchstones of this subgenre are more clearly *of* film than they are of its Mary Shelley original: the electrodes in the neck; the storm and its harnessing (Benjamin Franklin invented that much of the Frankenstein Monster as surely as he did the circulating library and bifocals); his ill-matched spare parts leading to the oddly out-of-balance, stiff-legged walk that caused so many schoolchildren to impersonate the Monster. His fear of fire is probably connected to his birth (as the rest of us are said to fear the sea from our origins in the womb). His need for sex and companionship is natural enough when you think about all that lightning power, but his problems with sex are equally understandable when you think of his walk, the electrodes, and of Doctor Frankenstein's sloppy workmanship (that problem of sizing, for instance: even Big Man Outfitters could have made the Monster more presentable)—all of these make him less than desirable as companion, much less as sex object. So the Monster seeks the company of the hospitable blind or the accessible child (see *M*, *Saboteur*, *Strangers on a Train*) because he knows society rejects him as a surrogate human. Such encounters persuade us the Monster is a companionable if misunderstood sort of fellow, and bring him to that very attractive dawning realization of self. He is like Milton's Adam, who had not been so could not know what he was. Mary Shelley was attracted to this quality, but failed to make us care about it. And, of course, the Monster's dawning sense of origin leads also to the atrocity against the child that so riles the folks of the village.

Unlike Wolfman Pictures, in which outgrowths of type and structure repeat throughout the subgenre, Frankenstein Movies (after the first one) move ahead rather randomly: the issue of age and youth seems a constant ingredient (the Doctor and the Monster of *Halloween*; Norma and Joe of *Sunset Boulevard*) and attempts at vicarious immortality or rejuvenation (*Sunset Boulevard*, *Murders in the Rue Morgue*, *Svengali*, *The Picture of Dorian Gray*). The tragic immortality of the Monster and the strangely unguilty Cassandra-like warnings of the Maker (*Halloween*, *Sunset Boulevard*) suggest that the pattern of ageless youth and recapitulative age runs pretty deep in the subgenre. The dominant fear, as with many Science-Fiction film monsters, is that an originally worthy experiment has run amok. If Benjamin Franklin brought us Karloff's Monster then Mary Shelley brought us *Rodan* and even *Gamara, the Invincible*. The fear of power unleashed is, of course, more a collective fear than the fear of heritable awfuls. The fear of science, fear of learning, fear of atomic energy or of unleashed electricity or radiation or tilted magnetism at the poles, or, for heaven's sake, of concussion,[3] are collective fears because in them social fears confront an antisocial force. We feel pity for the Monster assaulted by people and dogs in abstract pine forests, taunted with fire by misshapen dwarves; we do not feel terror, terror of the Wolfman's "There but for the Grace of God Go I." We could *be* the Wolfman, but we could not be the Monster because we have always, for ourselves, been. The Monster, as Mary Shelley made clear, like Adam, sprang full-formed, already mature. We cannot become him. But we can abstract ourselves being him (as we did when we were kids, arms in front of us, stiff-legged, staggering after our screaming classmates), and maybe more important, we can abstract (and accept) that he Has To Be Destroyed. Wolfman does too, but *he* (in his human remission) longs for cure. Not the same Has To Be Destroyed we feel about Dracula. Dracula's got to be stopped as an epidemic has to be: everyone he bites can bite another. But a For-the-Good-of-Society Has To Be Destroyed. The Monster makes messes and kills children. The Wolfman bites and (it is suggested) rapes. Dracula bites and spreads disease.

---

Two friends of mine wrote a musical version of *Dracula* and their talk about story first raised in my mind many of these issues. The Count led (or perhaps we should say, leads) a life outside society. He combats his loneliness by evangelism and initiation, drawing others into his society to make it more populous. He's a count and even more distinctly aristocratic than Larry Talbot. He's foreign but he emigrates, usually to England. But his is the least interesting of the subgenres before us, probably because, unlike Frankenstein, all Dracula movies have a close kinship with the original literary texts—in trappings, dialogue, sequence, characters, and so forth. The novel and the play have a far greater role in forming Dracula movies than the movies have in making available its submerged psychological truths; so dramatic enactment chills itself into formal abstraction. It garners our giggles and impersonation (who has not twitched a cape?), but we don't identify with Dracula's plight. We can't quite work ourselves up to his enthusiasm even for the capes and fangs, much less for being undead and sleeping in a coffin, or infecting everybody else. (For a particularly unattractive view of this life, see *Near Dark*; George Romero's Dracula, *Martin*, is positively chummy by comparison.) That's why we empathize with Dracula's hunters, with them hunt him down, ignore his screams as the cruel stake is driven home.

The accidentals are Transylvanian earth (see *A Song to Remember*, "Polish earth"[4]), the stake, the coffins, crucifixes, garlic, wolfbane, aversion to the sun, a need for blood, the fatal lure of promised eternal sex. These are firmly fixed, as if in concrete, by the dramatic source. But fears are more powerful than we might have thought and oddly double: fear of the soul-theft that Dracula will perform on us (especially if we are women playing the piano in filmy gowns), matched by our fear of the death-in-life he offers and maybe even a fear of the immortality he holds out. So what, Jonathan Harker says, if we have to live on flies and bugs: we will live forever. As I say, somehow that's not quite appealing enough.

In a sense the Mad Doctor (*Doctor X*, *Secrets of the Wax Museum*, *The Abominable Dr. Phibes*, *Mask of Fu Manchu*, *Metropolis*, *Star Wars*, *Back to the Future*, *Buckaroo Banzai*, *Brainstorm*, *I Was a Teenage Werewolf*) is a function within the other subgenres: Maria Ouspenskaya's gypsy is the Mad Doctor of *The Wolf Man*, Praetorius in *The Bride of Frankenstein*. Even von Helsing in *Dracula* shows some sign of being tempted across the Border. The Border, of course, is the same as that for Frankenstein, the Bounds of Nature, sensible and practical science on one side, what no one should dare to do, on the other.

Mad Doctors are led to excess by their obsession. They neglect legitimate work, are maddened by the applause and honors they see being conferred on the clearly inferior minds and second-rate science of the "straight practitioners" (here we veer

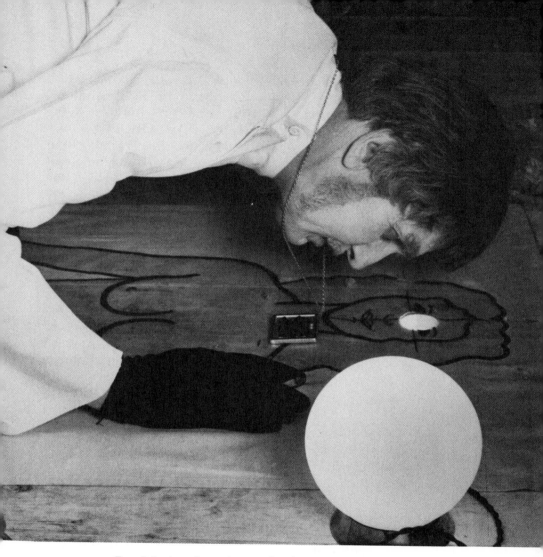

HORROR: Careful planning, the mark of a good Mad Doctor:
Vincent Price in *The Abominable Dr. Phibes*, 1971

closest to the Inventor Movie, which I've suggested is sibling to the Mad Doctor). The intelligentsia, the Establishment, make Mad Doctors mad, then, by conferring honors on the second-rate and failing to value what was once the best within its Academy. The Doctor is driven beyond the Bounds. Mad Doctor has its own charms. Its disease leads from the treatment of human ills of one sort or another (they tend to be M.D.s), through the temptations of technology more frequently than those of science, into the production and spread of cruelty, torture, ills, deformity, death, and really peculiar behavior, to say nothing of wonderfully loopy useless inventions such as the "synthetic flesh" *Doctor X* is working up in the lab. Or *Dr. Phibes*'s chart to guide him in boring the hole at the proper point in the floor so as to trickle through it attar of brussels sprouts so it may fall directly on the head of his victim nurse in the room below, so the locusts will be attracted to it and then go on eating her as she sleeps. Mad Doctors are systematic. Once beyond the Bounds, the Doctor will do whatever is necessary or rather whatever comes to hand to:

a) wreak revenge, especially on the Academy for driving him out;[5]

b) complete his demented experiments;

c) embarrass his daughter or fiancée somehow, or even endanger her life; or

d) enlarge his bizarre collection (*Secrets of the Wax Museum, House of Wax, The Devil-Doll, Attack of the Puppet People, Tarantula*). The Mad Doctors are collectors and pack rats. *Doctor X* and *Dr. Phibes* have the most consistent taste, but they all seem to like *things*: gothic towers or underground galleries as laboratories, or pipe organs. This matter of taste makes a distinction clear in a sub-subgenre. *The Phantom of the Opera* is a mad lover, a mad musician. Lon Chaney is also a Mad Doctor, with inventions (bombs, breathing tubes, flood switches); Claude Rains has the consistency of taste of Mad Doctors, and the obsession, even a hint of the father/daughter incest. He kills to pursue his fatherly/loverly ambition for Suzanne. *The Invisible Man*, a near-Mad Doctor, goes for tricks and, of course, the ultimate disguise, but is distinctly different. He *seems* to be a Mad Doctor, but more like a Jekyll/Hyde. Also Mad Doctors prove that secrets will out, frequently to our embarrassment and dismay and that of our daughters. Mad Doctor then turns rogue and jokester (like Marlowe's Faust or *The Invisible Man*). Having nothing to lose he sees in random or in jesting violence just one more outlet for his frustrated, undervalued, and now totally unhinged genius.

His domestic life (the daughter, the fiancée) is on the surface as normal as yours or mine. Of course, with the wife nowhere in evidence we wonder more about incest, especially when the Mad Doctor is played by Vincent Price. I suppose daughters and fiancées are more prevalent than wives simply because their innocence provides an excuse for incredible dumbness. Wives are smarter; they couldn't live with a Mad Doctor without asking better questions than the fiancées and daughters we see.

The hallmarks we have seen before: electricity (especially that directed through electric chairs); Bounds of Nature (suggested in his last report to the Academy, which so upsets that august body); lab coats, bubbling flasks, and glowing fluids; glittering deaths. This subgenre could be the most fun of all if it had a really sound center,[6] but generally everything decays into process (announcement, exile, excess, madness, final experiments, debacle, and death sometimes accompanied by the Fall of the House of Usher). *The Abominable Dr. Phibes* is an exception to this, of course, because he starts out dead (which is perhaps the abominable part). There's little realization of madness on the Mad Doctor's part and even less sympathy on ours. Mad Doctor is in the spirit of Edgar Allan Poe (the masquerade in the Chaney *Phantom*, *Dr. Phibes*'s house). We can be amused at him or gasp at the ultimate experiment, but we have trouble participating or believing in it. The film seems to know this, and this seems just to drive *it* beyond the Bounds. At least a Dracula (usually) takes itself seriously.

But just because a Mad Doctor Movie is not as empathetic or as psychologically affecting as Wolfman does not eliminate it as an effective and powerful generic force. I've already pointed out the connection to Inventor Pictures. *Flubber* and *Son of Flubber* are comic testimonies and *Dr. Strangelove: or How I Learned to Stop Worrying and Love the Bomb* suggests the viability of the subgenre in a very different satiric vein. Mad Doctor has plagued scientists as no other has: that alone might be sufficient redeeming social value for any subgenre: to have set up so convincingly the suggestion that anybody in a white coat is up to no good can't be all bad—indeed for a culture badly in need of such checks and balances to its cherished myths of the good scientist Mad Doctor has served us well. For the fear attendant on this subgenre is the fear of soulless science or of process uninformed by redeeming human purpose. Hal, the computer of *2001* (and *2010*) is a Mad Doctor: that should give us pause about whether this generic element applies to contemporary life. And there is a Mad Doctor dimension to Doctor Movies, a subgenre of the Women's Picture (see *Men in White*, *The Citadel*). The similarity tends to emerge when the doctor, to prove his serum or treatment or cure, goes Beyond the Bounds either to experiment upon himself as guinea pig, or something worse (*The Fly*, a combined subgeneric mix in the earlier version, in the Cronenberg film is a combination of Werewolf, Mad Doctor, and Jekyll and Hyde).

When Robert Louis Stevenson completed the first draft of *Dr. Jekyll and Mr. Hyde* and showed it to his wife, Fanny, she made one of her few completely unambiguous contributions to literature: she suggested that maybe it was all in Jekyll's mind. No need to wait for Edmund Wilson to come along years later (as he did for *The Turn of the Screw*) to make a twentieth-century masterpiece out of this one: Fanny put it in the text. But it's unlikely that the story's deliberately intended psycho-

logical dimension is what has given this story its filmic persistence: more likely it's that Hyde is catnip for actors and that it
is, as I have suggested, a combination-of-ingredients of the
other subgenres:

1) He brought it on himself. He's a Mad Doctor converting
himself into a Frankenstein's Monster: he's his own creator and
creation. BUT

2) the antidote is getting weaker. The Monster is taking over.
The Doctor will not just be killed but obliterated. Patricide and
suicide find here their happy and perhaps inevitable union.[7]

3) The Monster/Doctor connection has some of the overtones
of Siamese Twins (*The Fly*, de Palma's *Sisters*) or the good and
the evil twin so beloved of the Women's Picture (Bette Davis in
*A Stolen Life*[8]), Comedy (Bette Midler and Lily Tomlin in *Big
Business*), two TV mini-series (*Master of the Game* and *Hollywood
Wives*). No need for a fiancée/daughter for these; twin brothers
and sisters do the wimp work just fine.

In the Wolfman what leads to pity in the Mad Doctor leads
to extermination of the innocent not by the guilty but by the
reflexive process that grips this particular Mad Doctor—or perhaps worse, by the course of disease, acceleration of madness,
decay of constraints (if we read what we see in strongly social
terms). Dr. Jekyll is also a traitor to the name of Doctor—that's
why his opposite number is called Mister.

The accidentals are indicative: the elixir (immediately recognizable or it would not so easily have become a part of Tom
and Jerry and Bugs Bunny cartoons); the cape, evening clothes,
and walking stick; the bachelor pad—not only a space for
Hyde's luxurious comfort and sexual convenience, but a tunnel into Hyde's world, a tunnel away from dinners and drawing rooms and Mayfair fronts, through the back door to the
lab, an avenue to back streets and low life. Friends and servants help Jekyll, cover for him. He is, after all, doing nothing
more than any gentleman might, as an escape from the ten-

sion of his work (and Victorian social strictures), fulfilling the macho dream of prostitution and snuff-sex, the customary Victorian way (or so some scholars tell us). The habits of the rich, the kinship of the professional class with aristos, the shame of science, are also characteristics.

The dominant fear here is fear of self: one may succumb to just what one has devised or concocted and gulped down voluntarily and gulps down again and again, or to an escape from everything one stands for into everything one dare not allow one's self to have: one can even escape the fear of sex and respectable betrothal into the mayhem and violence of sexual bondage and misogynist rape.

There's an odd sidelight to this in an instance of late-genre breakdown: In a movie called *Dr. Jekyll and Sister Hyde*, Jekyll recognizes his unwilling desire to turn female just as his closest associate recognizes Jekyll's desirability as a homosexual lover.

The Jekyll-Hyde story has low-life in common with other subgenres—the gypsy camp in *The Wolfman*; the Bandbox in the Slums of *Werewolf of London*; the Yellow Bird sung by Angela Lansbury and the suggested sadomasochistic den in *Dorian Gray*; the whores the Mad Doctor uses for guinea pigs in *Murders in the Rue Morgue*; the low resorts in *Six Hours to Live* (which joins the Mad Doctor subgenre only through the benefit of a resurrection apparatus, for its scientist, far from mad, is almost cuddly). Low-life stands as an emblem of man's lower appetites and betrays the Victorian roots of many of this genre's literary forebears. And brings to the fore again the power of snobbery in Horror.

What I have been citing is part meaning and narrative and part image and design. There is a way in which the objects of Horror Pictures—the accidentals (bandages of the Invisible Man, the Mummy's cerements trailed out a door, footprints of the Wolfman, crucifixes, the Doctor's glass and electrical devices in *Frankenstein, Doctor X, The Abominable Dr. Phibes*, the underground crypts and labs of Rotwang in *Metropolis*, his desk lamp) take on a life of their own. Design becomes an independent fabric of sequence and belief on which we can fix even as we engage ourselves in the psychological power of the narrative. It is perhaps one genre (another would probably be Science-Fiction Film) in which we most freely accept physical object and technology as substitutes for event, partly because the Horror Movie works on a rather distant and abstracted form of empathy. The narrative is more idea or mnemonic jingle than story; we inhabit these movies by a series of speculations about ourselves and our world rather than by any tangible moment-by-moment experience of that pine forest, lightning on the roof of the tower, coffin in the vault. It's what makes them so much fun to watch alone. Come to think of it, it's what makes them so much fun to watch with a full audience. Out loud we may make fun of them, but that's to cover for the inward naked victim they can make of us.

Taken to its limits the diseases of these subgenres have a broad allegorical base: the Faust legend. A man trades the givens of his life—his soul, his well-being, his sanity, his immortality—for an extension of the self beyond the Bounds of Nature. In *Hangover Square* Laird Cregar's composer finds in his curse (the musical theater) some of the same jokes Faust found in his. As Mephisto says, he can give Faust more than he has the wit to ask. And Faust's behavior once the bargain has been made proves his point: Faust wastes his time in silly japing and jesting, tweaking the Pope's nose, just like Aladdin wasting his wishes with his lamp. This finds echoes in *The Invisible Man* and *Topper*, and in the reappearances of the rotting victim in *American Werewolf in London*.

But what separates things like this from the usual meaning-mongering of literary criticism, that equation of genre = story? I have combined many movies into single summaries with a purpose: the strong distinctions between these subgenres and the repetitions and refrains in accidentals and in verbal material suggest again that the proper metaphor for genre is not formula but language. Genre isn't made by following rules, but by the infinite variation of interchangeable parts. When a cloud passes over a full moon in a movie (*OSS, The Exile*, or *The Onion Field*) we are shoved into Werewolf, or when a man holds up a cross at arm's length toward another character (*Hamlet, Richard III*) we are shoved into Dracula. When a monster, any monster, gets up again after being fatally wounded (*Halloween, Red River, Friday the 13th, The Terminator*) we find ourselves in a Frankenstein. Our recognition of this shove, our immediate ability to know where we are, is a generic recognition. The ground rules of subgenres are strict but they exchange elements and habits rather freely.

This is an important principle, one that has its most significant application when it comes to genre units. In language, variation as well as regularity teach us to talk and read—flexibilities, not absolutes. Any number of stories can be enabled by the same subgeneric or generic structure. Story seems variable when compared to our constant ability to recognize genre, genre gives us an ability to know what we watch, to read clues, to understand where we are. As with language, we can speak and read more than we know the rules for.

The boring part of genre study is that which combines a group of stories or heroes or settings or climaxes so as to point out the likeness of one crooked Indian Trading Post agent to another or one taxi dancer to another. More interesting than this is to discover why such a diverse group of stories can be identified as a genre or a subgenre, and what is the coherence in these genres or subgenres that is common knowledge to audiences, moviemakers, and sometimes characters on the screen. Horror is portable and we can read it as Horror even in small fragments without its interrupting our coherent sense of the movie we are watching or its genre—Western or Women's or Costume or Joan Crawford.

Some summary pronouncements:

1) Horror is all about sex.

2) Horror is intensely personal but (generally) distantly empathetic.

3) Horror is hung up not just on tasks, but on class. That Horror tends to be European gives a clue to some of this.[9]

Perhaps sex and class are too thorny to appear in the midst of our recreational (as we say) vehicles: they need to be disguised in the fantasy trappings of Horror, the alien clime of Transylvania.

In *Bigger Than Life* Nicholas Ray takes a nonfiction piece about steroids written by Berton Roueché for *The New Yorker's* "Annals of Medicine" and gives us the Wolfman's change in gradual drug-induced stages. The father terrorizes his son in a comparatively mild way about throwing the football, then in a sudden obsession he forces him to drink his milk (stretched to unbelievable tension by Ray's brilliant use of CinemaScope); finally he emerges as a monster, ready to kill the kid apparently because he's read in the Bible about Abraham and Isaac. It is a Wolfman picture down to the hair on the hands, all accomplished in the context of a Fifties Family. More: sometimes a subgenre as a whole has usefulness beyond the *conscious* employment of its hallmarks and objects and accidentals: it is equally useful as a framework for knowing what's going on in a very different sort of movie, apparently distant from its kind. When Buster Keaton in *Go West* doesn't recognize what's wrong with his obsessive attachment to a single cow he's on the generic track for Wolfman even though the picture's genre is Comedy/Western.

Elements, fragments, pieces can have a life of their own, can bond to each other with the ease (and some of the mystery) of chemicals seeking their valences. This is the real gift subgenre offers: not to provide us with lists of possible stories told under a single generic rubric, but to suggest that genre once divided into subgenres is further reducible to generic or subgeneric fragments, any one of which can become a genre unit and prove almost completely independent in practice. Where any of these appears first is sometimes mysterious (who first thought of Igor's torch, of the Mad Doctor's triumphant hysterical laugh?). But mystery of that genesis sometimes leads to certain meaning: the genre enables us always to know where we are and what we are watching even when we don't know how it will add up or what it will mean in the end. We can imagine what we are seeing from what we know, and for a time go along with where the movie takes us for however long it takes. This is how we read and speak English, more English than we have rules for; this is how we know where we are in a Werewolf Picture.

What is Horror good for? To give us an excess against which we can judge contemporary terror; to give us an extreme measure against which this terror or chronic fear may seem the less; to give us a metaphor for unspoken fantasies and nightmares of sex; to show us things (like Hal of *2001*) Horror didn't at first even know it was aiming at; to make laughable the very unlaughable real and present danger or threat of our lives out here in the audience. It gives us diseases which prepare us for, maybe sometimes even inoculate us against, the diseases that we meet.

# 5. JOBS, GEOGRAPHY, AND RITUAL
## Assorted Genre Fragments

---

*"Didn't we pass that rock a way back?"*

—Harry Carey, Jr., in *Wagonmaster*

I have been accused of seeing a genre beneath every bush. This is probably a natural result of my elemental view of genre. There are a lot of different kinds of movie—a Psychiatrist Movie, a Hartford Movie, a Pirate, a Betty Hutton, a Joan Crawford, a Desert, a Jungle, a Frozen North Picture. This does not mean that any of these looms large in the development of movies, but it is another way of saying that sub-sub-sub-subgenre is not a good way to examine generic problems: instead of insisting on a complex compound, take the watch apart and see if the parts still tick. The Hartford Movie does; so does the Joan Crawford. Three families of these elements—geography, professions, and rituals—will, I think, demonstrate elemental anatomy.

Places in movies are located in our cosmos or in the cosmos of the movie—or else in a blend of the two. For instance, when John Ford moves the cavalry or the stagecoach or the wagon train round and round in Monument Valley it is not moving through Arizona, nor does he want us to think of it there. Monument Valley becomes a figurative space, a visual trope that aids us in knowing the people who inhabit it and the story their actions convey, because by it they are both placeless and also firmly placed. As the place is understood so are the people known: known people in an understood place.[1]

But in *Easy Rider* Dennis Hopper and Peter Fonda undertake a motorcycle trip through the West to New Orleans. That they pass landmarks of our country in the wrong sequence (or entirely off the track) is irritating in this movie's context because the movie has not managed to make much of anything of its space (large or small: in the frame or in its geography), or to make anything like the artifice, the spatial vision Ford makes of Monument Valley. *Easy Rider* just assumes that we won't know or that it doesn't matter.

I think it does or does not matter according to what any particular movie has made of geographical or fictive space: we know we are Americans as well by either sort. Fictive space is a staple of some Costume Pictures (*The Court Jester*) and of Empires (*The Man Who Would Be King*, *Four Feathers*), but most magnificently, of the Western (*Rio Bravo*, *El Dorado*). This king of genres is less obligated to any map than it is to what Western directors, such as Walsh, Hawks, Ford, Boetticher, and Mann have made of spaces they found there and made into their films' visions. The dark canyon, the cooling rocky stream, the threatening mound of rocks, the protective mesa. Place certain is different. Either this sort of landscape becomes a metaphor for nowhere, as background to presumptively timeless events (the stage to Lordsburg of *Stagecoach*, the desert of *Zabriskie Point*), or else it affirms a local habitation and a name (*Saigon*, *Lisbon*). Sometimes place certain becomes mythic (the beach before Valencia in *El Cid*). Any of these can be generic.

There is an analogue to this in one shape from the Costume Picture involving time and timelessness: a movie set during the Civil War is a Costume Picture; if it is set before the war it is a Southern Picture; if after the war, it's likely to be a Western.[2] (I would say, with Basinger, that it's never a War Picture.) In between is the War itself, that very very Costume-

Picture center of battles and issues. But this center is a less certain and more imaginative temporal space than either the space for antebellum romance of Western Expansion (*The Buccaneer, Gorgeous Hussy, Rio Lobo, The Iron Mistress*) or of Atrocity Picture (*Mandingo, Drum*). What comes after—the postwar return to the business of the Frontier and the Gilded Age —suggests a moral or historical construction. Once they are in films real places can become either certain or imaginative, fixed or expansive, depending on how they are handled. But note how many places certain have been extended by movies to become places imaginative: Macao, Casablanca, Berlin, Saigon, Marrakech, Pago-Pago.

Two of the most certain of the many places certain of American film are Los Angeles and San Francisco. They were always readiest to hand for filmmakers, but movies do not always see even these two as places certain and factual, or they have not always been made to seem so. *Greed* is (in part) set in San Francisco, but the movie doesn't really become a San Francisco film. *San Francisco, Vertigo,* and the 1978 *Invasion of the Body Snatchers* are San Francisco films, as are *Bullitt, The Lineup, The Killer Elite,* and *Point Blank*. *Ella Cinders* is (in part) set in Hollywood, but Los Angeles is still just Hollywood—it hasn't yet become Los Angeles in our imagination and was kept from becoming so for a while yet. Movies at this time are generally imprisoned on studio streets in the soundstages or what is easy to get to in Los Angeles. Moviemakers didn't want to let on that what we were seeing was just funny old Los Angeles, after all. As a result L.A. becomes a rather familiar Nowheresville, anonymous city (*The Public Enemy*). By the time of *The Long Goodbye, Farewell, My Lovely, American Gigolo, The Late Show, Day of the Locust, True Confessions, To Live and Die in L.A.,* we have the legitimate L.A. Movie: high living, drugs, too much money, not far from the border, crazy religions, creepy crimes, black-and-white cop cars, run-down neighborhoods, buildings in Spanish stucco, aging hoofers, the recent past.

Some of this is no more than habitual cliché, but many generic elements begin life as local-color clichés or stereotypes. In *The Long Goodbye* there's a meeting of some of the old Hollywood elements in a new Seventies L.A. version: the hood has a lot of henchmen and they all seem to be weightlifters (bringing full circle *The Big Sleep*'s puny Jonesie); the detective keeps a cat (both a joke on Philip Marlowe and a gesture in the direction of the comfy old Angelino). In this new L.A., Malibu has stepped up to the present from its use as location in *Humoresque* and its use as place certain and place mythic in *Mildred Pierce*: the 24-hour-a-day gatekeeper, the up-and-down-the-beach drop-in cocktail party (see *Rich and Famous*, *The Long Goodbye*, *S.O.B.*, *That's Life*) the drying-out hospital. But people still walk into the sea there. As is apparent from this, things associated with a given geography in place-certain subgenres are not necessarily strictly geographical. (*Humoresque* is supposed to be set on the East Coast; we see a California Beach.) But Malibu is both geographical *and* generic, place certain and place mythic.

Perhaps even when some location is by its surroundings geographically certain (as in Marlowe's eyrie apartment and the hood's high-rise of the 1974 *The Long Goodbye*), others just as readily identifiable escape such certainty because the movie's space overwhelms the geographic space, the movie takes over. Nina van Pallandt drives her car on a recognizable street at night as Marlowe runs after it, but the sequence is not geographical—that is, certainty doesn't just come with the territory, it's a matter of what the movie *does* with it that's generic. The driving sequence inhabits the space of the movie, the space of L.A.'s imaginative cosmos, as surely as the Parthenon at the end of *Nashville* is a part of that movie's expanded cosmos. *The Long Goodbye*'s supermarket and bar and real-estate woman are of the expanded cosmos. *S.O.B.* confirms the strength of the L.A. and the Malibu place-genre. *The Late Show* confirms its types.

Some development of place-genre unit moves beyond convenient location. The enormous Chinese population of Los Angeles makes an entirely adequate Chinatown, but it never figures as prominently as it does in San Francisco films. This is because San Francisco is for place genre more exotic: San Francisco Movies feature the import-export and antiques trade, great wealth (*Bullitt*, *Mildred Pierce*, *The Maltese Falcon*, *The Big Sleep*), fogs and the waterfront, the bridge, Yellow Peril.

As to New York, *On the Town* and the *Godfathers* I and II, *Saboteur*, *The World of Henry Orient*, and *Rich Kids* are New York Movies; *How to Marry a Millionaire* is not, but it uses the geography. New York movies dwell on the alienated face in the crowd, ethnic background, insiders and outsiders, canyon dwellers, hobos (in the Thirties) and (now) the homeless. *A Tree Grows in Brooklyn* and *Arsenic and Old Lace* are not Brooklyn Movies, but *Saturday Night Fever* may well be. Borough genre is less surely, but nevertheless clearly, defined.

*The Third Man* slides easily from the Vienna the Waltz King called home to postwar criminal corruption. Paris, I suppose, has always been its own genre, as London, Honolulu, Hong Kong, and Berlin between the wars. Nashville and Lisbon were perhaps never slated to make it in more than one movie. *Lisbon* discovered that the place-name had more to be said for it than the place itself: it never became that foreign clime rife with romance that its name promised. But *Saigon* survived such a place-name exploitation to move on to become place genre because of our sad war there and what it made of the town long after Alan Ladd had departed (*Good Morning, Vietnam*, *The Deer Hunter*).

Some of this certain/mythic stretch depends on a Great Shift —something in genre history similar to a vowel shift in language history. Before the end of World War II we knew (and cared) little of what Italy or Germany or even France (beyond that strip along the Seine of Paris the movies love) really *looked* like. They, we felt, looked like what the movies told us they did (compare the Venice of *Top Hat* to the Venice of *Summertime*). In *Hitler's Children* Kent Smith calls on a timid journalist and we are given a front porch right out of Indiana—front hedge, clapboard house, and all. We wouldn't have thought of doubting it in 1943. But once the war was over, pictures were shot on location and the acceptable look for such places changed utterly. We are told that we are in Berlin. Our knowledge of what an earlier Berlin looked like (established in *Hitler's Children* with period newsreel footage) was less than certain. Once we had the postwar movies—some more like travelogues than they ought to have been—it took Billy Wilder's *One, Two, Three* to give us a new mythic Berlin, much of it in the old studio back-projected manner. And a Scorsese to make Manhattan artificial again (*New York, New York*). Another turn: subjective concentration on locations and carefully matched sets in *Taxi Driver* artificialized into a new shape for Nowhere; soundstage sets did the same for *New York, New York*.

Nowheresville raises another question: beyond the visual trope of the empty Great West where can movies be set when they want to depict Nowhere? or a significant Anywhere? *The Last Picture Show* and *Bonnie and Clyde* suggest that West Texas is a candidate for this, a survival perhaps of a bit of that feeling which attaches to Texas West of the Pecos, Judge Roy Bean Country. And the flats of Death Valley (*Greed, Blowup*), the heartless metropolis of L.A. high-rises, or the empty-streets menace of burned-out New York borough (*Fort Apache, the Bronx, The French Connection*). Nowhere is Dorothy's Kansas (*The Wizard of Oz* and *Return to Oz*): three straight lines with a tornado reaching down from the top through the middle to the bottom. A more articulate version of this is the several places certain in *Badlands* which that movie and its skillful voiceover make into expansive metaphors for an empty and lonesome America.

Much of the search since World War II for new locations has brought us potential for new generic landscapes, but few have caught on.[3] *Wise Blood* and *Southern Comfort* set up an expectation for rural Georgia and some new uses for the South, but it hasn't developed. Probably this failure is a consequence of the Southern Picture hangover, a powerful subgenre by no means dead. The antebellum Southern Picture from *Gone With the Wind* to *Mandingo* is perhaps the more familiar half of this double subgenre, but Faulkner, Tennessee Williams, Robert Penn Warren, and the Southern Literary Renaissance led to a New South Picture—*Baby Doll* and *The Long, Hot Summer* and *The Story of Temple Drake* and even *Night of the Hunter*—and these in turn promoted a new Southern Gothic Horror—*Hush, Hush, Sweet Charlotte* and *Suddenly Last Summer* and, in a way, *Deliverance* (the South really *has* swamps). Blacks had to be (needless to say) done in a different way. Don Siegel's *The Beguiled* is a brilliant blend of bellum and New Southern Gothic suspicion (in its attitude toward incest, for instance).

New York is too big a generic problem to do justice to, but Washington is simpler. The format is established by the Costume Pictures (*Tennessee Johnson, Gorgeous Hussy, Santa Fe Trail, They Died with Their Boots on, Wilson, Mission to Moscow, Ten Gentlemen From West Point*). Frank Capra does what no one else could do: he makes legislators human and their limestone city real in *Mr. Smith Goes to Washington*, as surely as Preminger objectifies them in *Advise and Consent*. World War II makes the place untidy in *The More the Merrier*. *The French Connection* uses Washington's open spaces as Nowhere. Only recently some of the values (in *Being There, All the President's Men, No Way Out, Suspect*) particularly associated with *place* have emerged. *The Day the Earth Stood Still*, of course, moves the Washington Picture into the future.

Hitchcock understood Washington and gave us that knowledge in a single shot: Robert Walker stands on the steps of the Jefferson Memorial watching Farley Granger's car pull out of sight in *Strangers on a Train*. We watch Walker as Granger does, receding, a scary solitary figure against a sterile monument.

Hitchcock here, as with everything else he does, is a special case but perhaps a case in point. Like Ford he knows that it is necessary to understand what place certain can do (*Saboteur, Vertigo, North by Northwest, Strangers on a Train, Frenzy, I Confess, To Catch a Thief, Foreign Correspondent, The Lodger, Blackmail, The Thirty-nine Steps, The Man Who Knew Too Much* I and II) before taking up the placeless (*Psycho, The Birds, Rear Window, Rope,* or *Family Plot*, a seamless blend of the Los Angeles and the San Francisco movie which results in mutual cancellation of place certain). In a sense no Hitchcock film is really *within* place-genre or really without place (Bodega Bay of *The Birds*), even as no Ford film belongs in any genre but the genre of the Fordian. The Master-genre of the Hitchcockian overwhelms all other genre in his movies and Hitchcockian always *seems* possible to find on a map, notwithstanding that it is mostly the product of artificial filmic device. In some of his high points —the Statue of Liberty (*Saboteur*), Mount Rushmore (*North by Northwest*), the British Museum (*Blackmail*)—the artificializing of the familiar physical landmarks is made into a new kind of visual allegory and we realize what mastery of place and space and volume is involved in place certain. He makes a familiar picture postcard (*Frenzy*'s opening) into a new terrain to explore. And it's all tricks. Hitchcock knows that persuading us we are in a place certain is far more important than shooting in a place certain.

But when we move in the taxicab from Cary Grant's office to the Plaza Hotel or along the Hudson River in the train ride to Chicago in *North by Northwest,* or on the train between Washington and Forest Hills in *Strangers on a Train,* we are as effectively exposed to artifice as we are to the factual geographical certainties, even as we move toward Bodega Bay or off the main road toward the Bates Motel (the Baltimore of *Marnie* and the placelessness of Bodega Bay in *The Birds* are both the product of perfect glass shots and matte work).

If places certain were no more than travelogues neither the

extraordinarily pleasurable masterworks of Hitchcock nor the ordinarily pleasing *Late Show* would be possible. Or if genres were nothing more than cowboys and kissing movies.

The Florida Movie is distinctive if attenuated, and I think it is a place genre independent of Southern. It seems to be getting more prevalent of late (*Gator, Porky's, Scarface* (II), *Night Moves*). Drugs and Cubans, great wealth and sexual corruption now dominate. What made the Florida Movie such an odd duck to start with (*Coconuts*) was that Hollywood thought of Florida as somehow its rival for the public's affections, and this rivalry set the Florida Movie off center. Maybe it's the way movies about television were in the Forties and Fifties, as opposed to the way movies about movies were a bit earlier: the portable-swamp phenomenon functions in the Florida Movie —tending to stories of Ozark-like Redneck isolation (*Wind Across the Everglades, The Yearling, Gator Bait*), or tales of land greed (*Empire of the Ants*, in which the giant ants attack in Florida but eat their prey and spray their pheromones in Southern California), or wide-open gangster stuff (*Key Largo*) and drug stuff (*Scarface* II, *Night Moves, Blue City*). Some of these are no more Florida movies than *Ella Cinders* is an L.A. Movie, but their common concerns suggest there is such a thing as place-genre. *Distant Drums* is Costume, *Dead Reckoning* is Crime, or near-Noir. But Coppola puts a Florida movie into *Godfather II*, TV tables in the the sun-deprived Florida Room of Hyman Roth. And *Health* is a Florida Movie.

Road Pictures did not all star Hope and Crosby. *Easy Rider* is a Road Picture (one thing that makes its laissez-faire sense of geography so irritating). Road Pictures prove the point, not just of place certain and Nowheresville, but of the power of interchangeable parts. In *Vanishing Point* Barry Newman heads west from place certain. In the desert he becomes less and less interested in delivering the car (even with the obsession of driving a heavy car a long distance[4]) than with the Nowhere of the Desert and its nutty Sixties inhabitants. His inevitable death (or, as it turns out, transfiguration) comes at the hands of stupid and venal State Cops. He hits the roadblock (the assembled plow-fronts of payloaders) and disappears. In *The Gauntlet* Clint Eastwood sets out to deliver from place certain to place certain a prisoner to testify at a mob trial, discovering along the way that the cops he works for are more of a threat to him than the mob members she'll help to convict. The structure is that of the picaresque novel, but in film, instances of both Action/Adventure and Comedy that take this form tend to concentration (Self, Hero, Quest) rather than diffusion, as in the Picaresque. Heroes fall in love or undergo male bonding in these movies. Prevalence of the American Desert in Road Pictures perhaps drags Quest Picture over from Westerns this scenery evokes and adds it to this spunky little genre. *Two for the Road* is a Road Picture about love, Martin Scorsese's *After Hours* and William Friedkin's *The French Connection* are urban Road Pictures that take place mostly on foot. *Badlands* is a Road Picture of domestic violence, *It Happened One Night* is a Madcap Heiress Road Picture, *Midnight Run* is without doubt the best recent Road Picture, although the genre appeals to contemporary directors. John Hughes's *Trains, Planes, and Automobiles*, Jonathan Demme's *Something Wild* and a significant prelude to *Melvin and Howard, Mad Max Beyond Thunderdome, The Sure Thing; Silver Streak*, and *Runaway Train*, as well as *The General* are Road Pictures about trains.

There is a Hartford Movie: *Parrish*. Makes Hartford look like Madison Avenue. And, I suppose, *The Adventures of Mark Twain*, although the Hartford place is nowhere made certain *or* expansive. There are a lot of short New Haven Pictures (*Valley of the Dolls, Night and Day, All About Eve, Splendor in the Grass*) that show consistency in brief place-fragments: Gothic architecture, pizza parlors, singing at night.

More significant than such unglamorous places certain are big categories of place so powerful they can be thought of as whole genres (the Desert, the Mountains, the Jungle, Outer Space). The Desert is seen in a lot of readily classifiable genre formats: War, Empire, Women's, Musical, Thriller, Western, Costume. But when men and women are trapped there, the larger genres are forgotten and the actions and timing are dictated by other genres (War, Swashbuckler, Women's, Costume, Musical, Comedy, and oddments like *Captains Courageous* and *The Old Man and the Sea*—Fishing Movies, I guess: there's a Fishing Movie in *Jaws*, *To Have and Have Not*, *The Breaking Point*, *Jaws II*, and a little one in *Lord Love a Duck*). The Mountains never quite catch on as firmly (*The White Tower*, *The Eiger Sanction*); only *The White Hell of Pitz Palu* stands out in my memory, and that's not even American.

The Frozen North is an odd but (like the Cuban Musical Number) strangely plentiful glob of genre, probably its own. There is a Penguin Movie (*Cry of the Penguins*), Eskimo Movie (*The Savage Innocents*), and even a Sniper Movie (*The Quarry*). There's *The Call of the Wild* and *The Fatal Glass of Beer* and *The Gold Rush*. The South Seas, the Jungle (War, Women's, Tarzan, Costume, Musical, Professional) are early independent genres —and probably each does something completely new. Like the Desert, each makes its own generic shape out of borrowed pieces with which it festoons the all-consuming location.

*Things to Come* and *Destination Moon* are design triumphs of imagining the unimaginable. But since 1957 and Sputnik, Outer Space has had an amazing expansion and evolution. *2001* makes a spiritual center where perhaps none exists, but a commendable bit of generic pioneering nonetheless. The Jules Verne strain (*Journey to the Center of the Earth*, *The Time Machine*, *20,000 Leagues Under the Sea*) makes a retro trip of time-travel, trying to combine in an ironic view Verne's factual ignorance of space and our relative sophistication about it (see chapter 1, New Things). *Alien*, *Aliens*, and *Outland* move a new age toward our own—space trash, the junkiness of space (in the

Seventies) now that its presence and our presence in it have become banal. The place of dreams has been supplanted by the familiar pessimism.

---

Places are different from Professions. It's the difference between characters and setting, but more. Places give potentials for action; Professions set ground rules. Professions are a subgeneric ground bass to genres, genre units, fragments, parts. As I suggested in chapter 2, the Inventor Movie is tied in strange ways both to Mad Doctor and to Composer. The Composer (And Then We Wrote) in turn ties itself to Costume and to Musical (as does Singer and Actor and Band Leader and Ballerina). Journalists early and late were tied to *The Front Page* format—this movie probably has more credited and uncredited versions than any other shape—together with *Dracula* it's a genre-freezing work of art.

Moviemaker is its own genre, and Star (*The Oscar, Sunset Boulevard, The Legend of Lylah Clare, The Goddess, The Star, A Star is Born, Mommie Dearest, The Big Knife*), as is Doctor and Academic, but Doctor is tied to Women's by the frequency with which they cross (*Magnificent Obsession, Dark Victory, Woman Obsessed, Not as a Stranger*). Psychiatrist is different (*Now, Voyager, The Shrike, Spellbound*) and ties to psychological thriller and suspense. And because of the low esteem in which our culture holds intellectuals Academic is almost always comic (*Horse Feathers, Animal House, Bringing Up Baby, Getting Straight, The Lady Eve, Ball of Fire, A Song Is Born*).

Soldier and Sailor and Marine are a part of War, even though there are instances between the Wars in which these have an independent generic nature (*Hell Below, Submarine D-1, Hell Divers, China Seas*). Spy is tied to Thriller (*Secret Agent, Five Fingers*). It and Detective, Cop, Lawyer, Thief, Killer, are a part of Crime, although there have been some signs that Lawyer (partly through the influence of television) might take off on its own. Lawyer is certainly an ingredient in the Conspiracy

Picture, a Crime subgenre coming on strong since the Kennedy assassination (*The Domino Principle, The Killer Elite, The Parallax View, The Kremlin Letter, Winter Kills*).

Ad-Man had a brief vogue in the days of the Gray Flannel Suit and the Huckster. Professional Rich Man is a pursuit in itself, a staple of Comedy, Western, Women's, Musical, and Costume, specialized in by everyone from Rudy Vallee to Buster Keaton. In each of these genres the "profession" of rich man finds a different role (*The Navigator, Duel in the Sun, The Set-Up, Funny Lady, Lola Montes, Trading Places, Diamond Jim, Arthur*). Restaurateur oddly ties to both Women's (*Mildred Pierce*) and Gangster (*Scarface* I), but can be found all over the place—in Adventure (*Only Angels Have Wings, Raiders of the Lost Ark*), Costume (*Unconquered, Ten Gentleman From West Point, Forever Amber*), and Musical (*Holiday Inn*). Madams have their firmest base in Western and Costume, although Women's is littered with Madams and ex-whores, as are latter-day War and Crime. Politics and Government Service (as I suggested about the Washington Picture) is a problem haunted by the spectre of *Wilson* and graced by Frank Capra and Otto Preminger (*State of the Union, Mr. Smith Goes to Washington, Advise and Consent*), given its ultimate *Walpurgisnacht* by the Marx Brothers in *Duck Soup*.

More teasing than these easy ones are some tough cases. Why do movies think of Sculptors as solemn (*The Agony and the Ecstasy*), when magazine cartoons see them as funny? Why are architects (*The Fountainhead, Towering Inferno*) blessed with a sacred calling in movies—or else reduced to murdering the residents of their buildings by the use of shoddy materials? Architects turn allegorical on their own (perhaps with a little help from Henrik Ibsen), probably for some of the same reasons that Professor and Doctor and Lawyer become allegorical —or, really, generic—rather than descriptive.

Why are Playwrights figures of compromise (*All About Eve, Author! Author!*), Actors creatures of vanity and excess (*Sudden*

*Fear, Stage Fright, A Double Life*), and Actor-Directors (*The Band Wagon*) worst of all? Painters paint in ways they never would (*The Agony and the Ecstasy, Prince of Foxes, The Picture of Dorian Gray, Lust for Life, The Moon and Sixpence*) but they do spend quite a bit of time doing it. Painting is a process (*The Horse's Mouth, The Picture of Dorian Gray, Prince of Foxes*) seen in the clear images of successive stages and developing completion; process is always present, even when stages of that process make no sense at all out of how you go about making a painting.

Not so Writers, always treated so foolishly by movies—even good movies—unless they are Journalists, folks of action. Most writers I know testify that they have never, not once, ripped a sheet out of their typewriters, crumpled it, and thrown it on the floor, or broken their pencil deliberately (except when talking to their agents on the telephone, never while writing). *Youngblood Hawke* gives us a world of swank garret studios in Brooklyn Heights, a cocktail party at which a critic, having apparently committed his critique to memory, succumbs to a popular clamor that he recite it in the author's presence. *Rich and Famous*, although it does pretty well on the accidentals of success (most notably seen in Candice Bergen's wardrobe and apartment), has a terrible time showing us Jacqueline Bisset's work beyond the National Book Award Committee meetings and what she Has To Say About It. And this is a good movie. Worse jobs are done in *The Great Gatsby* II or *The Adventures of Mark Twain* or *The Bride of Frankenstein* (it has Lord Byron). In *Mark Twain* a Tom and Huck about the size of Teenie-Weenies or Puppet People foregather on Twain's writing desk to urge him forward (but it turns out It Was Only a Dream). George Sand (*A Song to Remember*) wants us to think she's a more serious artist than Chopin but she doesn't seem to work nearly as hard. George M. Cohan in *Yankee Doodle Dandy* is shown writing music to words but never seems to get around to writing the book to go with these songs. *The World According to Garp*

does in the typewriter scene one thing well: it renders the loneliness of that lonely craft, and it shows that longhand is no
way to travel, but it does nothing much to distinguish the
mother's work from the son's except to note that she has it
easy and he has it hard—like Bergen and Bisset in *Rich and
Famous*. Both can see their books in the show window (see
*Suspicion*) and talk to their publishers. They don't seem to need
agents.

Or why is it *not* thought absurd for the critic to be shown
reciting his column when we can't watch the writer writing
but only ripping ruined sheets out of the machine, blocked
again? Forest Rangers and Fishermen and Salvage Workers and
Grocers and Linemen work, even Office Workers (how much
more do we know about Janet Leigh's work in *Psycho* than we
do about James Franciscus's in *Youngblood Hawke*?). Probably
Writers are shown only when frustrated because movies think
writing is a sacred mystery—or because screenwriters think
fiction writers are so good and holy that when they come to
depict the act of writing (beyond, of course, that wonderful
fiction of the ripped-out page), they fear they might vulgarize
the holy mystery. Or they think its words aren't action. Surely
they cannot think they aren't work.

I have written of the problems in silver-screen science (in
chapters 2 and 3); there's some of the same difficulty with computer whizzes. Either the movie wants to show us Young Tom
Sawyer at the keyboard (*Jumping Jack Flash*) or bore us to death
showing illegible screen formats (*Rollover*) or make computers
into a kind of black magic or crime (*Power, War Games, The
Fly*). The presentation seems to be at its best early on (*2001*),
and in decline now that computers have become a household
appliance.

In a sense the root of my complaint has an easy explanation:
as I already said, some things are easy to show visually,
generically—others are difficult. But is it easier to drive a locomotive than to write a short story? Buster Keaton shows us

how to drive a train and if we tried our hand at it just after watching *The General* we at least would not wreck the locomotive. Or fly a jet, better narrated by *Firefox* than is the writing of Franciscus's second novel in *Youngblood Hawke*. Perhaps more to the point, take the computer simulations of *2001*, *Tron*, or *Rollover*.

The professions crisscross traditional genres as place-genres do. To understand them will not help us to understand genre's ability to categorize and make art common and accessible for all, but they can help us to understand how genre is made. For genre is not a category or basket into which we can dump whole movies, but composed of discrete pieces which used in one combination may make a Western, in another add up to a Musical, in a third, mix it all up and become Western/Musical/Women's/Horror—body parts for which the connective tissue —not the parts—frequently decides the result.

---

Place and profession rest on our sense of real things in our supposedly real world. Ritual is an attempt to reach beyond this world, to make movies approach a world beyond our own. It is hardly new to point out that movies are filled with rituals. Much of the writing about Westerns (especially about John Ford) dwells on this. I suppose my own favorite undefined, open-ended ritual in film is *The Searchers*: a file of Indians (watching, waiting, they have time) and a file of whites under Ward Bond's command ride parallel, each file taking the progressive, dynamic form of the land forms they pass across, heads in relationship to land and hills and sky in a pursuit that doesn't need to/doesn't dare to run.

But another just as arresting (and I am trying to spread the definition of ritual to include some unconventional elements) is the hanging (or rather, near-hanging) of Robert Harron in *Intolerance*. Even in this silent, the audience already knows what events leading up to an execution by hanging will be included—the priest in the cell, confession and communion, the long march to the gallows, hesitation at the foot of the steps, the hood for the head, guards and wardens and clocks and watches. But like the blanks in the firing squad's rifles in other movie executions, here there is an odd element of official anonymity introduced: guards are lined up, each with a razor poised over a triggering string, all to cut at once, none to know whose cut string will sever the life only a few feet away. The hesitation of the razors over the strings is metaphorical, profoundly filmic, expressive at once of the guards' nervousness that they will have to do it and our fear lest reprieve will come too late (we see it on its way). It is so powerful that I find myself every time not knowing if Harron will be spared or not.

In a sense such rituals—times out of life, moments of suspension, cosmic hesitations, reaches beyond—are what we come to the movies for. We seek to watch a bettered life, sloppiness and meaninglessness resolved by clear framing and clearer cuts. Ritual in movies conducts a higher discourse: just this much shall I show you, and just for this long, then no more, it seems to say, but see my power. Rituals confront characters and communications with another world. In other words, as ritual is to these participants, so are movies to us out there in the dark.

Rituals are also superchases, generic elements with multiple potential to bond themselves to other elements in the picture and beyond the picture, connections capable of revealing to us distant meaning, or of connecting very efficiently elements of a movie with other elements—its own, or those from other movies. Ritual is something movies learned from plays, more remotely from grand opera, more remotely still from the Greeks and from religion—movements, gestures, timings and involvements with carefully chosen spaces that speak to something beyond this work, beyond their world on the screen or ours down here in the dark.

Busby Berkeley moves us up in the air in what may be the most ritualistic of all camera gestures, an overhead shot of a big number. What we watch in Berkeley's movies is carefully planted bits of rehearsals, phrases of song. We remember well other Berkeley numbers we have seen. But when we move up above them we know we have arrived in a sky of pure expression, a Never-Never geometry of near-identical women, choreographed and geometricized beyond body and crowd into a wonderful dynamic mosaic. Even without the climactic seal of this shot, Michael Bennett was able to steal the Berkeley ritual for the finale of *A Chorus Line*. We knew where they were headed, but we didn't really know how good it would be when they got there until we saw it for ourselves. Places and professions give local habitation and name to sets of generic conditions that go with each territory; rituals take us out of such situational determination and most surely connect to other rituals we have seen, on the screen or wherever. And movies are so innocently/guiltily powerful that in Riefenstahl's *The Triumph of the Will* Hitler and his deacon and subdeacon, just for a moment, approach the high altar of Nazidom with our almost automatic collaboration by virtue of the camera's borrowed spatial gesture and the familiar grooves of movie ritual.

Initiation into the male companionship rituals of the flyers' enclave of *Only Angels Have Wings*—not speaking the name of the dead pilot, going ahead and eating the steak he ordered before he crashed, the two-headed coin—are widened to admit Jean Arthur once she has herself proved professional with her singing and piano "specialty." In *His Girl Friday* Rosalind Russell is already well inside the male preserve (as she is in *Flight to Freedom* as Amelia Earhart). But ordinarily women move through rituals as decorative priestesses or talismanic virgins. In *Cobra Woman* beautiful women with slit skirts and high heels move through the clearing to an altar (that turns out to be a swimming pool) and our mind runs on, not to deacon or subdeacon or even to Wonder Woman, but rather to that posture of beauty queen that Esther Williams so perfected, graceful in the water by virtue of God and underwater photography, graceful on the land only with the help of posture training and the director's keen eye for ritual space, ritual passage, a ritual approach.

Something of this sort of timing, phasing, ritualization, is present throughout movies. Our recognition of what is likely to come next is anticipated in a ritual unit, made completer than the dramaturgy of a play's or novel's denouement ever could be because we watch it in *their* space, the space of these realized figments. The Cossacks move down on the Jews as we had been told they did, as we heard they might, as we knew it would be. The Indian threatens the white child with a cold expression conveying by the immediate cut that follows or by the shadow falling on the child, or by the silhouetting of the Indian against a glowing sky, a rape, a scalping, a capture more certain than we could get from a graphic representation. A simple rhythmic logic in these rituals is perfectly realized in the best of film, and works according to the laws of genre even in the worst. We move beyond their attendant movies and beyond imprisonment in the self.

# 6. BREATHING THROUGH A REED
## Prison and Escape

*"Whoever heard of a birthday party in a cellblock?"*
—Andrew Prine in *House of Women*

There is a wonderful Prison Picture near the middle of *White Heat*. Raoul Walsh (who made a few Prison Pictures in his time) finds new delights in old material: in the Machine Shop we see not only Cody Jarrett's disabling headache, Fallon's (played by Edmond O'Brien) big chance to cement his undercover buddyhood, we also see another inmate, in an Inside plot on Cody's life, drop a piece of heavy machinery on him and discover it was arranged by Steve Cochran, Cody's rival for leadership of his gang on the Outside. In the mess hall we get the sound of regimented seating, regimented eating, the whispered question down the table line and the answer back that Cody's mother is dead, his resultant headache and fit of violence, as he stands on a table like a fire-crazed Frankenstein's Monster and takes on prisoners and guards alike in a punching spree. On visiting day we have a deaf crony of Cody's (incidentally having a great conversation with a shyster) engaged to lip-read Fallon's phony wife the Treasury men have sent in to communicate with Fallon. But perhaps best, there is an Escape Picture within this Prison Picture that has pretty nearly everything one could want. Cody has been declared insane and is in sick bay awaiting the visit of the psychiatrists who will commit him to Another Kind of Institution. His buddy, a trusty sent to feed him in his strait-jacket, smuggles him a gun as Doctor, Guard, Psychiatrist, and Another Psychiatrist—each and every one—is shown to be, as if by chance, busy looking away from the trusty passing the gun to Cody. There follows the successful getaway ("Get in the back and act loony"). There is something in the deliberate artifice of this passage that seems to me essential in the Prison and Escape Picture: the allegiance and empathy structures are so tried and sure that calling them up seems to have a ritual rather than just an informational character. We sing along with the folks on screen.

This is one reason the Prison Picture is so curiously mercurial. Prison is an independent genre within the Crime Group: the Escape Picture is a function of Prison. But we can also find Escape and Prison in almost any other kind of picture: and there they take on their own form and function (the escapes of *White Heat* or *The Count of Monte Cristo* or *The Mackintosh Man* or the escape sequence of *The Hurricane*; the Prison Pictures of *The Adventures of Robin Hood* and *Bringing Up Baby*)—genre units which seem to drag the rest of these movies out of their given genres and into Prison or Escape. The Prisoner-of-War Picture is a nearly independent subgenre of the War Movie and is also oddly independent of Prison Pictures in general. Evidently being imprisoned for a national cause changes the ground rules profoundly, even as being condemned to death does ("Concentrates" the "mind wonderfully," says Doctor Johnson). The Death-Row Picture seems to be independent of Prison, and although it seems illogical, Death-Row seems to make most sense as a category of the Women's Film (*I Want to Live!*, *Intolerance*, *The Book of Daniel*, *A Tale of Two Cities*). Because the genre is so mercurial, to bring all of these classification categories—genre, subgenre, genre unit, subject matter—back together for discussion under the rubric of Prison and Escape may be a good idea. There are similarities and relationships between one category and the next that come to be of particular note just when they fail to bridge these mysterious gaps: it's a genre which seems as interesting for things that do *not* work the way other genres do as it is for things that do. Why should Prisoner-of-War differ so profoundly? How can something as dire as a jail cell be so often used in Comedy or Musical? The Prison Picture fails to unite itself, so seems different from other genres. But it has great power when it turns up in those other genres, as does Escape.

The first question about Prison is a poser: Why should anybody want to watch a Prison Picture? There is a simple answer: as Hitchcock says, we all hate cops and fear imprisonment from childhood (although few of us had a father as bent on convincing us of this as Hitchcock's was).[1] I think it's more complex. I think we want to watch for some of the reasons we want to watch a Werewolf Picture: if I had to be a con, how would I act? As during World War II children would say to each other (or to themselves), If I have to be a refugee, what should I take with me? In other words, coming into the movie we have made a big fantasy jump, from the certainty of unjust accusation, trial, and imprisonment (even as in the Werewolf we feel strange powers without having to recall we were bit by a large vicious animal). Prison seems to be powerful in the geography of the imagination—the world of Just Suppose—even if we never pursue it far enough to know what crime has put us there. Guilt probably has something to do with it, and paranoia. (Why should guilt be adduced here rather than in the Western? or in the Women's, which much more frequently than the Prison Picture turns on guilt?) But almost as certainly it's something about our need to feel unique, one, only. This is strongly invoked as we watch a Prison Picture. I think we have an almost spiritual need for such a thing as Prison Pictures: not just because we are all guilty, but because we all have a nagging fear of universal unjust punishment.

The mechanical uses of Prison Pictures are perhaps more

difficult to sort out. Prison—or Inside, as they call it—is so surely a world independent from Outside that how one got there doesn't really matter except as it provides the prisoner with an identity card, credentials for the Inside similar to money and power in the Outside World. Murderers are kept at arm's length because they have nothing to lose; child molesters are (generally) shunned; burglars are chummy. We sometimes watch the check-in routine (nowhere more tellingly than in *Escape From Alcatraz*, climaxed by the Horror lightning flash); check-in signals the passage from Outside to In. Getting there can be attended by all the initiations and familiarizing routines we find in the draftee routines of the early World War II Combat films. After the check-in comes staying on (making terms with, settling into Inside—prison society). Eventually the movie sometimes gets to the point of Getting Out (by release, pardon, escape, or death).

Inside is an absolutist world, because its rules are binding, artificial but final, like those of the Desert (not enough water, mirage/delusion, great distance, rescuers that fail to spot you, the blinding sun, the cold at night) or of the Army, or of the Army in the Desert. Absolutism spreads through every part of the Prison Picture. He was driven to suicide, they say, as we see the shadow of suspended feet in the cell (*Brute Force*). The routine of the day makes this point more clearly than similar routine does in other genres: getting up, meals, exercise, social time in the cell, work time at the jute mill (*The Big House*), road crews (*Cool Hand Luke, I Am a Fugitive from a Chain Gang, The Hurricane*), machine shop or laundry (*White Heat, Brute Force*), sewing machine or home-ec class (*Hold Your Man*), social time in the cell (*Women's Prison, House of Women, Brute Force, White Heat,* etc.), and bed check (*Escape From Alcatraz*). Routines are the glue for the events of each individual movie, the convention of routine is a supportive structure for passing the time. Breaks in the routine—visits with the warden (in *Brute Force, Escape From Alcatraz, House of Women, Women's Prison*), visits to the Infirmary (*White Heat*), and (more important) Visiting Day (in virtually all titles)—loom almost as large in structuring generic shape.

Character is perhaps as important in Prison and Escape as it is in Western or Costume (see chapter 1), maybe even more so than in War, a genre which it sometimes closely otherwise resembles. The cast of characters is too diverse to be surely categorized but some types emerge again and again. The Warden is seen in two varieties: Old Warden (kindly) and New Warden (cruel) (*Birdman of Alcatraz, Escape From Alcatraz, Brubaker*). His Deputy or Executive Assistant is frequently (in the event of a kindly or ineffectual Warden) something of a Nazi (*Women's Prison, Brute Force*). The Guards or Screws are good, bad, strong, weak, corruptible (*Birdman, Brute Force*). Parole Board and visiting psychiatrists are something like the witnesses for executions, more possessed of their lives Outside than they are interested in what's going on Inside (*House of Women*). Reporters wait outside or are on investigative missions as significant as the lawyers' quests for new evidence (*Birdman, I Want to Live!*). The doctor is either rigid (he's on to those malingerers) or a bleeding heart (useful for escape) or both (*White Heat, House of Women*). The chaplain is a weak link, useful in escape or a sympathetic ear. He is, of course, a constant companion on Death Row (*Intolerance, I Want to Live!*). The society of Prisoners is certainly more attractive than the institution's Establishment. The Head Honcho is probably riding for a fall (especially in recent rape-conscious Prison Pictures, *Scarecrow*, for instance). The Young Blood in the old days was always asking for it, just waiting for his comeuppance (*Brute Force, Riot in Cell Block 11*). These days he quails before the inevitable, almost initiational ritual gang rape. The Nance is quite often an assistant to the Doctor, and useful for escape (*White Heat* and in the prisoner-of-war hospitals: *The Bridge on the River Kwai, King Rat, Empire of the Sun*), or a friend who may warn a con he is about to be attacked with some kind of homemade weapon (*Escape From Alcatraz*). The Inventor most frequently is found working on escape attempts (*Bad Boys*). The Boxer tends to be a Good Guy (*Runaway Train*). The Undercover Cellmate is generally not sympathetically drawn (see the complex instance in Edmond O'Brien's stellar performance as Fallon in *White Heat*). The Dealer can obtain anything for a price (see Eaglebauer, chapter 7, or Milo Minderbinder of Joseph Heller's *Catch-22* or King in *King Rat*). There is an Old Man (*Escape From Alcatraz*) who has been here so long that he knows how to get around the customs and rules of the Inside society and is a law unto himself. Then some of these functions can get mixed: in *White Heat* the Old Man is the deaf communicator of the underground grapevine because he can read lips; the Old Man of *Escape From Alcatraz* is an artist, matching his abstraction from the system with an abstraction from the prison's rehabilitative work. In that movie the Nance is a Mouse-Keeper. The cruel warden of *Escape From Alcatraz* is a lot like the second-in-command of *Women's Prison*. Then there are the kids, the traitors, Good Blacks, Boss Blacks, pushers or suppliers, former Messrs. Big, power brokers, lawyers and other messengers from the power structure Outside.

We spend our time Inside learning the ropes, outwitting the screws, scheming the riot or plotting the escape or countering the revenge. We talk to shyster lawyers ("You couldn't get me off if I was pardoned"[2]), girlfriends and wives and fake girlfriends and wives (for the undercover cops), and tend pets (cockroaches, mice, rats, birds). But with all this activity and company, with the routines and the powerful spiritual camaraderie that is ours as soon as the great steel doors close behind us, it still comes down to that question, Why would we choose to spend our time in a Prison Picture?

I think some of the appeal of these movies is connected with the Depression. The empathy for the inmates the movies of the Thirties seem to demand of us is different in kind from, say, *Birdman of Alcatraz, Riot in Cell Block 11*, or *Escape from Alcatraz*. We may be following someone we know is a criminal (George Raft in *The Big House*) or someone we know is innocent: the movies seem to have in common an assumption that we will ally ourselves with whatever the inmates plot—escape, revenge, murder, or whatever. In later movies (after *Riot in Cell Block 11*) this seems not to be the case. The recent failure of one television series (*A Place Named Mariah*) and the appalling racism of another (the Fox Network's *Women's Prison*) might suggest that the audience's sympathy for cons, willingness to go vicariously to jail is now less useful or responsive to our needs than it once was. As with some other genres, the oneness of our then-unified society in the Depression seems to bear a lot of weight in this matter.

But perhaps more significant than this is how the prison geography works upon us. A genre doesn't (as I have said before in these pages) enable bad movies. It enables both bad and good, but more important, it enables us to make new movies in our heads. Its patterns produce expectations as we recognize this generic element or that. Any set of expectations makes possible a happy surprise when a good movie comes along that can surprise us with variations, new imaginary rules, and new exceptions to the rules, rules we could never have imagined before we saw this movie. As soon as we see the light shafting down upon the cells (in those grand glass shots, projections, painted drops, and sometimes even fully realized sets, in latter days even prisons themselves, *Point Blank*, for instance) we are prepared for the routines, the characters, the exercise period, escape attempts, assaults, riots we have seen before. Our empathetic imprisonment is accomplished by the genre's mechanical signals.

Some of this is not very different from High School Pictures: limited places to go: the halls and lockers, the stairways, the gym, cafeteria, classrooms, playing fields, band room, shop.

P R I S O N: Melodramatic architecture, *The Big House*, 1930

Prison is similar, except that activities undertaken in prison are under more severe limitations. The possibilities of the cell, once explored, become a concentration of our attention; we measure the steps to the infirmary, or in the yard, or down the hall and toward the Chair. When we come to something we have successfully anticipated, we have expected it because of a collaboration between generic hints and recognitions with a strictly organized geography.

What happens that we did not expect is probably another clue to why we can like Prison Pictures. We do not have to be masochists to anticipate discipline or punishment: it comes with being a kid. Since this is a world separated from the Outside, the outwitting of screws and regulations and wardens is a part of what happens we could not have expected. Another part is that Prison is so free of the Outside it can become a surreal fantasy world of threat. And violence, abuse, and torture.

The Inside has, as anyone who has even visited a prison can attest, absolutely nothing to do with Prison Pictures, Hollywood's idea of prison. But Prison Pictures are as popular Inside as War Pictures were with Douglas A. MacArthur. Their fantasy works on the same wave length as the cons' reality operates upon, so that the excess in the movies is evidently recognizable to those Inside subjected to the real thing.

This surreal fantasy is released in a peculiarly powerful way when women come on the scene. Prison has as strong a connection to the Women's Film as Doctors and Hospitals do: it is a part of the many Nemeses that hover just out of sight in that brooding, haunted world of Women's Pictures. But when women come to prison there is a rich vein of irrational event. In the first place, the Matrons are visions of Mother (or rather Stepmother) as dreamt by the punished child. In *Hold Your Man* the many matrons seem to have been enrolled in some mad religious order, clanking about complete with uniform capes. It is an image of woman in charge not that far removed from *Rebecca*'s Mrs. Danvers, each with keys she will not let out of her sight. *Women's Prison* gives us Ida Lupino's definitive Matron, a vision out of Nazi lore, keys at the waist, smart skirt snapping, and eyes to go with it. Her cruelty is as much the product of our imagination, the product of the discipline that's gone into her characterization, as it is of anything she actually does.

The presence of women also brings about a strange geography. In *Women's Prison* the Women's Prison is oddly hooked on to the Men's by a narrow corridor we can just barely see into. So that when a man escapes, it is, of course, a husband of one of the female inmates, escaping only to reincarcerate himself in the laundry of the Women's Prison, where he manages to impregnate, of all people, his wife. Women's Picture has to collaborate with the Code to come to such an irrational development. But the Code is perhaps generic, itself a lot like Prison Pictures, too: absolute punishment is meted out for committing an infraction, however slight, while clever dancers go free. Jean Harlow's prison in *Hold Your Man* rehabilitates the girls much as high school might, with home ec classes far grander than high school, a stove for each and every girl, and special uniforms to wear for that class only. The girls probably make cupcakes, too. In *House of Women* trusties go to work as housewives for the Warden. But then, this is an extraordinary institution: children (usually a central, sometimes offscreen feature to the Women's elements of Women's Prison Pictures) are Inside and there is a birthday party ("Who," the Warden asks, all too disingenuously, "ever heard of a birthday party in a cellblock?"). Strange, but no stranger than us sitting there watching it all, with delight. It's probably the only picture to turn on defacing of a photo of Troy Donahue, too. Only in the Prison Picture.

In these pictures Outside is run up against Inside. But there is a reversal. The faithful woman waiting outside the walls of

Folsom Prison is, if condemned to prison, faithful in a different way when she's Inside, taking the punishment meant for Her Man, or the punishment which never would have been hers had it not been for him. For the Prison Picture, Outside is a world in which money can be made and life can go on, but when Prison is mixed with Women's, Outside is a vale of tears: life goes on Inside but it is more of the same she had Outside (*Hold Your Man*). Outside is more clearly coextensive with Inside in the Women's Prison Picture. The female convict has scarcely more hope once she gets out that she will ever escape what? her lot? the sentence she has chosen for herself? The most powerful image of Outside/Inside in men's Prison is the cons who still walk as if chained even after they are freed in *I Am a Fugitive from a Chain Gang*. This is in turn almost a metaphor for women convicts in movies, serving sentences, as they committed the crimes, for the sake of the rotten men in their lives.

Our attentions as audience are focused on the immediate solution of a problem, an engagement that becomes the spine for our empathy and allegiance. What is the problem to be solved in a Prison Picture? Generally the problem turns out to be an Inside problem. For *Birdman of Alcatraz* Burt Lancaster first sees the birds as companions, then as something like science. The function of the Telly Savalas character is that birds keep Robert Stroud (Burt Lancaster) from going coocoo. In prison the prevalent fear (and the frequent public nuisance) is madness: to protect one's self from it is the point of activity. In *Brute Force* cons combat cruel and vicious keepers to keep up their spirits and make it possible for them to go on. Outside problems—in *Brute Force* and *Women's Prison*—are sometimes resolved by suicide, which becomes an Inside problem of morale. Outside problems are sometimes adduced (*Bad Boys, Women's Prison, The Big House, White Heat*) as reasons for escape, and escape then becomes the problem to be solved. In *The*

*Onion Field* the autodidact lawyer (complete with steel-rimmed spectacles) pursues a different form of escape, legal redress. But there are more movies trying to deal with doing time than there are movies that deal with escape—spending the time, making it pass, finding some Inside occupation which will take the mind off what is out there.

---

The difference between this and life in the World War II Prisoner-of-War Camp is striking, although fear of madness is present there, too, and the frenzies of activity to ward it off take on, if anything, greater variety and ingenuity. In Prisoner-of-War Camp necessities are different because ground rules and the geography are different. In Prison Pictures escape is a resort of the very desperate or the very foolhardy. In POW camp it is everyone's duty. So in POW Pictures escape becomes one center of story, and (as with Prison Pictures in general) survival in this artificial society another. In POW, the Outside exercises greater control over Inside than in Prison Pictures. Military rank (an Outside value system) is strong and sometimes cuts through Prison's sense of a Different World. Only in *King Rat* does Outside military rank seem ineffectual. Probably this is to a point (both novelistic and filmic): to set up King for his comeuppance once the war is over and his whole system of economic and power dominance will disappear with the shortages that have empowered them. In *Bridge on the River Kwai* military rank, hierarchy, and the discipline that goes with it are shown up as mad. Colonel Bogey's need to keep order among the troops and his own sense of identity in captivity lead to his (mad) decision to drive his men to complete a Japanese military objective; morale-building is made literal: building the bridge, making its conflict more powerful as this comes to loggerheads with William Holden's and Jack Hawkins's mission to destroy the bridge. This leads to a perhaps too-pat paradox: does Alec Guinness leap for the explosives plunger because he realizes the folly of his ways, or fall on it accidentally (ironically) still not knowing the madness of his military rigor?

Geography imposes some other differences: generally Japanese camps are in the jungle, far from civilization (*The Bridge on the River Kwai, King Rat*), Nazi prisons are in castles (following the great tradition of *Grand Illusion*: *The Colditz Story, Escape from Colditz*) or in muddy woods (*Stalag 17*) or not far from the frontier (*Grand Illusion, The Great Escape*). Some Prison Pictures involving camps or military guards (*Cool Hand Luke, Scarecrow, I Am a Fugitive from a Chain Gang, Papillon, The Hurricane, Prisoner of Shark Island, We're No Angels*) parallel POW Films more closely than they do Prison Pictures, suggesting that geography—geography of living quarters in this case—*is* generically determinative. And perhaps something of the social matrix —maybe a hangover from *I Am a Fugitive from a Chain Gang*. So in POW we find a powerful subgeneric detail which can dominate more important subject matter and end up changing a picture's generic identity.

As escape is the center of attention in POW prisons, planning and scheming for it take over some functions of time-passing routines. John Sturges's *The Great Escape* is of course the great example of escape planning. In this movie Prison Picture meets Heist. The prime Heist Picture format is probably that of *Topkapi* (although the shape is present in earlier examples, it is probably at its most elegant finish here). The scheme is laid out in such a way that we as audience can be engaged in the details and process of each part of the heist —each participant's role in this teamwork effort unfolds as carefully planned and timed-out behavior which makes absolutely no sense without the addition of the Big Picture. So we watch each small part of the Master Plan building toward its own perfection still not really knowing if the single performance for which all this is rehearsal will work or not—or even knowing what the sequence of the various parts may be, how they fit together, what each will accomplish in relation to the whole. It is an ideal format for suspense, something I have called omission suspense in fictional narrative:[3] we know everything except the one or two details necessary for understanding, so we await the understanding that only performance can give. In *The Great Escape* these rehearsal/performance parts are enhanced even more by a series of last-minute crises: Donald Pleasence's blindness, Charles Bronson's claustrophobia, miscalculation of the length the tunnel must be. A simpler version of this is subtly worked in *Empire of the Sun*: Basie turns out to be charting out land mines when he sends Jim out for small animal trapping. So we have the thrill of worrying over Jim with the irony of Jim's devotion and slavish obedience to his mentor, all going for nought because the Japanese guard changes the nature of the suspense by catching a glimpse of Jim in the grass and then chooses to ignore him. The empathy patterns are similar. The elaboration of each part, then all parts in *The Great Escape* is parallel to this more particularized version.[4]

Escape, though, is probably far more significant in its occurrence beyond the limits of the Prison Picture and the POW subgenre. In Ford's *The Hurricane* we have an instance of a small Escape Picture that motivates the whole movie which contains it, a short Prison Picture with a stunning escape sequence which makes of a somewhat conventional South Seas Picture (or a pretty good Disaster Picture) an unforgettable generic triumph. Terangi, the native first mate of a white man's ship, free spirit of the islands, punches out a white man in a bar and his wimpish skipper turns him over to the civil authority. As the rest of the movie is concerned with the rigidity of deLaage's (played by Raymond Massey) civil authority as Governor, this is thematically apt. But as soon as Terangi gets to prison and meets the evil jailer (John Carradine) an ordinary thematic rehearsal is liberated by Ford's genius to become something much more powerful. Terangi takes a header off the cliff where he is on a road gang and tries to swim to his ship. Each attempt leads to viler and viler durance vile until we are sure his spirit is broken—he attempts suicide in his cell by hanging (shadow on the wall and all). But this is only a ruse for a final successful attempt, which leads to yet another escape under water in the local village where he is discovered stealing food and water from a store for the long canoe trip to his island. He does everything but breathe through a reed, and in a film notable for beautiful images, Ford goes even farther in giving us a flash on the knife as it cuts the canoe's moorings, reflections on the water, mists of obscurity, the guards' flashlights as they probe the store for a sign of Terangi.

Escape, like Horror, can turn up at any time and take over whatever is happening on the screen. Something of the same guilt which seems powerful for Prison Pictures must be operating on us. It is easier to understand why we want to watch Escape more than Prison. Escape sequences built into other films of some genre other than Prison (*Band of Angels, Objective, Burma! White Heat, The Stunt Man, The Adventures of Robin Hood, Robin and Marian*) are far more frequent than Escape Pictures (*A Man Escaped, The Great Escape, The Colditz Story, Victory*). Most of the Prison Pictures I have listed involve some kind of Escape sequence, but Escape does not dominate Prison in them. Perhaps it is our need to be cool operators, or look cool, and the movies' need to make us, empathetically, escape in a cool fashion, that is central to these films. We are very close to the escapees—I suppose as close as we ever are to identifying absolutely with what we see: pursuit is near, capture is menacing, our need to get away is just. This is the rich vein tapped by the popular television series *The Fugitive*. On the lam is how we imagine ourselves, and our skills and duplicities, our swiftness and cunning, are never more surely tested or more surely made parallel to the action on the screen.

Breaking the bonds usually comes first (see *I Am a Fugitive from a Chain Gang*). Contrary variations can be seen in *Sabotage*

P R I S O N: The beginning of an escape sequence: Paul Muni in
Mervyn LeRoy's *I Am a Fugitive from a Chain Gang*, 1932

and *The Stunt Man*: in the first Robert Cummings fools a blind
man (who turns out to have detected the handcuffs anyhow),
in the second the environs of a movie company on location
provide a perfect cover for the fugitive. Escape through the
swamp may come next. It can involve escape underwater (although this may come along at any time) featuring either holding the breath or breathing through a fortuitously discovered
reed, but water is also effective for deflecting the impact of
bullets by the fact (frequently established in Escape sequences
by underwater photography) that water damps bullets. Drying

out is next. There is also Confusion of identity by a friendly passerby (useful for Working Behind Enemy Lines in War and Espionage Pictures) and being forced by anxiety of pursuit to take on odd tasks and to assume role disguise (the impromptu political speech in *The 39 Steps*). Later come furtive reunion with a loved one and arrangement for safety abroad, with (along the way) close calls with authority and brushes with recapture. The best moment of all Escape (or perhaps even of all Prison) Pictures comes in *I Am a Fugitive from a Chain Gang* when, during such a furtive meeting the girl asks what he can do now to survive: "I steal," he says, and the light on the screen disappears, the happy accident of a power failure on the set that is, of course, art. Hitching a ride or hopping a freight car are frequent features. Fugitive action, though, is not so much a matter of action or narrative as it is a series of exercises in subjective empathy. We are each of us brought closer to discovery and unmasking, only to be reprieved at the last moment by fortunate accident or fortuitous whim. The virtue of the unit, I suppose, contrasts to the cockroach race, where the event is totally disconnected from us and from the narrative: it can be plugged in and function at any point without disturbing the surface of the narrative. With Escape Underwater our identification is so firm and so complete with the character on screen that the placement of the sequence is as absolutely connected to what goes before and after it as the cockroach race (see chapter 8) is absolutely unconnected.

The Wolfman subgenre has this power; bits of Horror tacked on to Westerns (*The Searchers*) or Women's (*Possessed*) or Musical (*Meet Me in Saint Louis*—Halloween—and *Singin' in the Rain*—the dancing partner in Donald O'Connor's "Make 'em Laugh") display the same kind of force. The film reviewers who latched on to the phrase "mere escape" were addressing a fundamental truth about film: we go to the movies to get away, and are never so successfully away as when we are there. Prison Pictures are perhaps an oddly perverse escape genre, but Escape is its perfect metaphor. Nowhere else in movies are we so completely identified with a figure on the screen as we are with the con or the POW escaping underwater. Escape sequences are the metaphorical proof of our need for what only movies can give us, and the actual proof of the curious way movies can find to give us what we had not the wit to ask.

# 7. LET'S BURN THE SCHOOL
## The High School Picture

*"You girls were really shitty to Carrie."*

—Betty Buckley in *Carrie*

High School is so simpleminded a genre. To say we have it because it's the kind of picture kids would go to, to say that its form is the kind of thing kids will like, or that Teen Splatter (High School's near relative—any violent death or psychotic killer movie involving teens or high school) features the sort of mayhem teens talk about, to say that Carrie's revenge is the kind of revenge teens might seek is not tautology, but probably defines the essence of the High School Picture. It's like that: flat-footed, forward, kind of dumb. But if we are to locate any force in these pictures, we will find it in their content. It is an appalling statement, but a sad fact, that form has failed to make a significant contribution to this untidy group of new elements. As the High School Picture is anarchic and spontaneous, so disorder and mess are appropriate to it: something of the kind of haphazard free association some Silents had. When the moviemaker of a Silent found a fire in town, he filmed it and changed the script to fit the fire. The High School Movie is unwashed in this way. What organizes them is what they have in them, the point of view they take, and their acceptance of chaos. Teenagers can be repellent humans but they are very appealing animals, and they're funny. These movies have an appeal much like their subjects: they are gawky and clumsy and untidy. Acne, while not universal, is certainly not unknown. The sad, neck-braced child of *Sixteen Candles* who cannot get a drink of water from the fountain is Carrie without the power. *Jennifer the Snake Goddess* is Carrie specialized. Plato (Sal Mineo) in Nicholas Ray's *Rebel Without a Cause* is a potential Carrie. Born victim struggles with potential pyschopathic misfit/killer: in the case of Plato, victim wins; usually it's the mad teen.

High School Pictures, though, call up something primal in all of us. William Faulkner's stories about children are so effective because they understand that we have all been children and they use that understanding effectively.[1] High School Pictures tend to be about public high school, but they know this: even if I went to private school I can be every teen in this picture. I can be (because I have been) victim or failure or nerd; I can be (because I have dreamed it) psychotic killer or avenging angel or Splatter monster. This primal force is more important than anything else about the High School Picture, it is at the heart of this crude genre.

We can learn much about the High School Picture by taking seriously its sister the Splatter Picture, never applying an argument to High School without thinking what it might mean if applied to Splatter. Both share the audience's desires: both provide just the sort of movie their audiences come out to see. And since content rules here, similarity of function may be the same thing as similarity of form. They are bonded by a common fear. The teen has little imagination of death beyond the extreme imagination of disaster they call being mooshed, but teen *fear* runs much deeper. *I Was a Teenage Werewolf*, for instance, a powerful incipient High School Picture, shares some characteristics with Splatter, with Concert Movie, and with Mad Doctor. The Change, those moments when Werewolf passes from human to beast, parallels puberty's confusion and horror. Teen Fearster Pictures turn on fears of loss of identity, abandonment, failure to fit in, getting caught while screwing, all those things we used to worry about *all the time* instead of just now and again. To be a teen is to be the potential monster or a potential victim in a teen Horror. High School is a horrible place (and high school is so often a setting for Horror) because it's filled with fears set up on overgrown legs walking about the school halls, going to lockers, changing in the gym, dissecting cats. Carrie wreaks her retribution for all of us: the teen turns. Jason, the ultimate too-young nerd, seeks satisfaction for offenses committed against all of us when we were nerds. From *Friday the 13th* to *Friday the 13th II* he moves from some kind of dead to some kind of alive. Never mind that it makes no sense: Splatter and High School Pictures are both haphazard: not for them the strict ground rules of Horror.

Splatter may involve High School but not necessarily; High School may have Splatter's violence but not necessarily. *Terror Train* (college) is Splatter, *Sixteen Candles* is High School, *The Class of 1984* is both. So Splatter is not a true subgenre of the High School Picture, but rather a mutant that shares most of its drives and shapes, a crazy brother, a dark risk of the High School Picture: at any time it could become *this*. Because the two hold fears in common, the moral structures of both (absolute judgment, absolute memory, absolute revenge) are similar. Both have simplistic (or at least simpleminded) narratives. Strange to say, this simplicity and flat-footedness can sometimes (*I Was a Teenage Werewolf, Rock 'n Roll High School*) give us moments of elegant abstraction. Even the crudest and unhappiest teenager, after all, can sometimes surprise us with moments of animal grace or direct humanity. The unwilling affection between Mr. Hand and Spicoli in *Fast Times at Ridgemont High*, the child practicing alone in the gym (*Citizens Band, I Was a Teenage Werewolf, If....*). The familiar geography of automotive shop, band room, bio lab, gym, showers, lockers, perhaps accentuates the force of such moments, mixing spooky trappings (we were unhappy then, and fearful) and memory support.

This is lugubrious stuff, but in its midst there is an even more depressing characteristic of this genre's world: the misunderstood teenager is in a sense worth more dead than alive: dead we have pathos, the athlete (or virgin) dying young; alive we have energy, anarchy, blurted-out truth, recurring skin problems.

It's not the kind of thing Aristotle would like much, but it's very likely the genre our times deserve; it's certainly the genre the subject deserves. Fast foods R us. Our proper Michelin Guide deals with why Wendy's is better than McDonald's. Fast food is the category: sloppy, greasy, untidy foods in unmemorable feasts barely distinguishable one from the other. A memorable Big Mac is a contradiction in terms. So *The Breakfast Club* wants too much to be liked: *Rock 'n Roll High School* has tonal problems—it never finds a single way to deal with both Eaglebauer and Joey Ramone; when Spicoli isn't on the screen *Fast Times* is a mess (too much Abortion Picture *and* too much Male Virginity Picture). But these movies offer the plenitude Fast Food offers: you don't like this? wait a minute and another will be along: drive in to the turnaround and call it out. The way we remember these movies and tell one from the next (*Teenage Werewolf*, *Rebel Without a Cause*, and a few others excepted) is by minor tonal or structural consistencies or by those sudden graces. The girl in the neck brace who can't get her mouth to the drinking fountain wouldn't show up in *The Breakfast Club* because there aren't enough kids in that high school (like *Blackboard Jungle*). They wouldn't burn the school in *Fast Times at Ridgemont High* because, for all this movie's anarchic push, the authority of the teachers is unquestioned.

It's true, but all too easy to say that the High School Picture had to be because there was a massive teen audience, still growing. Too easy and just not good enough. Genre responds to culture and related market phenomena, but not because audience speaks its demands and then genre results. Genre evolves in a much more complicated exchange; its relationship to worlds outside itself is a tangled web. If there hadn't been a teen audience the genre could have been as stillborn as the OSS Picture. This is true. But the High School Picture does not *come from* the audience. The High School Picture comes from movies we already have: movies come from movies. It takes this new shape—High School Picture—because of audience.

The High School Picture is tied to cultural phenomena as surely as the Combat Picture of World War II is, but it is tied to phenomena less consistently marked, and it doesn't evolve as surely as that genre.[2] We can cite some things that had to happen in American culture before the High School Picture could develop: the Pill, a revolt against authority, Sputnik, and the educational reforms of the Sixties. Most important, we had to have rock music before we could hear the High School Picture. Without it we would never have shifted to the point of view of the kid. High School comes from Family Pictures, not those pictures made for the family audience—not films now rated G—but that near-genre centered upon the American family, and from an even fuzzier near-genre, Americana— movies that show community and its smaller counterpart, family, in a sometimes nostalgic, rather soft-focused image of America caught in some more or less timeless Golden Age (or, more recently, caught in a dystopian vision of products and roadsides). Americana was a less defined genre than Family, a clustering of themes and manners, not a center around which might develop a shifting, organic, self-inventing genre. Americana we still have with us, but in the same rudimentary stage of generic development.[3] Family itself never grew as a genre or changed or evolved because it was too tied to a *subject* (and thus too message-oriented) to become a proper genre. Instead Family moved out of movies to television. If the Western had been as intent on selling horses or cactuses or stagecoaches as the Family genre (both in movies and television) on selling love or absence of love, we never would have had even *Cimarron*, much less *The Virginian*. The B-Western wanted to sell its load of clams and didn't develop. *Bigger Than Life* and *Rebel Without a Cause*, exceptional Family Pictures, have been enormously influential in the development of other movies.

Before youth culture came along there were some Family Pictures we would have to call ur–High School Pictures. They are pregeneric pictures looking for a center and characters, for some way to be—in other words, trying to find some dependable genre units they can plug into place. The best known Family Pictures are the Hardy Family pictures. Shortly after *A Family Affair* Louis B. Mayer discovered the perdurable qualities of Judge Hardy's talks in his study, Mickey Rooney's tears of frustration, his double takes, his slow burns. Or maybe reports of the box-office receipts from *A Family Affair* made Mayer rush in to MGM and devise the Hardy Family series on the spot. Genres are no more made by studio executives than by audience demand (see chapter 2). More Inventor Pictures were made (and new outlines for them concocted) after executives saw box-office receipts for the earlier ones, but they didn't invent them in the sense I just said. In any event *A Family Affair* and the Hardy Family Pictures that followed were pregeneric, more formula than genre. Ur-genre hadn't yet found out how to be generic.

*A Family Affair* was about what in grade school we used to call Civics: a bad construction company challenges the civic probity of Judge Hardy (Lionel Barrymore), and each member of his family bears some of the brunt of the Judge's unbending morality. One daughter's marriage is shaky and she fears his disapproval, another has a blooming romance with a hireling of the bad builders and *she* fears his disapproval. Andy, the youngest, has his first encounters with the ever-elusive Polly. There are odd bits of gangsterlike threat and a political convention to renominate the Judge. A mishmash. But Louis B.

Mayer is no dope: for by the time of *Love Finds Andy Hardy* (1938) Lionel Barrymore is replaced by Lewis Stone, civic probity is gone, and Andy is everywhere. *Love Finds* has music, a dance (not yet a prom), and a wrecked car (Andy is fixing it up to become his beloved jalopy). Features are falling into place even though this will never manage to be a High School Picture. The dance (as in *A Date With Judy*) is held at the Country Club.

By the time of *A Date With Judy* very little else has changed: there are now two families, with contrasting social levels reflected in their houses, servants,[4] and manners, caring and neglectful parents. The role of parents separates Family from High School Picture. Parents dominate Family Pictures (Lionel Barrymore, Lewis Stone, Wallace Beery in *A Date With Judy*) and center our attention on the office. Family is a grown-up world. In High School Pictures parents are always just leaving home (*Risky Business*, *Reckless*), or nowhere to be seen (*Fast Times at Ridgemont High*, *Rock 'n Roll High School*), or idiots (*Lord Love a Duck*, *Rebel Without a Cause*), or mad (*Carrie*, *Jennifer*). After they leave or run amok we in the audience are free once again to become kids. This youthful point of view (p.o.v. teen) will be a significant balance point in formation of a new genre. But not just yet. *A Date With Judy* is still firm in its adult p.o.v., but by this time many features of High School are falling into place. There's a car, an older man (or rather, an older soda jerk, Robert Stack), a drug store. The issue—the movie's drawing card, its problem to be solved—lies more surely in Wallace Beery's threatened adultery with Carmen Miranda (she's giving him lessons in Latin dance, but these two are surely a match made in heaven if ever there was one) than in whether the school show will go on the boards or whether Judy will wear the wrong dress. And Xavier Cugat—no matter how many of the teens on screen ooh and ahh—is no Bill Haley, "Cuanto la Gusta" no "Rock Around the Clock." It's not even "Dear Mr. Gable."

*Margie* is the next memorable approach to High School. We have the right High School geographical spaces, a nostalgic youthful Cause ("Get the Marines out of Nicaragua"—that is, if we can ever get this national nightmare behind us so it can become nostalgic), first love, graduation. There is even a high school p.o.v. We're almost there.

Given the audience these movies sought to please, there's little wonder that nothing much was going on. MGM catered to teens who were thought to have no mind of their own. They were, of course, quite busy going to other kinds of movies not made for them, but *A Date With Judy* and *Margie* were movies one could see with one's parents—or rather, the kind of movie parents who didn't really approve of movies could take a child to. *Their* movies (see chapter 10). What is missing is the kids' point of view. Cannot the Crime Picture be free to be seen from the point of view of the Law as it is from that of the criminal? Why then must the High School Picture eschew maturity? The student point of view I think is essential: the High School Picture gets off on, is energized by, possible, potential, or realized teen anarchy. And I think this leads directly to High School's essential strength, its relentless energy.

*Blackboard Jungle* is:

1) a film version of a best-seller;
2) a star vehicle for Glenn Ford;
3) a Problem Picture, Juvenile Delinquent subgenre;[5]
4) a postwar picture;
5) serious.

All this gives the photoplay its preachy adult center. *Blackboard Jungle* is some kind of watershed: we must have rock and roll in order to have the High School Picture and it has Bill Haley and the Comets doing "Rock Around the Clock." They danced before the Battle of Waterloo; they also danced in the aisles of *Blackboard Jungle*. Rock and roll had come; High School could begin. But they did not dance to Glenn Ford's tune: it was to the spirit of resistance in Bill Haley's music. This movie doesn't have the brains to use the music's power: it plays the song over its credits. So *Blackboard Jungle* can't lay claim to have founded the High School Picture, or even to have founded the near-genre with which it is more closely associated: Juvenile Delinquent Problem Picture. *Blackboard Jungle* is not yet High School because of that relentlessly adult point of view.

Glenn Ford deplores the anarchy he finds at Manual High: kids should pay more attention to their elders. Ford's a vet, returned to find not only that he's changed, but that his job isn't exactly the one he left: now he must pacify the homefront. The enemy is the kids: Manual High School is filled with students in control. Well, not very filled—there aren't a whole lot of students in this school. And the students are played by actors rather long in the tooth for students who play out their roles in the manner of unruly men of a World War II unit gone awry. It's as if they had returned from the war too. Because no one at this point knows how to do anarchic classrooms, the movie reaches to the Combat Picture for a generic element we will recognize, and plugs it in even though it doesn't really fit.

Glenn Ford first tries what he knows, the way he used to teach. He cannot be heard, so the idealist in him succumbs to the pragmatist: *audio-visual*: he brings in special equipment to record their colorful speech. He doesn't even do this as well as his spiritual heir on TV, Mr. Cotter. The students break up the jazz record collection of his still-idealist colleague Jonathan Edwards (Richard Kiley), and they nearly rape his fellow greenhorn Miss Hammond. Mr. Dadier (or, as they say, "Daddy-O") turns defeatist. The movie has a washroom scene, a classroom knife fight, a victimized nerd, an overturned car (mysteriously flipped over by a too-swiftly passing jalopy), a street crime, an alley mugging, an assembly, a schoolyard threat, and teachers' coke-and-smoke room despair and apathy, led by, of all people, Mr. Murdock (Louis Calhern), the cynical history teach. But the picture is never as good as this catalogue might suggest. The embarrassing introduction of Miss Hammond in assembly (she is a woman, unfamiliar, and apparently unwelcome in Manual), followed by a surprisingly violent near-rape in the library, Louis Calhern as dapper phony, a promising appearance of a Dachau-guard disciplinarian (Emil Meyer), the youth gang, the bar, the wonderful geography (all the rooms are clearly labeled and Manual High School has a room for *everything*), all prove to be incidental. The movie doesn't want to give us the framework for rebellion its music suggests—that might get the new genre off to a characteristic start. *Blackboard Jungle* has to wait for *Class of 1984*, a near-remake, for its promise to be fulfilled. It seems ashamed of some of its startlingly diverse and delightful elements. It's not just *Blackboard*'s stultifying direction, its adult point of view or pulled punches, or even the failure of the world of 1957 to be enough like our own. *Blackboard Jungle* can't make generic sense of a genre that isn't there: it can't spend cash it thinks is worthless.

One mysterious bit of this movie, however, is firmly tied to the future genre: the story of the wife (Anne Francis) looks as if it came out of a World War II or Korean War Combat Picture. It dwells as such pictures do (primarily movies about the Navy[6]) on domestic unrest while the man is at sea. In *Class of 1984* this symbolic narrative can be brought to a conclusion at the story level: the toughs carry out their threat against the male teacher by beating, raping, and nearly murdering his wife. In *Blackboard Jungle* Anne Francis miscarries because of the student threats, or rather because she's worried about their threats and her husband's absences, or something. But her unexplained miscarriage is enough to introduce an element the High School Picture will use and use again later on: the Abortion Film. Anne Francis is here to give Glenn Ford someone to tell his troubles to and to ask the Problem Picture's favorite Fifties question: Do we want to bring children into a world dominated by such toughs? Do we want to have children who will be like them? After such an idealistic victory in 1945, is this a fit homecoming? *Blackboard Jungle* cannot find the energy of this, anchored as it is in its adult point of view.

After *Blackboard Jungle* came more Problem Pictures about teens (*Blue Denim*); true High School is still a long way off. So it might be more efficient to get at the new genre through a *locus classicus*, *Fast Times at Ridgemont High*. It is classic even though it never seems all of a piece. This may well be a characteristic of the genre: High School encourages us to admire a thing yearning to get there more than getting there. Like a high school sophomore the High School Picture appeals to us in an unexpected way. What is there to like about this gangly, spotted, in-between teenager? The answer is energy and potential. Unleashed anarchic spirit. It's too much to expect High School to be aesthetically whole or under control as well.

*Fast Times* came along at the right time. Just as *On the Waterfront* made people who hadn't done much thinking about movies think about the American movie and what it had become since World War II, so *Fast Times* made all of us think how many other movies we'd seen that looked just like it, how many of these it was better than. High School was easy to recognize, just as genre is, but before *Fast Times* this didn't seem so apparent.

*Fast Times* is inchoate; it will never make it on story or unity. It moves right along, but the way one moves through a mall, looking here, stopping there, buying something cheap and thinking about buying a lot more. It works like an anthology film: we'll have this, next this, then this. Short subjects rather than spine. It's about as organized as a meeting of the Future Secretaries Club, as structured as band practice, and it doesn't seem much to care. The movie starts out in the mall, as a matter of fact, but we never get to wander around in it.[7] We get to the high school by accompanying some of the characters we have met in the mall.

Spicoli, not much more than a stock character, becomes the movie's most important organizational principle by virtue of

HIGH SCHOOL: Faceoff at the pass: Sean Penn and Ray Walston in *Fast Times at Ridgemont High*, 1982

Sean Penn's brilliant comic performance. Spicoli as hero is a bit out of date, which I suppose is part of his charm: he's out of Beach Blanket and Surfing Movies of two decades before, but his performance, like those of Jamie Lee Curtis and Molly Ringwald, makes this little genre his very own. We develop an empathy with him: how reasonable the appeals of anarchy when compared to the idiocy of fuddy-duddies. Fuddy-duddies here are represented by Judge Reinhold on the student level and on the faculty level by Mr. Hand (Ray Walston).

The anthology continues with short subjects: we get a Male Virginity Picture; Female Virginity Picture and Abortion Picture starring Jennifer Jason Leigh; frustrations on the job and feckless sexual fantasy starring Judge Reinhold; presumed maturity and a rather incredible love for an absent older man, starring Phoebe Cates; wrecking the tough's car (borrowed by Spicoli and the black tough's younger brother) followed by a ruse to cover it up in a vengeful football game.

With one exception, the Abortion Picture, all these shorts are pretty good movies. The source of the Abortion Picture, like the first cockroach race, is shrouded in the mists of film history. It didn't begin in *Blackboard Jungle*, it just came to high school then. Probably it was Women's, perhaps a pseudo-instructional forerunner of *Mom and Dad*, about teenage (or at least out-of-wedlock) pregnancy that considers abortion as a way out of the lonely disgrace society uses to punish unwed motherhood. In earlier movies the solution was a happy decision to put the kid up for adoption or a harrowing resort to a back-streets practitioner who offered infection, blood poisoning, death—the specter of the Botched Abortion. The deliberate (*Leave Her to Heaven*) or accidental (*Gone With the Wind*) pitching of one's self down the steep flight of stairs was a do-it-yourself Abortion Picture. Next came medical ethics (*Not as a Stranger*), and with abortion legalized, feminist self-determination. We still had retro Botched Abortions in Costume Pictures (*Racing With the Moon*, for instance, made Costume because the movie hinged on a Botched Abortion). The hint of Women's remains in the challenge to the father to agree to accompany her. Earlier Women's Pictures (*Doctor Monica*, see chapter 9) show female friends more reliable than the partner. The Male Virginity Picture of *Fast Times* is not as bad as some, but it's still too long: it sacrifices energy to Neanderthal pacing. Compared to it Phoebe Cates should win the William Blake Prize for combined Innocence *and* Experience. Her cute demonstration of a blow job with the carrot from her brown-bag lunch in the school cafeteria is characteristic and believable: we'd be better off watching the movie this lively short really belongs in than we are watching the one we find it in.

All the movies in the mainstream of High School Pictures (*Grease, Rock 'n Roll High School, Pom Pom Girls, Christine, American Graffiti, Ferris Bueller's Day Off*) follow *Fast Times*'s *locus classicus*. All are episodic, all survive on rock and relentless energy. The arrival at school is a stream of students in profile, then the stream shot head-on, then from the back as the students mount the stairs. We meet at the lockers, have a token classroom experience, get down to business (sex and humiliation) at the lockers, (sex and gossip) in the cafeteria, (sex and showing off our terrific line) in the library. Then break for the gym or the playing field. Later comes stuff at the hangout, Inspiration Point, a bit of touching home life (generally siblings, *sans* grown-ups), the Prom. All this depends, as does the magician's legerdemain, on what the other hand is doing, on distracting gestures, fast shuffles, no-reason transitions. We bump into a familiar face in the hall we can recognize and identify and it is as likely to be someone from our own past as it is to be a character we've seen earlier in the movie. The High School Movie depends absolutely on this automatic identification and recognition. What we see is barely removed from what we suffered at that girl's or that bully's or that teacher's hands—humiliation, triumph, momentary regret, tearful farewell. We didn't leave it without scars. Any High School Picture seems certain that it depicts *our* high school, that any one of us is one of its types: we know where everything is—shop is over there, band room down the hall, principal's office here near the center, just across the hall from the trophy case.

If we move from *locus classicus* to *locus in extremis*, from *Fast Times at Ridgemont High* to *Rock 'n Roll High School*, we find more of the genre's strength and even more of its disorder. *Fast Times* is more central than *Rock 'n Roll High School*, in part because it has sacrificed its spontaneity. *Rock 'n Roll High School* is spontaneous almost to the point of looking unfinished. The arrival montage is accompanied by music from an overturelike sound track, continued in the schoolyard piped throughout the school over the public address system by Rick Randall (P. J. Soles). She commits anarchy right from the start by trying to put life in the school by means of, yes, music. This movie tries for a rock anthem principle (they don't want us to have *our* music: see *American Hot Wax*).

It's not the protagonist but ancillary characters that make this movie tick. The *Rock 'n Roll High School* principal reaches a satiric extreme (she may even be borrowed from Ida Lupino's Nazi warder in *Women's Prison*). Once she has introduced us to her laboratory mice and the special earphones (even if we can't yet predict it), the movie will end in burning down the school. Excess is this movie's middle name.

More extreme even than the Principal is Eaglebauer, a triumph of character, secure in his Milo Minderbinder GHQ at the rear of the Boys' Lavatory—a GHQ with fixtures. The bathroom door admits us to another world, a Twilight Zone as clearly removed from real high school (if there is such a thing) as the Principal's mouse and rock music experiment is. In Eaglebauer Andy Hardy rides again. He is as intent as Andy, fastened on complex schemes for worldly wealth and beating the system (without the distraction of pursuing Polly, which ate up so much of Andy's time). Higher criticism might ask if Eaglebauer *is* a student. He seems to have been around too long. He has even taken up some teaching tasks—the kind of thing you might learn in the washroom—but the washroom is, after all, his office, or his corporate headquarters or Combat Information Center. In a lot of ways he's an older man, older man as nerd—and nerd[8] is certainly the most significant new character type to emerge from the High School Picture—the clothes are bad, so is his complexion, and he talks through his nose. (There's also a second nerd in this picture, rather unaccountably an out-of-touch-quarterback nerd.) Eaglebauer's also the pusher. This suggests another appeal of the High School Picture: step around the corner in the hall and you can be in the world of Eaglebauer, or of the mad janitor (*The Breakfast Club*), or of the science class conducted at gunpoint (*Class of 1984*). Some familiar spaces are not just enriched in the High School Picture, they are made magical.

The boys' lavatory seems rather close to Timothy Van Patten's hangout in *Class of 1984*: same kind of trappings and some of the same transactions. One setting, then, with many functions equals fast food: the economy of this genre is sometimes overlooked.

*Rock 'n Roll High School* could almost be a Musical except that the music is so bad (not, of course, a very able generic distinction), though I suppose this is a matter of taste. High School Pictures often use Retro rock: it's safer than something Right Now—by the time a movie gets made the Top of the Pops has moved on. Something of this retro spirit is spread throughout the High School Picture. Retro or revived music of an earlier time lets us identify ourselves with what is on the screen at the same time we can condescend to it as a bit old hat. But in this movie the problem is not Retro: it is the Ramones—particularly Joey Ramone, incredibly enough, this movie's sex object. He seems barely conscious. It's clear no one ran him through his lines so he might find out what was going to happen in the movie. The idea of bringing film stardom to the Ramones is lunatic: they are a mess. But the messiness of the Concert Movie near the end of *Rock 'n Roll High School* may well be what makes the movie work. Its energy gives this picture, for all its defects, an irrepressible forward motion. The Ramones and the concert are anarchic and this is an anarchic, not a runaway movie. *National Lampoon's Vacation* is runaway; *Rock 'n Roll High School* is systematic anarchy. Anarchy is not chaos.

The so-called John Hughes Trilogy (*Sixteen Candles*, *The Breakfast Club*, *Pretty in Pink*) is instructive to this point. Like *Fast Times at Ridgemont High*, *Sixteen Candles* looks like a classic: we are moved along smooth grooves of developing anarchy: Molly Ringwald's day begins badly when her parents forget her all-important sixteenth birthday (as we expect—or we think we know to expect—from High School Pictures) and gets worse as she begins the school day. A note passed in class is lost and then intercepted: her life is ruined. (How such momentary perils resonate with that high school sophomore within each of us these movies speak to!) But the movie loses its concentration and its sense of direction. We go to a party; some of the gags move in the direction of *National Lampoon's Vacation*. The grandparents could fit in better if this were a simple High School Picture anthology structure (indeed some *Twilight Zone* music sets up just such a magical potential). I suppose even the racialism we see reflected in Long Duck Dong, the visiting student from mainland China, is in the spirit of the High School Picture (but why not a student at the school instead of *au pair* to the grandparents?). The wedding of Molly Ringwald's sister is there, I suppose, to provide motivation for the parents' forgetfulness and to contrast its final, to our heroine's temporary, perils. But it all comes out rather like the football game near the end of *M\*A\*S\*H*: all the characters are there for a final rakehell event but it is so far off the subject of the movie that it goes nowhere and the end of the movie falls flat.

*Sixteen Candles* is mainline genre compared to both *The Breakfast Club* and *Pretty in Pink*. If Hughes were as good as John Ford I suppose he might have avoided (as Ford did, essentially by generic quickstep; see *Seven Women*, chapter 9) falling into so commonplace a genre and making it into a trap. Hughes's sense of genre is crudely manipulative. He doesn't give in to it, but genre makes him nervous. He seems to feel he can somehow improve the High School Picture, give it a fatal uplift, make it a better thing than he found it by raising its sights and bringing in elements from other genres. Sometimes this works, but not for whole movies.

So *The Breakfast Club*. What works best in this movie runs counter to the genre, the idea of teenagers forced to be with each other alone, away from the institutions of home *and* school (although they are confined of a Saturday morning in its spaces for punishment). Their class just now is each other: peer bonding. Five characters in a locked room, each prejudiced against the others. This brings up one of Hughes's innovations of the High School Picture: class warfare (not sophomores vs. seniors, but rich kids vs. poor). It's at the center of *Pretty in Pink*, tangential but important in *The Breakfast Club*, and at issue in *Ferris Bueller's Day Off*. It seems to me not to belong to the High School Picture: when he makes the school of *Pretty in Pink* into a small private school we seem almost to be having the explanation: he's making High School Pictures about private school. (This has lately been picked up by other directors: see *Tuff Turf*, *Less Than Zero*—the latter not really a High School Picture but dragged there by the commencement that opens it.)

How does such promising material fail? The performances of *The Breakfast Club* are strong, the direction of individual scenes as strong as anything in *Sixteen Candles* (or indeed, as anything Hughes has done), the story and visual ideas of this restricted school space, halls and library, tend to concentrate what we watch. But I think the dialogue turns dramaturgical and fails. Action, confrontation, conflict emerge from the lines and words, from literary text, rather than from film ideas or images. Action is off the mark and frenetic, never quite coalesces with what is being said, and musical numbers and dancing are brought in to keep our minds off the failure. (Hughes succumbs in a similar way to the parade rock number in *Ferris Bueller's Day Off*.)

Still, *Breakfast Club* with all its unevenness and stasis is head and shoulders beyond *Pretty in Pink*. This movie is so irritating it makes you worry about things you'd never have a chance to think about in Hughes's other movies. Jon Cryer (Ducky): why would somebody as smart as Ringwald give Jon Cryer the time of day, even out of sympathy? The movie's only answer: they are friends and they are both adolescent. Friendship looms larger in Hughes Films than in High School Pictures. If Ringwald's older friend at the record store thinks enough of her dress to get all done up in it, complete with Sixties hairdo, isn't it likely she'll get cranky when she discovers Molly Ringwald has *cut it up* to make an ill-advised punk sendup out of her favorite pink dress?

The dress may be more significant to the film than serving as climax or giving the movie its title, just as in the Women's Picture the red dress in *Jezebel*, *Queen Christina*'s unaccustomed female attire, *Rebecca*'s dress Joan Fontaine slips into (under the impression it will please her husband) demonstrate the force of the wrong or the signal dress in the Women's Picture. In the High School Picture other transfers from Women's Pictures work less well. Harry Dean Stanton in *Pretty in Pink* serves as an element of Women's Picture—the ne'er-do-well alcoholic, failed, or druggie husband/father. Though their house is out of *Carrie*, the situation, dialogue, and interaction are out of Women's Picture. Generally Women's takes over when it competes with High School (*Blackboard Jungle*, *Cooley High*, *Bad Boys*). Here it just slows everything down and messes almost everything up. The Father in *Jennifer the Snake Goddess* (also titled *Jennifer*), a cheap but peppy *Carrie* ripoff, is a throwback who embarrasses his daughter, but Women's Picture never occurs to us because the Father reminds Jennifer of her cultish talents out of the past, cautions her against the rich kids, mouths the Bible and listens to revival programs on the radio. Even taking into account its pink papier-mâché snakes, *Jennifer* is a better picture than *Pretty in Pink*.

---

Other High School Pictures only lead to an enforced sense that this genre is weak. Some of the Biggies—*Grease*, *American Graffiti*—don't seem on a second viewing even as good as *Fast Times*, and have far less energy. *Reckless* has its moments —sitting at the lovers' leap with the motorcycle, the arrival of the cycle at the high school, exploration of a new kind of secret place in the furnace room: one gets that itchy, anxious, furtive sense of private sexual fantasies, part and parcel of high school. But *Reckless* turns on individual fantasy and performance (particularly that of Aidan Quinn) and never gets around to generic discovery or even to generic rehearsal.

Some films that might otherwise be landmarks of the genre get sidetracked. *Splendor in the Grass* may be our finest period High School Picture. It has a wonderful bad girl at the waterfall, a historic debut for a very young Warren Beatty, and a great high school English class in Wordsworth. But Elia Kazan seemed to resent generic hallmarks at the lockers, the gym locker room, the big dance. We seem to glance and then look away. *Splendor* fails to be generically interesting just as *Blackboard Jungle* does: it's the adult point of view again. *Porky's* I think may founder on a different falsity. Here adult prurience makes the movie go, prurience at teenage raunchiness. When one steps back from it, this is just too kinky—really pornographic—to take up even for the length of a movie. It's not exhilarating or titillating, only enervating. *Risky Business* has a good star turn for Tom Cruise, and as I said about Sean Penn, the importance of these pictures as launching pads for really good, very young, very inexperienced actors cannot be overestimated. (It certainly plays a major role in why these movies make so much money.) But *Risky Business* doesn't spend much time on the high school business, figuring it has a much better thing going for it in the whorehouse business.

There are many attractive specialist oddments. *Satan's Cheerleaders* is amusing for about as long as it takes to read its title. *Jennifer the Snake Goddess*, as I said before, is not bad. It's a private school (as is *Pretty in Pink* and the dismal *A Separate Peace*). All three turn on an oddly distorted classist structure. Perhaps if *A Separate Peace* had the verve of *Jennifer* or that of *If....*, there might be a chance for the Prep School subgenre pictures to get a foothold. *Cooley High*, about an all-black high school, gets a good start and has a wonderful cast. Cooley High is cooler than most high schools. Sometimes everything rhymes ("All I know is that yo Momma's a ho," "Mr. Smith gonna have my ass for missin' class"), messing around with cars is more fun here, and school is more closely connected to the streets than most (compare *Blackboard Jungle*, playground roughhouse by comparison). It has an Abortion Picture and a high-priced sports scholarship that ends up in the toilet. The movie is intent on how special it is because this is a black High School Picture. So finally it distracts itself from the doings of the school into street life, urban violence, chases, the street-front hangout. Because its home has been established in High School Picture, not in the Street or Crime, the movie falls between stools.

Other sidelines: the Reform School (*Boys' Town, Bad Boys*) merges Prison Picture with High School, essentially destroying the young p.o.v. in its emphasis on the justice of this discipline which (unlike the Prison Picture) these movies seem intent upon our believing in. Prison Pictures seem to be agnostic about whether incarceration induces reform; Reform School Pictures have a need to believe. *Bad Boys*, though, has a science nerd who makes bombs out of radios and melts chainlink fences, and funny classroom and cafeteria scenes. (A general rule: cafeteria is funny; shop is not.) Military School (*Brother Rat, The Strange One, Taps*) tends to come out like POW Camp.[9] Compare Jocko deParis ("I'm Jocko deParis, not Charlie Chickenfeathers") in *The Strange One* with King in *King Rat*. The Performing Arts High School (*Fame*) I think bears a closer relationship to College Movies and Musicals than it does to High School. It could, though, have been a baleful influence on *The Breakfast Club*.

---

There are four triumphs in the genre, completely unlike each other: *I Was a Teenage Werewolf, Carrie, Lord Love a Duck*, and

*Class of 1984*. And there is *Rebel Without a Cause*, an auteurist masterpiece, perhaps beyond genre, but maybe responsible for inventing an important (and much imitated) part of it.

*Lord Love a Duck*, George Axelrod's aberrant classic, is *echt* Sixties. It strays from generic purity in its satiric aim—a little too formally pure and too highly organized for High School Picture's anarchy. Indeed, the movie's script is too good for a High School Picture. Roddy McDowall qualifies as a science nerd by his triumph in the guidance counselor's Rorschach Test (which she seems to know he'll lick her at and seems resigned to it: High School Pictures missed a good chance by not having more guidance counselors). Tuesday Weld's cashmere sweater club and funny parents qualify her as one of the most unforgettable high school girls of the entire genre. The principal and his office (always a touchstone for High School: watch for the potted plant) brings up another fact of life from the Sixties—the displacement of thousands of high school students from old Grover Cleveland to CONSOLIDATED highs, and the corresponding abandonment of old patterns and comforts: another thing to blame idiotic principals for. At the end the movie loses its way in Beach Party and Beach Blanket Movies, but finds itself again for a bang-up graduation—Roddy McDowall attacks the speakers' platform and the Principal with a pay-loader—putting the movie back on its anarchic (and its Sixties) track.

*I Was a Teenage Werewolf* is a brilliant exploitation film because it finds a new truth in an old place—the Werewolf Movie. Everybody knows any one of us could at any moment become hairy (see chapter 4). But this movie gives this truth a universal explanation—we are teens: puberty's demonic transformation gives new credibility to Horror. Injections by the Mad Doctor (a psychiatrist at the aircraft plant, a touch of postwar angst, and a hint of the movie's Space Slime) don't cause this lad's lycanthropy—the girl's parents' fears about his respectability do.

All the generic Horror trappings are present: the doctor has an Igor to assist him and Vladimir Sokoloff plays the Maria Ouspenskaya part; torches; help me, Doctor, please; and a nit-wit drug called Scopolomene.[10] The works. The class bell sets off this wolfpup's attacks. One victim sees her nemesis inverted as she hangs by her knees from the parallel bars, and this scene comments on something we knew but hadn't thought about much, the creepiness of gyms. And the vacant lot on the way home has never been both so down-home and so frightening. Perhaps the moviemakers were just taking an easy way out by using this familiar patch of the backlot weeds, but it works better in this picture than any stunted treetrunks and fog would. It's more High School Picture. *I Was a Teenage Werewolf* is mixed genre. The werewolf is more of a werewolf than the teenagers are teenagers because the generic format is better established for Horror, subgenre Wolfman. This movie doesn't know how good an idea it is pursuing: it's all there in the title. Werewolf is good because *it can happen to me*; Teenage Werewolf is better because *I remember how it was when it happened and they called it puberty.*

*Carrie* is a stunner, at once a high point of a peculiar director's strong style and a movie that almost perfectly straddles High School and Splatter—albeit extrasensorily, but then this seems (see *Jennifer, The Fury, Friday the 13th*) to be par for the High School course. *Carrie* is wonderful, a dropped box lunch, as someone said,[11] or rather a fantasy brownbag never packed by Mom. From its first shower of menstrual blood to the last grasp just beyond the grave, the movie takes the tack that every element of High School can find an excessive equivalent: the parent (see *Jennifer's* ripoff) is not only hopelessly out of it, but a religious freak. And she cuts up phallic carrots pretty funny, too. The vicious girl-clique consists of most of the girls in the school and not only are they as inventively classist as the girls of a Prep School Picture, but there's a ready source of blood

M I X E D: Scary gymnastics: Michael Landon in *I Was a Teenage Werewolf,* 1957 for their practical joke, a slaughterhouse located conveniently nearby. Carrie can burn the school with her eyes, and this is a picture that doesn't even need to save *that* for the picture's final climax. We don't need to take a class trip to the carnival, just follow Carrie home: it's right there inside her house.

It is, of course, balanced excess—about the best Brian de Palma has turned out. But its excess is off the beat. De Palma's precalculation seems wrong for a High School Picture, not because it doesn't touch all the bases, some of them in a way ("You girls were really shitty to Carrie") destined to become an industry standard, but because what we see coming is no broader anthology of surprises, no mounting anarchy, but more of de Palma's private fantasy. That, I suppose, is what we get for having an auteur director (if de Palma is one: I've never made up my mind[12]). To fuss about the shortcomings of *Carrie* in a genre happily represented by *The Blackboard Jungle* and *Sixteen Candles* is carping, though. The movie is well worth ripping off, and ripped off it has been over and over again.

Some of *Class of 1984* (I have already mentioned it as proper sequel or remake of *Blackboard Jungle*) is a good *movie* —beyond its generic virtues: the bad delinquent (Timothy Van Patten) bangs his head on various fixtures around the washroom so as to threaten the teach with the suspicion of having beaten up a student; he interviews a new drug flunky at the hangout ("Don't be a stranger, Cantino"); the Science teacher (Roddy McDowall) tries to act as if class held at gunpoint is a natural conclusion to how bad things have gotten to be. The music teacher still holds Van Patten in contempt even after he demonstrates, with a flourish worthy of a Hollywood Composer, that he is a dynamite prodigy and one hell of a piano player. But neither these patchy points of brilliance nor the way it completes, thirty years later, *The Blackboard Jungle*'s unfinished business are explanation enough for the power of this nasty little movie. Its point of view is tricky. We are asked, I think, to take the music teacher's side, but once he humiliates Van Patten in class and then trashes his car, the empathy structure becomes as slippery as in Fritz Lang's *Fury*. We must abandon empathy and this turns out to be more meaningful for us than if we had never hooked up with him in the first place. The end of the picture (Horror in the Shop, head in a table saw) is surprising even for jaded Splatter watchers. It gives us a healthy dose of teen hatred, a Sixties/Seventies phenomenon, in which ideological positioning is substituted for conventional movie empathy. Apparently comic trappings like the airport-style metal detector at the door of the high school take on a different, less satiric tone once we've been moved into the behavior-alteration segment of the picture. And this in turn makes of an exploitation High School Picture a rather frightening exercise in propaganda. It's finally the knowingness of the movie that is the most chilling. It knows that if we haven't seen *Blackboard Jungle* recently enough to see the parallels, the parallels will nevertheless sucker us in without our recognizing them; it knows we know the basic High School Picture; it knows we are ready to hate because we have come to this movie. This is in a way somewhat scarier than the automatic audience structures of *Porky's* or *Friday the 13th III*. This is a function of not anticipating something about the exploitation engagement, but of anticipating something about us.

So much has been written about *Rebel Without a Cause* and it is such a good movie that it seems almost uncalled for to claim it as a High School Picture. But like much of the cinema Nicholas Ray touched, its director may have invented a good portion of this genre—at least its heart. Anthology structure, quick association, rapid shifts of genre are here, but *Rebel* is serious where the genre prefers jokes, *Rebel* is profoundly characterological where the genre would prefer junky fast-food types, *Rebel* is high, the genre low. *Rebel* is always better than you remember it was the last time you watched it.

When this stranger (James Dean) walks into his new school, the arrival sequence is understood completely and instantly by

HIGH SCHOOL: Parents, strategically placed: Ann Doran, James Dean, and James Backus in Nicholas Ray's *Rebel Without a Cause*, 1955

Ray's camera for the first time in the genre. When we see Jim's red jacket, it is not just a wonderful period experience (like Warren Beatty's letter sweater in *Splendor in the Grass*), not just a chilling image (like the High School Picture in *It's a Wonderful Life*, that rollaway gym floor which so preserves in a single image our sense of frolicking at the precipice), but a perfect transference. As if for the first time the loneliness of each of us is made visible, available to each of us in this fragile, a bit too-old, eloquently tongue-tied Rebel dressed like an icon. His presence sits in our consciousness still.

Ray anatomizes his characters by giving us the parents (or in Plato's case, the missing parents), the homes, the new society that Jim, Plato, and Judy form on their own. As we look through our drunkenness and that milk-bottle bottom at the arriving, spatting parents, the transference is perfect and complete. High School is dropped as we get to that New Society at the mansion and the confrontation with Nemesis at the planetarium. In the manner of so many strong auteurs, Ray will deal with genre in his own way, and the Ray genre overcomes the resident genre. As soon as we see Plato holding the candelabrum on the curving stair we know we have passed into the movie's ending, and into a different order of meaning. Not only (had it not been invented) would Ray have been capable of inventing the cinema, he could have given it all its genres including Splatter. Plato is ready to go on to that, except that Ray has come up with higher calling for him. *Rebel Without a Cause* is not very useful as a guide to other High School Pictures, but it is an almost perfect ideal.

The High School Picture is still going strong: *Principal* rips off a bit of plaster from *Class of 1984* (and unfortunately, more from television); *In the Mood* is working the nostalgia trip; *Twelve O'Clock High*, yet another *High School Confidential*; *Porky's III* is just more of the same. The genre will dip, it will change. But it has responded to a need. We now have a genre appropriate to rock and roll, in its haphazard way a bit of anarchy for our very stuffy times.

# 8. THE COCKROACH RACE
## Movie DNA

*"The pellet with the poison's in the flagon with the
dragon; the vessel with the pestle has the brew that is
true."*

—Mildred Natwick in *The Court Jester*

A little bit of Horror can take over a movie of
any other genre. The clouds pass across the moon, interior
lighting takes on unnatural color, creepy music swells. Other
such generic elements are powerful, portable, and we can assimilate them at once. For instance, the cockroach race. Years
before I knew this bit of narrative was a portable generic fragment I knew it could be added at any point to a half-hour
television script to make of it a full hour script without advancing or visibly damaging the action, characters, plot, or sequence. Watching television, my family began to call these benign fillers "cockroach races." A literal cockroach race can be
found in *Stalag 17*, *The Big House*, *Today We Live*, a Howard
Hawks movie of World War I pilots and coxswains in party
and battle. In a cockroach race one character with no particular excuse claims he has a champion animal; challengers are
searched out and caught. The race that follows either gets interrupted (challenger or champion is stepped on, or else all
the bugs escape) or else completed. Then the main action is
resumed and cockroaches are forgotten. The cockroach race is

much honored in television (in *77 Sunset Strip, Miami Vice, Dynasty*), but its source is film: it probably originated as a cootie race in the trenches in some World War I silent.

But origin in genre is less important than usefulness and frequency, and the cockroach race is *very* useful; it turns up all over the place, in Costume, War, Prison, Detective, Women's Pictures, Musicals, and Westerns, and probably elsewhere as well. It is always at home wherever it turns up because it is perfectly portable, needs no introduction, and can be shoved into context without altering it in the slightest. When the race is over the script just goes on with what it was doing before the race began.

What then have we watched, and what good did it do us *or* its context? A clubby association of people; miniature sports rivalry; boredom that results in this desperate remedy; an event provided to bored people in a place in which active events are scarce. Perhaps more important than any of these is the sense that cockroach races have been before and will be again. Along with the folks on the screen we recognize how wonderful a truly silly diversion can be in the midst of a desert of ennui. The frogs in *Cannery Row* provide its cockroach race, the egg-eating contest in *Cool Hand Luke*.

Less tangible bits of action of even slighter moment than the cockroach race can become portable generic fragments —stripping of military rank (*Hell Below, The Story of Emile Zola, Across the Pacific, Northern Pursuit*), removal of a woman's spectacles (or a man's) (*The Big Sleep, Superman, Strangers on a Train, Now, Voyager, Bringing Up Baby, Rock 'n Roll High School, A Fish Called Wanda*), farewell at the train (*Summertime, The Big Clock, Since You Went Away, Now, Voyager, Casablanca*), the drag race (Andy Hardy *passim; Rebel Without a Cause, Grease, American Graffiti, Tucker*), or the fashion show, sinking in quicksand, escape underwater, a pop visit by the parents. Or simpler and slighter still, what I call "toad in the parlor": the unexpected visitor, generally concealed in a wing chair, waits in the dark for the arrival of the resident (*Big Sleep, No Man of Her Own, The Godfather, Gardens of Stone, All About Eve*). I say unexpected, but *we* know what it's there for. We have seen toads before. Recognition is the gift of genre fragments, as it is the gift of genre.

This recognition is both the gift of genre and a part of the language of genre fragments. The medium is not the message, but the recognition sequence certainly is. A generic hallmark on the screen triggers our recognition in the audience because of generic familiarity. The character there is brought up to speed and comes to know what's happening in the follow-through on the screen—comes to know what we already know, triggered by that hallmark. The relative timing of our recognition, and that of the character on the screen, is a fundamental rhythm of movies, as elemental as a heartbeat or a blink of an eye. There is another elemental rhythm that corresponds to this: how long it takes us to respond to anything a movie is revealing: the twirling parasol in *Sunset Boulevard*, the flash picture that comes to life in *Citizen Kane*. But for these the recognition of what's going on is sequential and doesn't appeal to much beyond the picture we see. Generic recognition is much subtler and more remote. We perceive genre in a much swifter way because it rests on connections, not objects or themes. Our speed of recognition acts the way an initiation sequence does in fiction, or the way our investment in one volume of a trilogy or tetralogy pays off in the next. The more quickly we get it, the more superior we are to Joan Crawford (deluded again by a man) or Mickey Rooney or a player as obscure as Grady Sutton, St. Petersburg, Florida's only star. The more such recognitions we pick up, the more our generic blood is up (or the better versed we are in the language), and the stronger becomes our desire to talk to the screen, to see our lives up there.

Generic recognition is more communal, more social than many of the other audience phenomena of film, and something of a badge of office for the familiar and comfortable moviegoer: once we've found out how to get into the spirit of it ("Polish earth!"; "You only have one wish left"; "Don't go in there!"; "What's that strange noise?"), we are hooked on that genre, indeed, on moviegoing. If we like movies, these triggers are supreme happiness. If we don't like movies or refuse to know them, we mistake these signals for literary meaning or ignore them, or remember them wrong. They separate the women from the girls.

They and the recognition they trigger and foster are the elemental quotient of genre, the slightest sufficiency of the biology of movies, the DNA of genre taxonomy.

Small or limited settings can become genre fragments, more closely integrated in story than cockroach race or toad in the parlor, or quicksand victim. But, for all that, they remain portable genre to genre, movie to movie, and are significant elements of generic interchange. The inside of a car (*On the Waterfront, Family Plot, The File on Thelma Jordan, Vertigo, Two for the Road, Bonnie and Clyde, They Drive by Night, No Way Out*); the engine room of a ship (*Shall We Dance, The Hairy Ape, The Sand Pebbles, Overboard, Fire Down Below*); inside the submarine (*Alien, Destination Tokyo, Destination Moon, White Heat, An Officer and a Gentleman*). The mythic outlines of Connecticut (*Bringing Up Baby, Rich and Famous, Christmas in Connecticut, All About Eve*) have been attested to by Stanley Cavell in *Pursuits of Happiness*. The generic point of a Connecticut Arden or Arcadia in screwball comedy is well taken. Cavell's sense of genre in this book is far more like Northrop Frye's than it is in *The World Viewed*, where he seems to be pursuing some of the points I am trying to get at here. But his sense of myth of locale is different from place-genre (see chapter 5). We could go on with the myths of locale, into San Francisco, L.A., and Florida, to say nothing of Myth Central, the Great West.

But I think the point is made: small places of setting, less-than-geographical places, are different: the geography of parents in the parlor (Andy Hardy *passim, Rebel Without a Cause, A Date With Judy, Long Day's Journey Into Night, I Was a Teenage Werewolf*), of the deck of a sailboat in a storm (*Mr. Skeffington, A Stolen Life*), the motel room (*The Gauntlet, The Hitcher, Broadcast News*), the space of a high school reunion (*Superman II, Peggy Sue Got Married, Something Wild*). Whole genres can be formed of such bits and pieces—genres that are like atolls, resting places for genre fragments, so many bits of flotsam and jetsam washed up on its shores from other genres. The Pirate Movie is one of these, the South Seas, and the Beach Blanket Movie. There were Pirate Movies before World War II, but when Pirate borrowed the Impenetrable Island Fortress from the Combat Movie it found a new format.

A cactus in a Chopin Movie could not function because the connective ends—what can join something to something else—just would not meet. We can't get there from here. This is less a matter of what goes together than a matter of what just won't work. But even though setting is vaguely geographical, the geographical metaphor is perhaps not as good here as the gustatory might be: think again of the menu. In other words, don't serve swordfish steak with mushrooms or candied yams: it's an antimenu. When we watch a Western we have an idea what to expect—spurs, whores, stampedes, quick draws, the bar in the saloon—what will be given us, though in part the wonder of Westerns is that they cannot be measured by what they contain. *Johnny Guitar* calls upon us to step up to a new kind of meal, each element of which fits all the others, but none of which can we (the first time we watch the movie) predict. The next time we see it coming, in whatever movie we spot it, we not only know this happened in *Johnny Guitar*, we know it as a potential for any other movie in any other place.

Cavell writes in *The World Viewed*:

I think everyone knows odd moments in which it seems uncanny that one should find oneself just here now, that one's life should come to this verge of time and place, that one's history should have unwound to this room, this road, this promontory. The uncanny is normal experience of film. Escape, rescue, the metamorphosis of a life by a chance encounter or juxtaposition—these conditions of contingency and placement underpin all the genres of film, from the Keaton and Chaplin figures who know nothing of the abyss they skirt, to the men who know too much (156).

In a good Women's Picture (*Doctor Monica, Deception, Sudden Fear*) we always know what has brought us to this point, this cliff, this particular promontory, but the course of getting there has never been anticipated: it has elements we find familiar, but the combination, order, impulse, impetus, are surprising. This is more than just a matter of variant usage: something in it has an essential free spirit of adventure—combination and sequence as experiment. There are unlikely combinations in genre that work like a charm. A woman in trousers is so useful and so portable a generic element (*A Song to Remember, The Plainsman, Jezebel*, and countless Westerns) that it is almost definitively *movie*, useful in most any genre. One can run on about *meaning* but this is not paramount to what we conclude when we see a woman on the screen in trousers. It is a generic element: use comes before meaning.

I have dwelled long enough earlier on icons perhaps, suggested that Lincoln is more portable than Washington, Stephen Austin (surely a strange choice for an icon) more portable than Quanah Parker, but not more so than Geronimo; and Liszt more than Beethoven—all for different reasons. Indeed, as I have tried to show, Liszt can move out of his lifetime (*The Picture of Dorian Gray*). Portability of such movable characters or human landmarks seems to depend on their recognizability —more than the force of historical significance or of individual character (witness Stephen Austin). Caligula had a decided vogue for a time but unlike Nero he wasn't physically recognizable, so he faded.

But as to portability, anonymous psychological recognizability is even more portable than famous faces: the woman who

shies from a man's accidental touch, the son who is too-dutiful, the woman who drinks a little too much, the too-willing big spender.

Take one of these types—the sailor in the grass skirt. We may think at once of its most familiar instance, Luther Billis of *South Pacific*. Or we may think it comes from World War II. But it is already turning up in the prewar period in service movies (especially the China service).[1] Its portability is proved later on in Beach Blanket and Prisoner of War Movies made after World War II. For Beach Blanket Movies the sailor in the grass skirt is an aging character type got into drag; in the POW Movie, the character is featured in a show held to cover an escape attempt or lighten the mood in a glum compound. The sailor may presage (or follow upon) a drunken brawl or a spontaneous musical number; or he can just do nothing more elaborate than humiliate females by the parody of drag. A grass skirt becomes excessive and so parodies women, rather than just (unsafely) imitating women. And the coconut brassiere and, especially in the Forties, the girdle. In other words, a sailor in a grass skirt can do all sorts of things. But more important than *what* the sailor in the grass skirt does is how quickly we *recognize* what he is doing: as soon as we see how coherent so crazy a figure can seem it becomes something we know on sight but, like the cockroach race, something for which we might well be unable to give a clear or accurate origin. Genre tracks happily along such immediate recognitions. We know more than we know we know, we can recognize things we don't know how to describe, we can know more than we know how to say. Just like the English language.

Such left-field characters are matched by even more isolated or limited fragments. The tall cactus in the Western. One cactus in the Sunday Morning Sequence of *My Darling Clementine*

COSTUME: An extraordinarily memorable woman in trousers: Merle Oberon in *A Song to Remember*, 1945 is so familiar and necessary to the composition that Ford moves it about from shot to shot. But the cactus doesn't turn up just in Westerns: see *Saboteur, Easy Rider, Vanishing Point, Paris, Texas, Raising Arizona*. Smoke signals on the horizon. The woman falling down at the plow once the man has gone away. Collapse in the snow storm. Thrown acid. The amputation. The gift for his wife or best girl the doomed cowhand or soldier or gunsel announces just before the stampede/terrorist explosion/machine-gun attack. The last payment on the mortgage or debt or car loan. The visit of the sniffy gallery owner to the new genius-painter's loft. The composer's visit to the music publisher. The face-off at the Western bar. The gun under the table. The arrival of the draft notice or the telegram from the War Department. The embarrassing drunk. The embarrassing dinner party or dress suit or mother. The wife's visit to the Other Woman (vice versa is usually not done). The sheet torn and crumpled by the blocked writer (chapter 5). The "snipe hunt" old hands devise for the greenhorn/tenderfoot/youth/raw recruit/student nurse. Will Aladdin find out in time that the wishes come from the genie who appears when the lamp is rubbed and will he manage to avoid wasting more than one-third of his wishes? The arrival of reinforcements as the old soldiers leave/look on/stand there, propped up, dead.[2]

A little freer, but still somewhat limited: marching off to war (Women's, War, Costume, Musical, Science Fiction, Comedy), birth of a baby (Costume, Epic, Women's, Comedy, Musical, War, Western, Horror, Inventor), the horseback accident (Costume, War, Comedy, Women's, Crime/Thriller). The chase is almost completely transferable from one genre to the next, as is the cute dog or chimpanzee or monkey, a cockroach race infinitely divisible into smaller parts (*Fury, Down and Out in Beverly Hills, The Thin Man, The Sea Hawk, Mogambo, Cobra Woman*, various Tarzan Pictures). The auction, the fashion show, and the deserted department store are more limited. The difficult journey beneath the earth is highly specialized (*The Adventures of Tom Sawyer, The Big Carnival, Them!, Les Miserables, The Third Man, Journey to the Center of the Earth, Nightwing*). There are some unaccountable oddments: the Cuban Musical Number turns up more frequently and in stranger places than even the cockroach race (*Godfather II, Hell Below, We Were Strangers, The Immortal Sergeant, There's No Business Like Show Business, A Date With Judy, My Sister Eileen*). Most of this is probably the studios' guess at contemporary chic (or contemporary tawdry) or perhaps just that they guess that what would most clearly mean musical number to the audience is *Cuban* Musical Number. But still the Cuban number in *Immortal Sergeant* is a poser. Escape through the swamp is so transferable and useful (*The Horse Soldiers, The House Across the Bay, Northwest Passage, A Song to Remember, Raintree County, A Lady Without Passport, Band of Angels, The Beguiled, Night of the Hunter, The Story of Temple Drake, Deliverance, Kings Row, Murder He Says, The Sea Hawk, Objective, Burma!, Southern Comfort*) that the swamp frequently appears where there ain't no swamps; see the swamp behind the house that fronts on a crowded and busy street (*Oil for the Lamps of China*), swamp on a mountaintop (*Woman Obsessed*), swamp at the frontier (*A Song to Remember*), Wild West swamp (*The Searchers*), convenient swamp (*Band of Angels*), and trysting swamp (*Raintree County*). Swamp, like Scylla and Charybdis, occurs when that's the next thing you have to get through, rather like life itself in that respect. And escape over the mountains, especially in World War II (*The Great Escape, The Sound of Music*). Transferability proves that these parts are interchangeable: genre—especially Women's Picture—can lead us where it wants without much effort, and readily takes us into loony Dark Valleys and Moments of Crisis, or brings us to the use of odd murderous implements (*Sabotage, Man Hunt*) with equal ease. From the most mundane and innocent, even lace-curtained, surroundings we are led in stages to outlandish moonscapes: one readily recognized event or action or thing leads to the next until finally we find ourselves completely out of the way, wandering in a land that could only *be* movie.

Such movable feasts might conceivably be used to construct a Movie of the Collective Genres. It would probably be busy, turn out to be a parodistic film of such perpetual and reflexive self-reference as the Seventies and, especially on television, the Eighties seem to specialize in. As with frequency of occurrence, potential for portability is less significant than usefulness of various fragments: the language which organizes all these spare parts suggests the richness of exchange from one genre to the next, and this is one reason it is so hard to define a genre.

For when we draw up anatomies of fragments or spare parts we are not cataloguing smaller and smaller subtypes of story (Western with cattle/sheep wars featuring a schoolmarm) or getting variant versions of what can happen in these movies. We are assessing a language of movable functions, interchangeable parts. And beyond that, getting at something that makes movies tick, makes them alive, the DNA factor. Describing what makes any genre work, trying to evaluate the freehanded use of these elements within its prescribed limits, gets us into a process of forming a language. Language mechanics makes genre a matrix for film meaning available to hack and *auteur* alike. And more than anything, makes genre study a serious and complex study, engaged in the heart of movie meaning.

Parts were probably what made genre so necessary a tool for American artists: any single part could provide a starting place in a New Land, and that is not just what Americans always look for. It's also what movies—and their directors—needed before they could figure out they might be art. Genre is what brought American film so far from its origins. So perhaps genre is the most important reason to reject the intentional fallacy for film criticism (Did he mean to make a great/funny/arty/

disjunctive/schlocky movie?) even more firmly than we do for literature (What did Shakespeare intend by the unweeded garden?).

Genre makes film independent of what the director set out to do. It can on its own make a film be one thing or another on its own. Did the director want a work of art or not? Who cares? With genre it is sometimes an irrelevant, and always a dubious, question.

There's a handy guide for the point at which the didactic element in a piece of literature gets in the way of art: does the "pamphlet" or "message" function of the piece determine how the sonnet is written—is the "pamphlet" hand doing the writing? Not so in genre. That's one of its beauties—even when genre takes over, the movie can still be its own thing, especially in the freer reaches of Women's or Western or Comedy. As long as the director doesn't think he's better than the genre.

Cockroach races belong: enjoy them. They are the heart of film.

# AMERICAN SCENARIOS

# 9. ALL SINGING, ALL DANCING, A MILLION LAFFS
## Musicals and Comedy

---

*Manicurist: I know you caught the bandit, Mr. O'Hair.*
*Fields: I know I caught him too, but it's no use talking to*
*these people, they're all nervous.*

—W. C. Fields, *The Barber Shop*

Now that we have looked at film genre in detail it's time to look at the way we look at movies.

If we lead lives that take their cue from film genre and we lead generic lives because we're Americans, we begin to do this early on. We first look at movies as children and as children we identify genres and respond to what they are, incorporate them into our lives. I did, taking it all in, going for punishment tours on the cannon in the rain in *Ten Gentlemen From West Point*, climbing the rigging in the storm in *Mutiny on the Bounty*. Childhood is a time of direct access, and no art ever knew its subject better than a movie knows a child. As popular art the American movie also knows, before it knows anything else, that it is American, and makes anyone who absorbs it completely know Americanness. Dream visions of running along the top of a train from a nameless Harold Lloyd movie, looking down on the crowd with Quasimodo in *The Hunchback of Notre Dame*, doing the dance with the stick in *Top Hat*—such visions take a child far along the road in wanting something else, wanting to get out of St. Petersburg, Florida,[1] wanting to be a part of the rest of the country, signing up for the American Dream. In a very strong sense (it's one reason everyone is an expert) genre is a kid thing. But as an *American* kid thing movie genre is even more significant, not just in nationalizing the kid's aims and desires—this would be little more than external decoration—but in internalizing American scenarios as mind-sets, expectations, predispositions, needs, wants, dreams, ideals, aspirations. Much of what I saw on the screen then is remarkably similar to what I see now, and much of what I saw in college I have turned away from. This is not because my dreaming then became the less, but rather because the American Dream depends, I think, on primal imprinting.

Some such genres are kid stuff and remain so: Pirate Movies were for kids: *The Black Swan*, the several versions of *Treasure Island*. *The Crimson Pirate* was released when I was in college and I revisited my childhood excitement at these swashbucklers. Burt Lancaster was better than Tyrone Power (at my collegiate state of development): it went beyond what Power could match of Lancaster's circus athleticism. Male bonding between him and his mute sidekick had replaced the love stuff of *The Black Swan* that as a child I had found slow, so *The Crimson Pirate* moved right along. (Is pacing one reason there is so much male bonding in Pirate, Action/Adventure, Thriller genres? Howard Hawks said movie story isn't a matter of Boy Meets Girl, but Boy Meets Boy, and it does seem the love stuff between guys is more prevalent in this sort of movie: see, for instance, *Nate and Hayes* for Pirate, *Butch Cassidy and the Sundance Kid* for Western/Adventure.)

Pirate doesn't really go anywhere, though, except toward degeneration—usually because it gets hung up in tongue-in-cheek self-consciousness. The Fifties was big on this. Degeneration, of course, was already present in the Forties; later Pirates (*Nate and Hayes*, *The Pirates of Penzance*, *The Pirate Movie*, *Yellowbeard*) just went on decaying. When its only evolution is toward decay, the genre is moribund.

Another genre I saw as a kid and found puzzling was Harem Pictures (*Road to Morocco, Arabian Nights, The Prince Who Was a Thief*). I think they got popular because of a now-defunct sexual fantasy—women kidnapped by sensuous desert men for their Fell Purposes. But the world caught up and passed this fantasy by: being kidnapped by people in burnooses no longer appeals. In its time it was a potent generic format for serious fantasy (*The Sheik*), or for G-rated (before there even was such a thing as ratings) fairy tale (*The Thief of Baghdad*), and comedy sendup (*Road to Morocco*, Abbott and Costello, Laurel and Hardy). Even though its evolution was retarded, Harem was generically better developed at its start than Pirate. It had a geography (the pool in the center of the castle room, the stairs to purdah), some ground rules (chase through the bazaar, usually ending in capture, guerrilla raid on the camp at the oasis), some characters (the blind beggar who saw, the prince or princess in disguise). But our sexual tastes changed, so Griffith's Babylon in *Intolerance* is a Harem source, and *The Wind and the Lion* comes near the end of this genre's listless development. There is even a docudrama TV miniseries, *Harem* (1986).

Kids enter movies through such simple genres, Harem and Pirate, Empire, Boys' Book, Girls' Book, Animal Pictures, Sports Pictures: to have a dog like Lassie, to know a horse like Flicka, to be at one with *National Velvet*; to run the race, make the touchdown, hit the home run (*Victory, Youngblood, Fear Strikes Out, One on One, Rocky*). None of these genres stuck with me: I was never any good at sports. I would like to think I was always too old for Animal Pictures, but I know it not to be the truth: I read shelves of horse books when I was little and went to see Animal Pictures. But I had a pet chameleon, black snake, and chicken, so parallels to Lassie and Flicka were distant. I didn't dig Animal Pictures the way I did *Jesse James*, or Sports Pictures the way I did *The Goldwyn Follies*. My kid genres were Costume and Musical and Western and Women's. It is important to assert here that there is a democracy of genres as well as a democracy of films within a given genre. We must not reject Animal and Sports Pictures: at any time they could evolve like the High School Picture. They haven't yet. They're just about where they started (unless *Equus* is an Animal Picture).

I think movies are frequently used for escape, but the kid sometimes needs to escape in a way different from the grown-up—sometimes just to another family that's not his own, sometimes to a place where people walk or dance on black glass floors, have cocktails, wear dinner clothes, stay up late. The first is represented by Family Picture, in which the survival or entity of, well-being of, the family is a central concern. Besides those I've mentioned earlier (chapter 7), *Author! Author!* and *Brighton Beach Memoirs*, *The Effect of Gamma Rays on Man-in-the-Moon Marigolds*, *Ah, Wilderness!* and *Long Day's Journey into Night* were adapted from successful plays—family concerns is one of the great subject matters of the American Realist Theater. Family is also significant as one of the genres in some of the most peculiar mixes of Mixed Genre; *The Little Foxes*, for instance, mixed Southern, Costume, Women's. Family shades off into another significant factor in mixtures—Americana. Altman's *Nashville* (also a Musical and a Comedy) and *A Wedding* are Americana; Jonathan Demme makes Americana: *Melvin and Howard*, *Citizens Band*, *Swing Shift* (mixed with Women's), *Something Wild* (mixed with Comedy and Road Picture), and *Married to the Mob* (mixed with Crime and Comedy). *Picnic* is Americana (mixed with Women's); *Chad Hanna* is Americana (mixed with Costume); *State Fair* is Americana (mixed with Musical); if there had never been an Inventor Picture, *Young Tom Edison* would have been Americana. *Judge Priest* and *The Sun Shines Bright* are Americana mixed with Comedy, but none of these labels is as significant as the primary label for these movies, Fordian. *The Egg and I, Mr. Blandings Builds His Dream House, George Washington Slept Here* are all Americana mixed with Comedy.

We need these labels if we are to take the position that every film has a genre because we have to clean house after we make all the piles that have clear genres and find we have some left over. We also needed these genres as a child to find our ideal other family, to help us identify what was so unbearable about the one we felt we had been put in by mistake.

The place with the black glass floor had another kind of family and as a kid I was torn between one and another —between knowing who I was and wanting to be quite other. Sometimes I needed to be surrounded by one kind of escape —taken into a different *normal* family for a change—and sometimes out of family altogether to the world of *Top Hat*'s Venice. Among other things, sometimes movies just want us to own them; sometimes this is enough.

What was going on in the country was a similar schizophrenic yearning (Did you ever have the feeling that you wanted to go and still had the feeling that you wanted to stay?). There were films that depicted shames of the nation and the nitty gritty (*I Am a Fugitive from a Chain Gang, The Public Enemy, Our Daily Bread, The Grapes of Wrath*) or troubled or close families (*Tomorrow the World, The Fighting Sullivans*). On the other hand there were black glass floors and high times (*Top Hat, Midnight*). The split, as has been observed, represented a response of ameliorative realism or of remedial fantasy for the Depression.

There were a lot of those black glass floors and those big white sets in Musicals, and for my particular movie generation the Musical was a firm center, so the Musical, and in particular the musical number, became an essential of life. The second movie my father took me to was a Musical. The first was *The Hunchback of Notre Dame*, which pleased and puzzled me. I loved going so effortlessly into the past, was pleased I could look at Laughton's ugliness and see what that crowd in Paris thought was funny about it even as I felt for him. I was puzzled (I think now) by how easily its complicated narrative passed from that movie into my head. But *Snow White and the Seven Dwarfs* and *Top Hat* were for me where self met its ideal form of meaning. I think Musicals give us who love them a self we might not otherwise know we have, and we get this developed self early. I remember my father warning me, "There's a lot of singing and dancing, and you may not like it." He knew I would love Musicals as much as he did, but he was a careful parent. (Later he dutifully warned me that *Pygmalion* was "pretty talky," as if that would stop me from staring transfixed at the screen even when I couldn't quite make out the movie except for the part with the marbles which I liked a lot.)

Musical numbers were an ideal way into meaning of these movies for a child: songs were sung in words of one syllable: short, direct. But we soon knew only their repetition and easy words were simple, aimed at the very stupid: we were very soon on to their sometimes complex double meaning and suggestion. All this was accompanied by a mnemonic tune. Most important, numbers were short; if we couldn't quite recall a full movie all in its proper order after just one viewing (I started staying twice through the feature at six when I began to go alone), a musical number could be put through the mind's projector with almost nothing lost. This total recall was a heady power because it engaged self directly in a world of fantasy. Numbers were not singalongs until we left the movie house, but then they became production numbers, something more than singalong, an access to direct participation. We could be as they were on the screen. I committed to memory Bill Robinson's dance with Shirley Temple on the stairs in *The Little Colonel*, "Buckle Down, Winsockie" in *Best Foot Forward*, Eleanor Powell dancing on the drums (a bit harder to bring back in detail, but we tried it on Sunday school tables). I watched as (how many? *all those*) Astaires stretched across the stage in *Blue Skies*. I knew it, I did it, so in a new way I *was* it.

And we carry this sense of them through later life. Our experience of Musicals is different from that with other movies. In *Swing Time* when I first sense how involved I am getting with Fred Astaire and Ginger Rogers in the "Pick yourself up, brush yourself off" number, on repeated encounters I suspect it is going to disappoint me just a little bit, because it's starting so haltingly—or maybe not quite be up to what I remembered. But as soon as the dancing starts I know it's all O.K. and I was wrong to have doubted it. For musical numbers we become collectors, handling yet again a loved object we hold as if it is ours alone; take it down off the shelf for another look, anxious that we have waited long enough this time so we won't go stale on it (we do, after all, know the tune and most of the words), anxious that since we looked last it will have lost its power to enchant. Musical numbers are why we watch Musicals. What remains of these movies other than the numbers is essential but not vital in the same way. Without the sense that the nonnumber portion of musicals is filler, we couldn't like musical numbers this much because without that space to accommodate their power we know the numbers wouldn't work.

The numbers in movie Musicals are a formal innovation in art—not like an aria in an opera, and operating not quite the way numbers do in musical comedies on the stage. I think they are the Musical's chief contribution to the way it makes American scenarios. Musicals are subversive in an old-fashioned way, as the burletta was to *opera seria*: they attack the formal orders of a movie's ideal narrative. This is an important part of their charm. The song cue is a self-conscious signal not just that a song is about to begin, but that the empathetic engagement a movie ordinarily makes with us is about to be suspended so we can participate intensely in the rhythmic and repetitive power of the lyric and music. If we love Musicals (and I say *if* because some perfectly respectable people find them beneath contempt) we relish this cancellation of the rules. It makes possible all of film's potential for expansion. The set can suddenly expand beyond the limits of the stage, beyond the space we have already seen as the cast rehearsed the number.

Of course if they're good they tell the movie's story and advance the action, but, more important, numbers are the stuff of Musicals' force, microcosms of their meanings, a medium for profound encounters. When Astaire sings "Never Gonna Dance" we know what a loss it would be if he *didn't* dance —the issue at hand is critical: self can be changed by the outcome.

Other numbers taught us to dance: if we could not walk out of the matinee into the awful Florida light knowing how to do "The Carioca" or "The Varsity Drag" we would not have been able to stand it. And the rousing, full-stage, full-cast finale of *This Is the Army* or the departure of the troop ship in *Up in Arms*: the crowds prevented much movement, but even standing still this was good stuff. And the Grand March number of *Yankee Doodle Dandy* (the one with all the Boy Scouts). This led to my lifelong disappointment in social dances I went to. (John Ford Pictures had taught me that dances featured grand marches, now two, now four, finally a line across the ballroom.) Newspapers had pictures of the grand march at dances in St. Petersburg, but not one dance I went to had one.

I ordinarily resist this kind of rampant nostalgia when I write about movies because I think it states the obvious, that a long career of movie-watching inevitably engages us on a primal level. I was talking at dinner with a friend this year at a college reunion, and she stopped in mid-paragraph to explain to a third party, "When you see as many movies as we do, the places in them become very important, and it makes us want to go there to visit." This is a message from an early self deep in Fantasyland. I appeal to nostalgia because this sense that a number reeled itself off just so I could make it my own, recall it totally, states a sense of movies that cannot be overstated: movies I saw happened just to me and only to me: a movie was mine as long as I was watching and as long as I could recall it and get it right. Neither innocence nor directness is lost when we grow older: we still see Musicals this way. When "Tangerine" is sung, or when Jeanne Crain sings "It Might as Well Be Spring," I know how to love. "Choctaw, Chickasaw, Chattahoochee, Chippewa" in *Good News* and "Moses Supposes" in *Singin' in the Rain* teach me again to handle tough words with ease. Once I can sing them I am as good as any well-schooled supporting player. This at my earliest consciousness appealed to the immature and undernourished imagination of a child working toward some adept, competent, or even elegant way to meet the world and express himself in it, and it passed through knowing adolescence into college intact. This innocence is never lost; I claim it still.

But latter-day Musicals are less satisfying and less innocent. Could someone whose imprinting Musical was *West Side Story* feel this way about numbers? I'd guess no because I hate that movie and almost everything that happens in it, and also because nostalgia is inherently egotistical. Fewer and fewer movies work on the kind of faith that Musicals of 1930–1960 had. Later Musicals (*West Side Story*, *South Pacific*) either imitate the shifts in Broadway musicals (big and bright is no substitute for feeling), or they indulge in a recapitulative fakery (the terrible Musical based on Frank Capra's wonderful *Lost Horizon*), or else they try (once Hollywood lost the knack for making numbers work) for revival of what had been but was to be no more. *A Chorus Line* tries in vain to find a structure based on old movies; *All That Jazz*, up against the same sort of problem, is perhaps more original, and almost successful. The Beatles movies and Elvis on film, on the other hand, are successful, a retro blend of old Musicals and new music. Richard Lester's *Help!* with the Beatles (and to a lesser and less successful extent Ken Russell's *Tommy*) anticipated a Great Shift that some years later would produce the video, a new form based on the Musical's old sense of number, but now with the rhythms and stories of successful songs picturized, hyped-up, and marketed. Videos have some sense of number as a small scenario.

Musicals—especially those numbers that moved us toward social accommodation by their ease, grace, articulation, and rhythm—made us Cyd Charisses and Astaires and, heaven help us, Betty Huttons: little old us. The formal innovation of the Hollywood Musical was a powerful force for adaptive fantasy: even if we were small, unfit, not cute, clumsy, we could for that three or four minutes imagine otherwise. The Musical has a great gift to give, in part because it has a great shape. Something about that imagining sticks with us, something about it makes us as Americans walk around with that confidence which seems to Europeans sourceless and mysterious, and to Asians, comic. About to burst into song.

Comedy is different—a political contribution to the idea of American scenario. In its own way it is as immediate, as directly accessed, as a musical number is, but Comedy is politically subversive. I don't mean that it is all satirical, or that it all works to construct some great political allegory, but rather that Comedy by its nature espouses a new politics, at least is an attack on the status quo, at most—the Marx Brothers— anarchic.

Why were Comedies so intensely felt by us as kids? I suppose because we were made to feel so at home in them, that they could (and did) happen to us, turned on what we had seen and known. Then using that familiar and conventional substance they proceeded to show us the way, educate us in the ways of democracy which were (and would be) ours.

What is the connection between Comedy and democracy? Perhaps it is the rhetoric of democracy that must always absurdly overstate its ideals or its virtue—or, at the very least, claim it really works. Its opponents are so ready to complain of democracy's crudeness, inefficiency, clumsiness, and lack of elegance that in order to claim for itself grace, ease, and competence democracy must misstate its condition. So we have self-ridicule and Comedy. But even without this undercutting of itself, there are plenty of ways to make fun of (and out of) democracy. Garbage men with power equal to the rich? (see Capra or Hawks or Sturges). Women with power equal to men? (see Hawks, see Cukor or Ford). Twenty-one-year-olds with more force than those in powerful middle age? (see Capra, see Demme). Are you kidding? Democracy, in its schoolteacher guise, will begin to explain, Well, of course the young can't with just a vote unseat all forms of power, but they do have the vote; Well, there's something like oligarchy, too; Well, wealth works its power outside governance. Overexplanation makes funny.

The chief kinship between Comedy and democracy I think lies in the doing. Just putting democracy on the screen and showing what it's up to is enough to raise a chuckle; show an extension or an extreme of it and you get a laugh. And because we're (well, sort of) free, we love laughing. The practice of Comedy is a practice of democracy because the situations Comedy turns on are tests of democracy; democracy is not just the condition for Comedy, it is the stuff that makes it up.

Of course the Comedy once built can move on to an unfunny result: in *The Gold Rush* the pathos of Chaplin's lonely tabletop dance with the legs/forks stuck in feet/rolls, in *Mr. Smith Goes to Washington* the rather tougher pathos of the common man who nearly makes it come right but finally has to be crushed by the Senate. Democracy (and this is funny) is barely possible. It goes without saying that the *results* of Comedy aren't funny. But the democratic sources are.

American themes in American Comedy are almost infinite, so I should add at the outset that I'm picking themes that work, some of them very old and close to universal: Aristophanes' *The Birds* turns on the way a man can become a machine and a threat to humanity, to be answered (and to be fought) only with a laugh. Henri Bergson identifies mechanism as a chief cause of laughter, and in film I suppose the most frequently cited example of comic mechanism is the efficient feeding machine on the assembly line of Chaplin's *Modern Times*, or even better, the tooth-cleaning mechanism. James Cagney's madly compulsive Coca-Cola executive in Billy Wilder's *One, Two, Three* is a man-machine: he combines the red-white-and-blue Americanism of his Cohan with the ferocity of his Cody Jarrett in *White Heat*. The Americans *and* the Germans in *One, Two, Three* reach a new level of self-definition: capitalist and National Socialist drives are made equivalent by comic pacing. Billy Wilder speeds up the action and dialogue to the pace of Howard Hawks's *His Girl Friday*. When people talk this fast and move this frenetically we think either of robots or of the wonderful mechanical jumps of speeded-up film (seen in Silents run at sound speed) or the electronic elision on our television screens every time we run a tape at fast forward.

Peter Sellers's collaboration with Stanley Kubrick and Terry Southern comes up with Dr. Strangelove (*Dr. Strangelove: or How I Learned to Stop Worrying and Love the Bomb*), a marvelous man/machine. I suspect the figure of Strangelove has its roots in Lionel Atwill's World War I amputee of *Son of Frankenstein*, which in turn is a source for Mel Brooks's *Young Frankenstein*. Again German is fed into an American extreme of character. Harold Lloyd's character in *Safety Last* is all-American, a nervous man/machine, beset and pursued and pursuing. So is Buster Keaton in *College*, simply imitating what he sees his fellow soda jerks and college athletes doing and ending up flat on his back. All he wants is to be just like everybody else: the mechanism of conformity.

An arcane example is Blake Edwards's *Victor/Victoria*, a movie that is all behavior and game. Both Julie Andrews's epicene sex impersonation and Robert Preston's aging drag queen play out models of gender behavior which become unpleasantly mechanical. He is simpler than she, a windup toy gone ber-

serk. She is a robot (akin to Maria in *Metropolis*), and her impersonation of a male female impersonator, necessary for her survival as a performer, lands her in trouble as a woman. The
more mechanically male (or imitation female) she becomes, the
more seductive she is to James Garner, so hopelessly in love
that he cannot see the signals she sends him from somewhere
not so deep in her real sex. This kind of mechanism (and a
similar ill-fitting adopted role) can be seen in Billy Wilder's
*Some Like It Hot* in Tony Curtis's and Jack Lemmon's imitation-
all-girl-musicians and in Marilyn Monroe's almost parodistic
(of Marilyn) Sugar Kane. Lemmon is a joke as a woman, a
parody of female, but so convincing that Joe E. Brown pro-
poses, and when told his mistake, replies, "Nobody's perfect."
Curtis is no joke at all, maybe *too* convincing, so he has to give
an impersonation of a near-sighted Cary Grant in order to persuade Monroe he's not the she Monroe knows very well:
they're chums. Sex role reversal has been attacked as misogynistic, an assault on women (see chapter 8, the sailor in the
grass skirt): these two movies prove it can be as generous
—and as independent—as any of the other assaults Comedy
can dream up. Men are as subject to being cut down to size by
it as women are.

The Comedies of mechanism produce a cautionary tale of
extremes: this woman becomes a machine, this man succumbs
to it because of this mind-set or that necessary impersonation,
or because she or he responds this way to the necessities of
the moment. Machines are cautionary, not emulative, resolv-
ing, or problem-solving, because machine undercuts everyday
human nature.

Not so scenarios for the Little Man, what William Steig used
to call Dreams of Glory (in Steig's case, kids: same thing).
These Comedies are little laboratories for democracy contrived
in some of the most extreme formats, to demonstrate and exercise the littleness of hero and heroine. In *The Gold Rush* Chaplin's littleness is measured not just by Mack Swain's greater

size but by his desperation: Swain is crazed by the snow and really, really hungry—hungry enough to see Chaplin as a chicken dinner on the hoof (or claw, I guess). Chaplin thinks he'd make a good meal even though he's scrawny. In classic victim response, the more Swain drools, the more Chaplin acts like dinner. Desperation of the Little Man is not that much different from mechanism: Chaplin is caught in the outsider's role by circumstances of cold, poverty, hunger, and the cruelty of others. Material for pathos, but the laboratory of Comedy makes it into continual triumph. Over these intractable odds little kicks of spirit seem effective. Democracy aspires to this: how we wish it might work as well as the movies do.

Buster Keaton's Johnnie Grey in *The General* is a technocrat, reared in a humble skill of engineer, but proud of his competence and flexibility in the mastery of his trade. He loves his locomotive (the General of *The General*), and this love comes into conflict with his love for a woman when she is kidnapped and his locomotive (with her aboard) is stolen by Union spies. To save it (as it turns out) is to save her; to save her makes escape back to the Southern lines with the machine more difficult. The littleness of the engineer is somehow matched by the movie's (and Johnnie Grey's) assumption that his girlfriend is a helpless dope, of no use at all in a train chase. She proves him wrong, but first she sweeps out the locomotive cab, and in tidying up offers Keaton a splinter to stoke the fires. (This inspires him first to throttle her, then to kiss her.) The payoff comes in her apparently silly scheme for thwarting the pursuing train: she ties a rope between two trees to stop it. Keaton wobbles both trees by tugging on the flimsy line, but she has the last laugh when her rope uproots two sizable trees, trapping some officers and men who are sniping at them from the front of the pursuing engine and they must stop to extricate themselves. The triumph of Little in this movie is

COMEDY: The Little Man (Charlie Chaplin) as chicken dinner for the other fellow (Mack Swain): *The Gold Rush*, 1925 multiplied: society keeps the engineer from enlisting (Keaton assumes it's his height, not his essential occupation, that keeps him out of the Army); Keaton applies the same strictures to the woman's inexperience. She wins out, as he has already won, by pursuing the hand as it has been dealt. He plays the engineer, and it becomes an image of such flexible heroism that when he turns soldier at the movie's end we feel he's betrayed the engineer we love. Keaton's truth to the human lies beyond both.

Frank Capra's movies offer obvious examples of the little man but less obvious than he might first appear. *Mr. Deeds Goes to Town* provides a hero (Gary Cooper) of apparently homespun simplicity, put to the test by everything American culture can throw at him. He proves not to be the pushover the big-city gal (Jean Arthur) assumes him to be, but remarkably resilient, as he demonstrates when he clears himself with the help of the people who testify at his trial. *Mr. Smith Goes to Washington* transfers similar initial condescension to a gratifyingly heavy Mr. Big (Edward Arnold)—a composite boss-figure combining industry, media, and politics, ideal as Smith's nemesis. Smith like Deeds is not quite the Little Man he at first appears to be: the worlds Capra devises are too dark. Opposing Deeds and Smith is a capitalist force of gravity that runs counter to the promises of democracy. Deeds's and Smith's hopes and ideals are good deeds in very naughty worlds indeed. Capra doesn't imply that either will be able to redeem his world from the powers of darkness Capra has equipped it with. But the scenarios give us hope—we see more good than bad, more of those wonderful screenfuls of supporting players Capra so skillfully uses than of wicked men in their gloomy and menacing offices. But it is a mature hope; for all their symbolic value and their power to rally, neither Deeds nor Smith has changed anything.

Mel Brooks's *The Producers* takes on another kind of dark world, a seedy margin of show biz dominated by Zero Mostel

COMEDY: The world and the front lines pass Johnnie Grey by: Buster Keaton in *The General*, 1927

as an enormous producer of enormous flops, so terrifying to the little accountant (Gene Wilder) he meets by chance because Mostel has already demonstrated he might just jump on him and kill him. The seediness of the world is partly of Wilder's making. He comes up with the suggestion to Mostel that producing a flop (what he does best) will make a great deal of money, if Mostel produces a guaranteed disaster (a musical called *Springtime for Hitler*), takes the backing he has gathered from little old ladies, and keeps it all himself. Wilder the Little Man ends up in jail with Mostel, but the dream of Mostel's friendship and the value Mostel has placed on him release Wilder from the bondage of littleness. Just by being a dream this Dream of Glory works. Sometimes we need nothing more than this for scenario: the sense that dreams, even dashed dreams, are better than nothing, or that others as well as we have loved and lost.

Blake Edwards's *S.O.B.* has another show-business scheme. A film director (Richard Mulligan), after more suicide attempts than we can keep track of, in a sudden flash of genius decides he can convert a losing G-rated bomb into an X-rated money-mint by getting the star, his Julie Andrews-like wife (played appropriately enough by Edwards's wife Julie Andrews), as she puts it, to "show her boobies." It works and the Little Man triumphs, only to have his wife and the grasping studio head (Robert Vaughn) take the movie away from him *because* he has made it into a success. The director is shot (literally) trying to steal (literally) his own movie. It nets for its Little Man only a beautiful Viking funeral. This scenario is a *succès de scandale*: by reversing a commercial product he never wanted to make in the first place, he turns it into a shocking excess. *S.O.B.* proves that ownership, far from being nine-tenths of the law, is only relative when it comes to talent: art probably belongs to the exploiter, not its creator. Another dark scenario from this supposedly lighthearted genre.

Scenarios for the melting pot are something like scenarios for the Little Man, more broadly applied than immigrant dramas: democracy's way of mixing it *all* up, master and servant, rich and poor, man and woman, young and old. There are, of course, some Comedies that turn on immigrants. Some of Chaplin's power over his times was surely that his getup —stick, baggy pants, worn shoes—brought him on like the immigrant he was: the little fellow was, at least in immediate appearance, a little foreign fellow. The Pink Panther Comedies take place in Europe, but Blake Edwards's Inspector Clouseau (Peter Sellers) plays upon our root feeling that the immigrant

COMEDY: Another foiled suicide attempt for Richard Mulligan: Blake Edwards's *S.O.B.*, 1981

(as they used to say, "our foreign-born") ought to act more like us (who have nothing foreign in our own background). This is also, of course, the basis of *I Married an Angel* and *Moscow on the Hudson, Visit to a Small Planet,* some of *E.T.* and other alien comedies—perhaps even of Lainie Kazan's Jewish Mother of *My Favorite Year,* certainly of Peter O'Toole's rendition of a boiled Errol Flynn in that movie. It's what makes *Star Trek IV* work: our friends the crew of the starship *Enterprise* are back on Earth, but it's Earth in our time, and they are completely foreign. These aren't triumphs over Mr. Big or of powerlessness over power, but rather of assimilation over characteristic essence, whether that essence is Italian, or French, or Vulcan. The lesson they teach is that overweening pride of the exceptional must be measured against the telling success of the average (or at least something a little *more* average).

Sometimes the melting pot assimilates with a vengeance. W. C. Fields and Alison Skipworth, in one of the short films of an anthology film *If I Had a Million*, set out to ram roadhogs with their heavy car. Only in America would a wronged party seek vengeance by motorcar. This is comic only in its inception: the implementation of the scheme is class warfare. The coming of the internal-combustion revolution was a libertarian breakthrough for the lower classes: by time payment they sought and found their cars; by car they found and sought their freedom from neighborhood, the isolation across the tracks. Fields and Skipworth, a headstrong pair, set out to ram roadhogs out of vengeance and a sense of injured democracy: it's their road, too.

I think Madcap Heiresses probably belong in this category (as they discover better who they are in the reflection of themselves they find in average people). In *The Philadelphia Story* Katharine Hepburn is less madcap than she is in *Bringing Up Baby*, and Grace Kelly in *High Society* is hardly madcap at all. The films turn on assimilation, whether the ex-husband (Cary Grant in the former and Bing Crosby in the latter) can cut the heiress down to size. In this instance, down to size is a matter of being less self-willed and more like the men who want her to love them. Hepburn is a pain in the neck to everyone—ex-husband, parents, friends—and we root for the ex-husband because it's clear he will be able to retain more of the essential woman in assimilating the heiress than his rival the rich dope will. At his hands Hepburn will get some comeuppance but not so much as to alter her essential charm. In other words, she will be brought into the population but stay something of her own madcap self.

The melting pot is a richer theme than *The Philadelphia Story* suggests. Leveling involved in assimilation sets up its own values to compete with the prevailing culture. In Clint Eastwood's

*Bronco Billy* the Madcap Heiress (Sondra Locke) is less nice than Hepburn in *The Philadelphia Story* and really bent on destructive behavior (as is Goldie Hawn, madcap amnesia victim, in *Overboard*). She is finally set to rights, not by exposure to the general population, but by being thrown in with Billy's troupe of anachronistic tent-show cowboys, who cling to Billy's old-hat ideals and hopes for the "little buckaroos" because he lets them be what they want to be. The melting pot brings Madcap Heiress to heel in a totally out-of-it world, leveling her to Billy's curious love for her. She not only comes to love him (a conventional result when Madcap Heiresses are brought into contact with their opposites, sane, everyday, unconventional males: see *It Happened One Night*), but she also comes to love Billy as the rest of the world does, because he's good. Assimilation is frequently followed by marriage or remarriage (as Cavell points out): once they are more like us we can get hitched.

*Bringing Up Baby* has, I think, the best Madcap Heiress of all. Hawks manipulates our attachments in a wonderfully rich empathetic structure, and Hepburn's performance (now perfectly sensible, now utterly impossible) makes us want to bring her back into the population real quick. Cary Grant's paleontologist, whom she traps into helping out with the pet leopard her brother has just sent her, is no place for us to turn for good sense: he's in love with the wrong woman, obsessed by bones "thousands of years old," and trying to get money out of people to buy more bones for him and support a museum to keep them in. So we first take the part of the Heiress, then that of the Paleontologist, alternately attracted to either (because it's obvious they can have more fun together than they can going their own ways), then repelled (because both are impossible half the time). Leveling involves our collaboration: the movie makes us want to bring both of them to their senses.

C O M E D Y: Madcap heiress joins the tent show: Clint Eastwood and Sondra Locke in *Bronco Billy*, 1980 (*overleaf*)

Assimilation is kept tantalizingly out of reach, up to nearly the last frame, as she, having finally found the missing intercostal clavicle, insists on returning it to David at his perch atop the Brontosaurus skeleton. Swinging the ladder in her joy, she destroys years of work as the whole thing collapses under them. What has come down is what stood between them (like the "Walls of Jericho" in *It Happened One Night*), what our collaboration in leveling has yearned to mediate, her nutty excess and his stuffy stodge. Leveling finds its best metaphor. Levelee (Leveler) collapses the world that stands beneath Leveler (Levelee) and herself.

Preston Sturges's *The Lady Eve* has a similar mismatch: the egghead (Henry Fonda, a herpetologist) is more accommodating than Grant and the Heiress is replaced by a vengeful lady gambler (Barbara Stanwyck). Centrism—the bringing about of assimilation—is thus much more erratic. In Hawks's *Ball of Fire* there's a more striking comeuppance for the intellectual when Gary Cooper the encyclopedia writer is assimilated through the efforts of the stripper (Barbara Stanwyck), a gangster's moll on the lam. Cooper is happily ensconced in all-male bliss (but they do have a housekeeper) in a New York brownstone (one of the best unit sets ever devised for a movie —makes us want to move right in) with a cuddly group of codgers, old farts, foxy grandpas—a dangerously cute assortment of hammy supporting players (Oscar Homolka, Henry Travers, S. Z. "Cuddles" Sakall, Tully Marshall, Leonid Kinsky, Richard Haydn, Aubrey Mather). Sugarpuss O'Shea ends all this, and under the cover of teaching the professor how to talk like the people, achieves her real aim, hiding out for a time. When push comes to shove she uses all of them to make good her escape so she can marry the gangster, but she feels like a rat, and even though she has forced the professors into engagement with the world outside, it is *they* who rescue *her*.

When we work within empathetic structures such as this we mediate. We are forced to judge excess by how it departs or deviates from a commonly held center line, so we may not want (except for the moment) to adopt the morality our collaborative mediation necessitates. By doing this we have already adopted a scenario of mediational negotiation. This cannot be a bad thing. Even without asserting that this scenario accounts for something in the American grain from the beginning —plenty of radical politics, social movements, reactionary response to progress, and an accompanying populism, centrism, mainline consensus-seeking—we know it accurately reflects another description of democracy. It is not, though, the situations or the conflicts of these comedies that bring us to a choice between centrism and extremism, but rather our expectation of what Comedy will offer, the shape of the way it works: we are given the options and know from the start that the outcome will be benign. We can enter into Comedy, however dark, with the sense that what happens will be mostly to the good. More significant to our rueful sense of the way American argument works is which excesses are brought toward the center: Madcap Heiress, excess wealth, and the selfishness of privilege; Paleontologist, egghead in his ivory tower. Too much money, too much thinking (see chapter 2).

There are some feminist Comedies about women who have already negotiated success in putatively male professions but who are now being resisted in the perfectly ordinary pursuit of their chosen fields. *Adam's Rib* (and to a lesser extent *Woman of the Year*) involves this competition; so do *Desk Set* and *The Solid Gold Cadillac*. Where do we in the audience stand in this? or rather, what would the movies have us see? The movies play both sides of the street, cozying up to our antifeminist sense that the woman got too much too soon and feeling superior in the feminist sense that the men are *still* dragging their feet. We may wink knowingly with the movie at the forward woman, but the format works against her: it is sure to hand her some kind of comeuppance in the end. The self-assured, self-determined woman (see Shaw and Ibsen) is of course much older than the suffragette, but this mode of showing women settled in a new self-sufficiency is more recent. Feminist advance is now a prevalent theme, and the sexes war on. Sexually aggressive women (*Something Wild, An Officer and a Gentleman, The Presidio*) are perhaps offshoots from this Comedy format.

Something of these movies, then, *is* part of the feminists' problem: it idealizes jockeying for position, give-and-take negotiations at the heart of mediation. *Pat and Mike* (like *Adam's Rib* and *Woman of the Year*), perhaps motivated more by the desire to have a Tracy/Hepburn vehicle than by the need for a particular format, shows us a self-determined woman safely corralled. Spencer Tracy, her manager, is so intent on his image of the woman athlete (Katharine Hepburn) as so much exploitable muscle on the hoof that he doesn't hear her very clearly when she corrects him.

*Unfaithfully Yours*, a brilliant comedy by Preston Sturges, matches a fantasy of perfect murder with the bumbling reality of failure. Rex Harrison (and Dudley Moore, in a very limp remake), an orchestra conductor, by the use of clever recordings (if he can just figure out how to make the machine work)[2] will apprehend his wife in the adultery he has supposed for her, and kill her perfectly in time to his conducting of Rossini or Wagner or whoever. He fails, but the object is wife-destruction.

This is misogynist, but it's not a patch on the most misogynistic movie ever, Buster Keaton's *Seven Chances*. Of course that's the trouble with Comedy: when we have to label it anti-this or pro-that we falsely limit its elusive universality and the necessary open season on any target. Even to call *Seven Chances* misogynistic is to be irrelevant to this act of genius in its life as an abstract object. *Seven Chances* offends universally, everyone and everything in sight—men, women, Jews, blacks, horses, trolleys, brides and bridegrooms, courting, the rich, the poor, lawyers, and country clubs. Keaton discovers he will inherit a great deal of money if he is safely married by day's end. His friend suggests that getting married is the easiest thing in the world and he should start out right here in the club (they are having lunch in the club) where he may meet women of his own kind. Keaton strikes out completely: women laugh at him, fail to get the message; his one success is with a precocious child who accepts his troth, but her mother won't permit marriage just yet. He trails several other prospects only to find them "inappropriate" (one reading a Hebrew newspaper is one of the movie's several racialist slurs). When another helper leaks to the newspaper that a millionaire in want of a mate will be at a certain church at seven, the brides descend in hordes. Bride-pursuit finally turns into rock-pursuit as Keaton's fleeing sets off a mad avalanche.[3] As I say, the movie has something to offend each and every person, but this is blended with such pure visual comedy that it finally comes back around to meet its offendees: the bride who has rushed out of the house so precipitously that she has time only for a veil of mattress ticking is a telling parody of woman intent on marriage at whatever cost; the pursuit by the brides (they finally take a trolley) becomes an unforgettable male bad dream formed on fears of marriage, male nightmare carried to a comically absurd extreme.

Leveling is more complex in *It's a Gift*, where we are engaged as W. C. Fields's allies in his battle against the world, against Californians and orange ranchers, all of which he brings to his comic level. A deeper theme is that of a Little Man trying to get by on the narrow edge of a pretty crummy business (see also *The Barber Shop, The Dentist, The Pharmacist, Poppy, The Old-Fashioned Way,* and most of the rest of the Fields *oeuvre*), beset by babies who destroy his premises with "molasses trouble," women who demand unreasonable amounts of kumquats, and a blind man, Mr. Muckle ("Look out, Mr. Muckle, honey"), who smashes through his newly re-glassed front door and destroys his inventory of light bulbs, evidently pretty often. Fields's wife makes him sleep on the back porch, an invitation to everyone in the neighborhood to harass him. (An early morning visitor calls up his name to someone in the apartment above Fields, "Carl LaFong." Then he spells it: "Capital L, small a, capital F, small o, small n, small g. La Fong, Carl LaFong.") He moves the wife and family and all to California and in the end triumphs on an orange ranch. Leveling brings the rest of the world into conformance with him. There is a delicate empathetic balance here: Fields gets us to accord with a set of values we might well reject if he espoused them with less carelessness. His haphazard existence appeals to us because it is marginal. It appeals because Fields is subversive of conventional aims and needs and values. *The Bank Dick* moves a little farther in this direction and *You Can't Cheat an Honest Man* perhaps farthest of all. The anecdote, even if it isn't true, about his writing the story for this movie on the back of a laundry list and selling it to the producer, is a perfect exemplar of the kind of leveling Fields produces: I shall behave just as I want and you will have to come around to doing it (whatever it is) the way I want. The human emblem for this is the company efficiency expert of *The Old-Fashioned Way*. On request Fields reaches up to the elbow into a desk piled high with important papers to retrieve just the piece of paper the boss is looking for. The office is powerless without him, but no one would dare suggest he clean up his desk.

I hope it is clear that not all this scenario—however democratic—is scenario to the good. Hollywood Comedy put down blacks, as surely as *The Birth of a Nation* did, with waiters and maids and chauffeurs showing their pearly whites, with otherwise sensible black men turning the whites of their eyes inside out at the mention of a ghost (for a contemporary version of this, see the limo chauffeur of *Die Hard* as he hears the building he's parked in is filled with terrorists). Hollywood Comedy as surely ridiculed women. Comedy can be as evil in its results as can any other scenario. Maybe this says no more than that democracy is nowhere perfect because its ideal is never quite achieved. Partly it's that hard knocks thump us down to size so we can live in this world with others. But it *is* a funny world, and Comedy is intent on proving to us that this kind of thumping does no permanent damage: just permanent instruction.

Musical gives its scenario in small, each number a microcosm for an encounter, a situation, a task. Its gratifying format sets up in us a disposition to expect working-out, even if toocareful finesse mars its end: excess complications part so that we can emerge into the light, the shape is significant to how we think things work. The scenarios provided by Comedy provide less of what seems to be a solution, are less overtly tidy, less sufficient of the moment. But Comedy is far more significant for our course as citizens: less individual, more social, less ideal, more like ourselves. By Musical we think we know what to expect; by Comedy we know better how to behave.

# 10. WOMEN'S, WAR, AND THE WAY WE WERE

---

*"What man would ever look at me and say I want you?
I'm fat—my mother doesn't approve of dieting. Look at
my shoes—my mother approves of sensible shoes. . . .
My mother, my mother, my mother."*

—Bette Davis in *Now, Voyager*

*She longed to know how she thought women in films
should fall in love so that their loves would come with
less pain than they did in life.*

—Gabriel García Márquez, *Love in the Time of Cholera*

In progressing from one kind of American scenario to the next we take what we can get. That is, I cannot
conceive of being imprinted by *The Brady Bunch* or *Lost in Space*
on TV, but my children were, and profoundly. Just so does
each of us put together a sensibility, build up everything we
are out of the attic's-worth of bits and pieces we found lying
about at the time, still at the time unconscious that what we
were doing was building, or learning, or taking it all in, later
incredulous that our experiences could be similar for everyone
who happens to be the same age, from the same place, subject
to the same stimuli, so different from everyone who is not as
we are.

After Musicals and Comedies the next movies I latched on

to when I was little were War and Women's: War Movies were
around by the time I was seven and eight; Women's we have
always with us. My parents never objected to War (there were
a few parents who didn't allow their kids to play with guns,
not mine), but for a time they thought Women's Pictures were
an odd choice for a child. They seemed to think they were
fundamentally wicked: they didn't like these films' easy ways
with divorce (a great no-no) and drinking (ditto). Parental approval of what we watch is no small concern. It touches upon
taboo: tales we can be told by parents; tales they wouldn't tell
us, Things We Ought Not To Know. Like other impressions of
the child in the dark, it stays with us a long time. Not that we
avoid what they wouldn't approve of, but that we find ourselves always either avoiding it or seeking it out.

The idea has more than nostalgic usefulness. Movies are divided between those they might choose (whoever or wherever
they might now be and whatever their taste) and movies they
would regret. We feel it still when we watch movies with our
parents, and we feel the converse when we watch with our
children. I suppose it's because film is so immediate that when
we feel them getting to us we project the effect they are having. We are, of course, as parents as dumb about the inner life
of the child as the child is about the inner life of parents. Had
our parents caught on to the inner life movies fed they would
have ceased to be parents and become like other people with a
sex life and a real past instead of those stories they liked to trot
out. Family is in the main a genre of which our parents might
approve, as well as Musical, Comedy, and Inventor; probably
Costume—though Costumes had some arcane drinking and
divorce and that kind of bad thing in them, it was still consid-
ered as educational as Classic Comics. Inventor, the most ap-
provable of these, contains something of the Mad Doctor; Family has some social worker's nightmares, as, for instance, Roger
Corman's *Bloody Mama*. This is a movie about a mother true to
her family to the death, Ma Barker, but such a movie! such a

mother! Before the credits she is held down by two lads we suspect are her brothers so a father figure can rape her. By the time the movie is over she has not only screwed one of the sons, but one of the son's male lovers. This is a movie I think parents would prefer their children not see—some would say anyone in their right mind would prefer no one to see. Yet it is clearly placed in genre (mixed Family or Americana, Crime, Southern) that might well pass the parent test. Parents priding themselves on their own enlightened state might watch *Bloody Mama* with their child. *Bloody Mama*, of course, was never made as a cautionary tale about family any more than it was made for the kiddie matinee: it was made for moviegoers who thrive on excess, violence, sex, and mayhem. Roger Corman was almost certainly cynical in placing this movie so firmly within the bounds of Family Picture or Americana (chapter 9), and too good a moviemaker not to know that *Bloody Mama* appeals to us by exciting our disgust and horror.

Parents, concerned about the noxious effect of bad dreams (and oddly persuaded that movies caused them), forbade the satanic indulgence of Horror Pictures. Horror was overtly subversive, shown in double bills at midnight when I was little ("We dare you to watch it all the way through"), as if they were some kind of devil worship, but subversive of something that held power no more, so subversive in a retro kind of way. We could by watching Horror Pictures offend the Puritan heritage of the country, but probably nobody and nothing else. High School Pictures give us a world robbed of the influence of parents and grown-ups. The Monster/Blood Rust/Wolfman/Mad Doctor point of view yields a different parental reaction. High School Pictures, as I have said earlier, prove subversive by virtue of their perspective: they attack the ruling adult world's status quo by showing us the anarchy of teens in control: teen point of view. Perhaps this is another proof, as Stanley Cavell says, that movies confirm their truth and ours by showing us a world complete without us, me, "that the present judgment upon me is not the last." If the world of the High School Picture is complete without me *and* without any parents at all, it is even better proof.

Any of the rest of the genres has a subversive dystopian element of some kind in the midst of its characteristic ideal. Horror and Crime would be lower by far on our parents' list than Women's and Family. What makes Animal Pictures (I include *E.T.*) and Inventor Pictures constructive is a norm set by parents ("Can I keep her, can I, can I?" "Only if you take care of all the feeding and cleaning up. It's your pet.") So any movies educate us in one or another sense of the word, either lifting us toward higher things or letting us peek at forbidden things behind the barn, even as experience (in a Puritan sense) can either bring us to the good or work toward evil.

So we went to War and to Women's, with our parents' blessing or without. War Pictures fall into a special parental category, our father the Commander-in-Chief. Combat Pictures were ready tools of propaganda, good movie soldiers working patriotic magic to bring us all to march to the same drummer. In the Forties they were intensely felt by the people who made them and intensely received by the people who saw them. *Guadalcanal Diary, The Story of Dr. Wassell, Bataan, So Proudly We Hail!* got us aligned, all going in the same direction, ready to fight. But what of *Battleground, The Story of G.I. Joe*, to say nothing of *The Steel Helmet*? The genre kept on growing, with the war and after, into Korean-War films trying to work the same format. What were we doing with World War II versions of the Korean War? or worse still, of Vietnam, movies that treated the Cong as if they were that old standby, the cruel and grinning Japanese Officer or enlisted man?

But while we watched the movies during the war that made the format, watched World War II Films during World War II, doubt was unknown. A contrary element (such as John Garfield in *Air Force*) was incorporated into the movies' characteristic fable of training, hardening, bonding, fighting. Garfield was a self-serving, undisciplined loner, unwilling to join the unit until push came to shove ("They're *shooting* at us"); he then took the side of his unit and the War Effort and became a hero. *Wake Island* has a milder version of this token resister in William Bendix. His decision not to reenlist is beautifully timed for December the Seventh, 1941, to remake his decision for him. As Basinger indicates, *Wake Island* blows up a collection of World War I things and geography, and, an amazing watershed film, gives new meanings to whatever meanings it can salvage from the old for new uses in World War II.

*They Were Expendable* is more disturbing. It presents its unit (a group manning PT boats, small craft) as a microcosm of Americans in a losing battle, suffering not just the physical affliction of casualty but the spiritual drain of defeat and (worse) the torment of doing nothing (in the words of *Mister Roberts*, "sailing from Tedium to Apathy and back again") while they wait for it. The movie finally deprives them of their weapons, as the Army drags the PT boats away on a truck. The force is divided, officers are flown home to fight again, and enlisted men (under CPO Ward Bond's command) are left to fight it out on the ground.

Combat Pictures have been treated by some dumb survey-historians of film as simple propaganda, something like training films. They are propaganda, but they are also fiction films. When we watch them today we are most conscious of their propaganda role, but we didn't watch them as indoctrination then. The training film I remember best from my time in the Navy in the Fifties was a blunt little number (called, I think, *The Officer of the Deck*) in which the new officer arrives aboard a ship that has just been through a crisis caused by an Officer of the Deck who hadn't minded his watch well enough: "So the O.O.D. doped off, eh?" the voiceover reports as he thinks, "That's not gonna happen to me." It became a joke with us, as did the VD films (grim though they were), because its spirit was indoctrination and it brooked neither interpretation nor inattention. Combat Pictures—and most fiction films—don't even try for that. We didn't watch them this way, and following them in this way is not what I mean when I call film-genre formats scenarios. Scenarios suggest, Training Films shout; scenarios make our world, Training Films insult us by sparse restraint, by their failure as participative fiction. Training Films come on as what we are told; scenarios become what we know.

Combat Films made American scenarios by encouraging us to assume a stiff upper lip toward Doing Our Duty or Doing the Right Thing. They made a new world we could inhabit and its world formed our expectation of what it was to be alive in a time of war. That's why they were so popular, so eagerly sought. In them the housewife, the child, and General Douglas MacArthur (who loved these films second only to combat newsreels) were one: all had the same sense of the same war. How grown-up the child felt when the Secretary of War came on in the newsreel and said, "What I am saying is that, up to this point, we are losing this war!" War Pictures convinced us of something like this: So war is finally come and this is what the world of war will be like. We became one with the movies of World War II, knowing why we fought, and ready to fight from our theater seats if it came to that. These movies create for us a sense of the world. We see always similar people (one of this kind, one of that kind, one Jew) pressured by similar adversity, each individually coming to similar low-key heroic actions, or resorting to similar halfway solutions, or falling short and slipping into self-interest and cowardice.

Some things we know from these movies:

—Diplomacy: we resisted because appeasement was wrong and these were Nazis.

—Peace and War: Later might be Too Late.

—World Leaders: Hitler was evil.

—National morality: we killed even though it was against our grain because the different culture of the Japanese (not to say the different color of their skin) made war, killing, rape,

and pillage second nature to them and we had to harden ourselves to their temper. Or so the movies said.

A single movie, a particular script or scenario, was less
significant than the whole shebang, the general expectation of
Next Things (What can we expect?), How Things Work. In
other words none of these movies worked on us as training
films would (those aren't movies), but as film genre works:
one film chase makes us know excitement, two make us expect variation, three bring expectation, delight in comparison.
Combat Pictures fit together so well that a sense of genre is
almost inescapable—it's better to die than screw the enemy
(*So Proudly We Hail!*), it's not good to hoard lipstick (*Tender Comrade*), it's good to mow down the enemy even if it means dig-
ging a grave to stand in while we do it (*Bataan*).

War Movies gave us many scenarios most Americans would
never have to use—what to do when tortured by the Nazis (*13
Rue Madeleine*), how to resist to the last man or peasant girl
(*North Star*), how to go on liberty (*Anchors Aweigh*). All were
grist for our mill. They did not just body forth a world, but a
moral sense of community. That sense remained in effect at
least for the space of one generation. It was very important for
anyone who saw a few of these movies. Most of us saw more
than that—many, most of them.

The Combat Picture was such an effective instrument of per-
suasion that its afterimage was a major factor in making movies about the Korean hostilities and the Vietnam conflict so
difficult. Having seen World War II as the movies gave it to us
at the time made it hard to figure out and respond to conflicts
not so simply reduced to good vs. bad. And it was hard to
conceive that society was now, years later, no longer as united
as the society from which we watched those movies then.

The kids of the Sixties and Seventies hadn't seen those pictures and were less than anything inclined to see things this
way. They knew what war was from television reporting (*LIFE*
Magazine had never gotten us quite *that* close) and what was

happening to people they knew. They were coaxed into *that* sense of what it was like to live in a time of war, but they knew, as we seemed not to, that war is hell. There were Vietnam Movies much later, but they did nothing to suggest that what they had seen on the news was wrong: they never provided an alternate scenario. Instead the scenarios adopted by one generation put it at odds with another.

Hollywood went on making War Movies during Korea and Vietnam. The Korean War Picture had a new element—brainwashing (see *The Manchurian Candidate* for a highly developed form of this). Vietnam War had another, the Heart of Darkness element, the product (as it turns out) of crossbreeding between war and the Private Eye's lonely voyage of self-discovery (see chapter 11) in Marlow's search for Mister Kurtz. In the film that comes closest to Conrad's novella, *Apocalpyse Now*, something of Private Eye and his lonely investigation into the underside of things is transferred to Vietnam, and in several other Vietnam Movies (*Go Tell the Spartans, Uncommon Valor, The Deer Hunter*), Vietnam's political uncertainties bring about the kind of transference we saw in *Blackboard Jungle* (see chapter 7) when that movie didn't know how to do a rebellious school gang. Maybe there is more generic crossbreeding and crosshatching than just Private Eye meets Combat: perhaps an older literary format, "going Native," the moral and spiritual compromise the Puritans faced when they saw the American Wilderness, transmuted into Going to Pieces in the Tropics (prominent in movies based on original materials by Joseph Conrad—*Lord Jim, Laughing Anne, Almayer's Folly, Outcast of the Islands*). So South Seas Pictures (*Miss Sadie Thompson* and *Rain, The Hurricane, Nate and Hayes* where it is blended with Pirate, even the Donna Reed plot of *From Here to Eternity*) take this as a shape for corruption.

---

Women's Picture was the kind of movie we went to with our parents, but they didn't always approve of them. This was because they sometimes just took us along (I had very few babysitters as I look back on it) with their friends, and these were what *they* wanted to see. This gave Women's an aura of the grown-up that War Pictures lacked. There were tuts of disapproval: Women's had more drinking than Westerns or Crime Pictures (but they didn't *like* Westerns or Crimes). There *was* a lot of drinking in them, and easy sex. I loved Women's Pictures, because I was sure they would show me how to live once I managed to get out of St. Petersburg, Florida.

The Women's Picture is a great umbrella under which many kinds of movies are made, and to assume that they are all set in the kitchen, that they are all like TV Sitcoms, or that they all degrade or uplift Women or push Women's Rights or any other simple thing is foolishness. Women's Pictures are almost as universal as humankind, and can be as abstract as Westerns. You can do virtually anything in a movie and have it come out a Women's Picture.

The Women's Picture is one of the treasures of American film. They are called Women's because in them Women come to the fore and because these movies were made for women, an audience once as secure as teens (although many men liked and like them). Women's Pictures are so important to American film and offer such significant American scenarios that they spread through and support movies of other genres almost universally: there are few movies that can be said to be free of their influence. A quick survey of the American scenarios invoked by Women's Pictures demonstrates how Women's slides into other genres:

Wife (*Mildred Pierce, Sign of the Ram, A Tree Grows in Brooklyn*)
Mother (*Stella Dallas, White Heat, I Remember Mama*)
Daughter (*Now, Voyager, Sixteen Candles, Doctor X*)
Whore-with-a-Heart-of-Gold (*From Here to Eternity, Stagecoach, Key Largo, My Darling Clementine*)
Career Woman (Donna Reed in *They Were Expendable*, Kay

Thompson in *Funny Face, Doctor Monica, Prizzi's Honor, Rich and Famous, Klondike Annie* crossed with Whore with a H. of G.)

Poor Woman (*The Grapes of Wrath, Sergeant York*)

Pioneer Woman (*Shane, Wagonmaster*)

Woman Pioneer (*Madame Curie, Flight for Freedom, Sister Kenny*)

Victim, Captive, Dupe (in the Harem, in prison, of the man's schemes and dreams: *No Man of Her Own, The Sheik, Broken Blossoms*)

Other Woman, Femme Fatale (*Fatal Attraction, Play Misty for Me, Now, Voyager*)

Rich Bitch (*Now, Voyager, Craig's Wife*)

Second Wives (*Rebecca*)

Unwed Mothers (*Fast Times at Ridgemont High*)

We can also organize these categories thematically:

You'd be so nice to come home to (Wife, Mother, Daughter)

One Woman Alone (Career Woman, Woman Pioneer, Pioneer Woman)

Against Her Own Will (Victim, Captive, Dupe)

Femme Fatale (Spy, Seductress, Other Woman, Rich Bitch)

Sidekick (Moll, Best Friend, Girl behind the Lunch Counter)

Ground rules for Women's are less certain than those of Horror. A woman is central; matters of the heart are never far away; something tends to disorder and the something that so tends is universal but as hard to define as the genre itself. It's as if the movies took that philosophical stance some housewives assume for the sake of sanity, that everything beyond this still point in the turning world is in entropy. Disorder frequently appears out of all due measure (what results when *Jezebel* chooses a red ball gown, for instance). It can come as an unexpected result to a series of mundane causes (Lana Turner's incomplete driving lessons in *Portrait in Black*). The results can run beyond expected measure. People who love Women's Pictures sometimes describe this excess as a point at which the movie goes off the wall: something simple happens and then something else, it proves to be decisive, and the picture takes a turn we never expected. So, for example, *Mildred Pierce* (Joan Crawford) gets out from under an unfaithful husband (Bruce Bennett), but then once she has pulled herself up on her own and begins to run her own business, her success attracts a ne'er-do-well wastrel (Zachary Scott). When he goes for Mildred's daughter things go off the wall. She might have been able to defend herself against him or even Another Woman, but not against her daughter. And now Mildred suspects the daughter has killed him. Women's Pictures surely inherit their sudden turn of plot from the popular fiction on which many of these movies were based. Later some of this excess, this cause/effect imbalance, became a challenge match between one and another director of these movies, as each worked to make his new project somehow stand out from the rest, or from the last one, find some way to split this movie from the pack.

The trouble with some feminist criticism of Women's Pictures[1] is that some feminists think audiences are made up of dolts because they take all Women's Films to be training films. They seem unwilling to assess the films as complex evidence emerging from a time certain, but instead insist that if the movie's not a part of the solution for right now, then it's a part of the problem. This can be worse for Women's Picture than as a polemic against other genres in that Women's Picture may appear to be teaching when it is not and appear to be doing nothing of the kind when it is providing most effectively its most powerful scenarios. No, I do not think that women and men all over America took *Mildred Pierce* as a script by which to confront their careless husbands and cruel daughters and bloodsucking other men. Women's Picture is the most oblique of all film genres (except, I suppose, for the Western), oblique in its *ways* and in how many interpretations may be put on its mercurial meanings.

Women's Pictures yack it up, although they're not quite as talky as Costume—indeed, the great ones seldom *seem* talky at all. But protagonists in them are far too heedful of what people say. The protagonist of Women's, woman and girl, early and late, sought and unsought, is always on the receiving end, always being *told*, and frequently ends up as much the victim of bum advice as she is of fate. Mildred Pierce embraces Zachary Scott's sense of finances to her peril. Sometimes (*The Sign of the Ram*) advice is one of the chief weapons of the wicked woman, certainly of the wicked mother (*Mommie Dearest, Now, Voyager*). Wicked women know a patsy when they see one.

This is simple obliquity. Take instead self-sacrifice, a teaching that apparently advocates passivity and docility, but which proves in the end to suggest exactly the opposite: self-sacrifice. These movies offer a new definition of heroism for the world. A protagonist in a Women's Picture offers something of hers— a strategic lie, her pride, her substance, her time, her reputation—as a sacrifice, hoping it will bring about some desired greater end—resolution of the marriage or divorce, a daughter's happiness, or a larger mission to the world (*Flight for Freedom*). Bette Davis in *Now, Voyager* gives up her claim to Paul Henreid so that he can reclaim the daughter Davis has salvaged for him with the help of Claude Rains. Joan Crawford in *Mildred Pierce* tries to implicate Jack Carson, and then herself to protect her beastly daughter (Ann Blyth): the sacrifice is made, but no one believes her. This is one of the advantages of sacrifice—you don't have to be believed for the sacrifice to work. When her husband falls ill Susan Hayward in *Woman Obsessed* is ready to ruin her own health by taking over in all his work (she falls down at the plow) in addition to her own work as mother and (perforce) as nurse. In *Seven Women* Dr. D. R. Cartwright, in order to save the other women, offers her body as a sacrifice to the rebel chieftain. And that's not all. She is a woman with a clear sense of who she is and what she means: dress is identity and her style runs to riding boots and trousers. So at the end of the movie she gets herself up in a white flowered kimono and an upswept Madame Butterfly look: she doesn't just sacrifice her all, she throws in what she has made of it and all it has meant to her.

In other words, in these movies self-sacrifice is not docile: it's a form of marking, of taking on a new identity. Force of habit suggests to us that failure of will or identity or courage is the medium of critical decision in these movies—in other words, that these are stories of women backed into corners. Seeing the movies proves this false. As the protagonist's identity rests on sacrificial marking, the courage evident in the sacrifice is a climactic act of self-assertion, not that far removed from Antigone's somewhat more active decision that brothers ought to have a fit burial. The will involved is more important than the courage, but this can look passive; these women's sense of who they are and (therefore) what they must do next is the most significant teaching of such sacrifice. Of course self-sacrifice can lead to victimization when adopted as a role model or assumed to be woman's lot or duty. But that's not what we ordinarily *see* in these movies: these are rather single acts of decisive women that become marking events—their cards of identity—for their whole lives. D. R. Cartwright and Stella Dallas offer extremes as examples, each becoming the opposite of all she has stood for, tough doctor as pliant concubine, Stella becoming even more what she was to start with, mother as sacrifice; both are as heroic as anyone the movies provide.

Self-sacrifice is more than a generic element; it is part of the primal understanding between women. Women in these movies may well be (indeed, usually are) men's victims, but they are always (at least afterwards) the other women's best understanders: wife understands secretary, or other woman, or (too patiently perhaps) daughter, and forgives and welcomes back the errant male (*Doctor Monica, Wife vs. Secretary, Now, Voy-*

*ager*). But these men turn out to be less important than they at first appear. Even when women have fought throughout a movie for something (usually one man), there can come a moment when all this is forgotten because of the higher law, the primal understanding between women (*Portrait in Black, Madame X, Gone With the Wind*). A moment of repose calls up sisterhood that seems to lie beyond rancor.

This is the hint of an ideal: once things are seen from some point of view other than the man's career-driven, affair-obsessed selfish monomania, the world is turned right and we see that such peace may be ours as well if we can just master the primal understanding of woman for woman. It can circumvent institutions, which—hospitals, law enforcement, social workers, parents and the family—have by this point already failed. This is one reason why Women's Pictures are so universal: they turn on fundamental human issues, matters not just of family and love, but fate and destiny, vocation and the heart, love and duty, free will and necessity. They suggest that only people persist, and even your enemies are people, if you can just get to that point. Women's Pictures incorporate a conversion of world view.

Why then do feminists complain of them? One good reason: often the course of the movie determines the course of the woman. This is not only depiction anchored in a sexist world, it describes a profoundly fatalistic system. Or maybe a quietistic system, if we can take seriously the understanding between woman and woman. The world is fated, but at peace with its fate. So this is so: then let us accept it. This was advice difficult to accept even in the time the movies were made, to say nothing of right now.

The bad side of this (taking what comes) is easy to ridicule. Why do these women always give in to the least hint of scandal (*Doctor Monica*), waver from their path advancing toward the New Woman when Mother calls (*Now, Voyager*), take the bum at his word (*Sudden Fear, Mildred Pierce*), surrender to guys

(*Women's Prison*)? And these are the good movies. Weaker women abound in Women's Pictures of the second rank. The good side is that these films also contain extraordinary women who make it possible for us to observe courage in unexpected ways (*Remember the Day*, *Tender Comrade*), to trace the course of truly remarkable people (*Seven Women*, *The Miracle Worker*, *My Little Chickadee*). Of late another part of this foursquare confronting has mostly been taken over by the television commercial: but always in the movies, even in the direst straits a woman can at least look her best, even when she is subject to the worst pressures imaginable and in the presence of a disintegrating life, as she is in *I Want to Live!*, *So Proudly We Hail!*, *Wife vs. Secretary*, and the Women's Picture contained in *They Were Expendable*. Or even in the Women's Picture that we so suddenly find ourselves in as we watch *The Grapes of Wrath*: the Joads are about to move out and take to the road; alone in the house, Ma Joad puts an earring to her ear and looks at her reflection in a bit of broken mirror. This is as much a part of Ma Joad's power as the Populist "We're the People" Earth Mother, and as American.

There is another most powerful lesson of these pictures: that every little movement has a meaning worth taking seriously. Women's thrives on significant mundane detail: Mildred Pierce's way with pies, Bette Davis's ivory carvings in *Now, Voyager*, Mother Jarrett's way with hats and eluding T-men in *White Heat*, the mad servant girl's ignored fears in *The Lost Moment*, Joan Fontaine's detailed suspicions in *Suspicion*. The concentration of Women's Picture, their obsession upon what is *small*, makes these details pay off. In *Stella Dallas* Barbara Stanwyck's wardrobe becomes almost an independent narrative, cultivating a complex double sympathy for her *and* her daughter: we feel for Stella as she strives in her daughter's behalf, but with the daughter we can regret her mother's clothes.

Women's Picture travels well: it crops up in widely scattered genres. To say that the "Women's Picture" of *The Grapes of Wrath* is a generic unit as it functions in that movie would probably be to make more theory than the situation calls for. But were *Gone With the Wind not* a Women's Picture the world would never have beaten a path to its door. Women's Picture has such wide borders, such a relaxed definition, and such a generous spirit that in even the most definitively generic pictures (the wedding in *Frankenstein*, the old lady's plight in *The Lavender Hill Mob*, Zasu Pitts's madness in *Greed*, the message in lipstick in *Saboteur*) we find ourselves slipping into Women's. A movie without a clear sense of its generic identity tends to revert to Women's (*Pinky* slides into Women's from Problem Picture, subgenre: Race; Anjelica Huston's story in *Prizzi's Honor* is Women's, as is the trip to the opera in *Moonstruck*; the opera in *The Lost Weekend* starts out in Women's but gradually gets overwhelmed by Problem; the cocktail party and the limousine in *No Way Out* are Women's). Women's Picture also knows what it is and can fend off attack by alien genres: an inattentive Western very easily can slip a cog and cease to be a Western; an inattentive Women's is just as careless and rapturous and free, but when it gets inattentive to business it is still Women's.

Castigated for being Politically Incorrect, undercut by parents because it seemed to condone divorce and drinking, the Women's Picture has taken a worse rap than it deserves. Most reviewers condescend to them ("soapy" or "true confessions"), but the simplicity and directness of Women's still triumphs. Mind you, there are boring Women's Pictures, infuriating ones, dull and cute, insipid and stupid ones. But these can be so characterized partly because the complex nature of Women's permits its characteristic elements to operate at their strongest and its weaknesses at their clearest. The very clarity of Women's Pictures has paradoxically militated against their being taken seriously.

*Doctor Monica* (Kay Francis) is busy at her profession and respected, secure in the love of a husband who we quickly perceive is smitten with love for another woman, and a rat. The only lack she feels in her life is that of a child of her own —ironic, for she is an obstetrician. When the Other Woman becomes pregnant she naturally seeks out Dr. Monica, who enlists the help of her friend the woman architect; together they will arrange for a discreet confinement. The Doctor will even settle the Problem of adoption by taking the child herself. Then Dr. Monica discovers by accident who the father is. She Goes Through With It, with the result that the child's mother is so in awe of Dr. Monica's strength of character that she flies off into the sunset (she is an aviatrix) to her presumptive death.

Bette Davis in *Deception* learns from her fiancé, a European cellist and composer, that he has made good his escape from Hitler's Europe and will meet her in New York. Once there he is surprised to discover that she not only has a very nice apartment, but very fine clothes, including fur coats. He soon learns she has become "the protégée" of a famous conductor, Claude Rains. Has she become Rains's mistress? Not in this movie. In the ensuing struggle (for Bette Davis's attentions? for the heart of Paul Henreid?) Rains at every juncture seems more interested in Henreid than he is in Davis. He takes the couple to dine in a fine restaurant (featuring I think the most agonizing torture-at-a-meal of all movies: Rains wear gloves) and commissions from him a cello concerto (occasion for Bernard Herrmann to compose one for the movie). The torment continually puts us in the place of the stranger coming into a room, sharing a meal. Henreid is not sure he understands this friendship: if this is a triangle, how does it work? Just what *did* Bette Davis do for those fur coats? *Deception* marks a high reach of elegance of the Women's Picture (Ernest Haller's photography is part of this, and the sets). At the same time the movie is a triumph of convoluted complexity and (with *Now, Voyager*) evidence that Irving Rapper is due for auteurist attention.

Both *Doctor Monica* and *Deception* are examples of the human

WOMEN'S PICTURES: Two parts of an odd triangle: Claude Rains and Bette Davis in Irving Rapper's *Deception*, 1946

complexity Women's can raise almost by second nature. They are soapy only at first glance. If we pause to ponder the issues raised and don't automatically reject their sudden shifts, we find their quality of immediacy parallel to our lives.

Nowhere is this primal simplicity clearer than in DeMille's 1915 silent *The Cheat*. DeMille boasts in his autobiography that he made it with one hand tied behind him, at the same time that he was filming another picture, *The Golden Chance*.[2] *The Cheat* is a treasure: simple, gross, and effective. Fannie Ward's extravagance in spending (for clothes, we are told as the movie starts, for parties) worries her husband. In a desperate moment she takes out what she thinks will be a short-term loan when it is proffered by a Burmese ivory dealer (Sessue Hayakawa). She is the cheat in question because she tries to get around the debt: when the loan is not repaid on demand he moves to collect, like Shylock, in a different kind, branding her on the shoulder with the brand he uses on all his ivory possessions. Her husband, breaking into Hayakawa's elegant Japanese house (proving how much fun it would be to break into one, crashing through the paper walls), kills a servant and wounds Hayakawa. The Husband is put on trial for his life and found guilty. As the judge is about to pronounce sentence, Fannie Ward struggles to the bench and exposes her branded shoulder. The outrage of the assembled crowd is so great they try to murder Hayakawa and the judge promptly reverses the jury's decision. Her sacrifice is (for the sake of her husband's life) to reveal to a clearly prejudiced world that she has been marked for life by another man, an Asian at that (see chapter 11). In our stunned confusion at this point in the movie it is hard to tell whether the branding has also been metaphor (certainly suggested by the rhythmic thrusts Hayakawa makes with the cylindrical branding iron, to say nothing of its shape), or if this is just grand guignol, racialist excess, or melodramatic denouement. How we arrive at that branding is as elegant an example as any other I can think of of the myriad winding ways Women's Pictures find to go off the wall. I suppose that the branding (and over the years DeMille shows a rather indelicate attachment to branding as a subject for film incident) is a shock in itself, but to have it come as a crisis in a movie which promises up to this point to be going to be about shopping, is an example of the way Women's Pictures can take in the slack and suddenly pull us up short.

Why do I like Women's Pictures so? I think it is different from the short circuit of psyche *The Wolf Man* works on us. There we immediately identify with Larry Talbot's disease because we are struck by how terribly familiar this outlandish change is, the hair on the back of the hands: in *The Cheat* we see what we have always known: that anyone can suddenly become someone other. I think not even a habitual devotee of Women's Pictures in the Thirties and Forties with twelve hankies in hand ever *identified* with everything that happened on the screen. My point about Women's Pictures' sudden turns is that the hapless member of the audience should *not* have been able to keep up—but he/she could. It was unlikely, but the movie accustomed us to such unlikely turns, sudden fortune, sudden grief. And there's something else about that sudden turn. Just so do our lives turn (see chapter 4, Horror and the way it enters our lives.) Even more. Being able—or rather, becoming able—to fathom those sudden turns is a learning experience profounder than any training picture ever offered. By them we become attuned to rather arcane subtlety: she has changed her outfit (*Wife vs. Secretary*); this furniture must all have been bought *at the same time* (*Craig's Wife*); she likes him/ doesn't really like him (*Mr. Skeffington*); she has taken a loan from a Burmese ivory dealer (*The Cheat*); she doesn't know her baby is dead (*Way Down East*); he is lighting her cigarette, but he is lighting *two cigarettes at once* (*Now, Voyager*). To be able to negotiate these twists and turns we must come to these movies with a flexible attention, an eye for visual detail, and a keen recognition of generic hints. This secretary is dressing too well; the matrons in this prison seem severe; he said he was working late at the office; but the child will notice, won't she? Just such signs as our life provides, so in turn, after we watch we read our lives better. The force of Women's aligns our process with its process, makes its signs our own. This of course is a profound measure of the power of genre, and of sure American scenario.

Women's Pictures turn on clothing, the hint of gesture, gossip implying infidelity, a sign of wealth, a whisper of class. Not only *Stella Dallas* or *Back Street* turn on class; so do *Mildred Pierce* and *Suspicion*, *Sign of the Ram*, *The Little Foxes* and *Mr. Skeffington*, *Kings Row* and *Seven Women*. These two last seem a bit anomalous in the context of Women's Picture, but that is because we are accustomed to underestimate Women's. Instead we should recognize that the Women's in Mixed Genre Movies is not a measure of their weakness, but of their strength.

*Kings Row* is now best known as the movie in which Ronald Reagan says "Where's the rest of me?" after his legs are cut off, and because he took the line as title for an early autobiography, surely one of the most curious choices on record. It should instead be known for its moments of unforgettable imagery: the haunted birthday party behind the cast-iron fence in the shadow-shrouded front yard, the remarkable public attack on the macho doctor (Charles Coburn) who is willing to kill rather than admit his medical error, the disturbing picture of insanity and the strongly felt threat of its inheritance that drive Claude Rains to suicide. The movie, like its title, is indeed very soapy, but it absorbs us more and more in spite of ourselves, in its images of the claustrophobia of small-town life.

*Seven Women* is probably the best example of Ford's abstract auteurist use of genres—many genres at once—escaping the dependence on any single genre. This is personal cinema of a master who must have had a pretty good idea that he was coming to the end and wanted to redefine a whole lot of things including, as it turned out, genre and personal cinema.

Our first (inappropriate) temptation would be to see *Seven Women* as a Western set in China: desertlike terrain, bandits' horses rushing about under the titles, friendlies and hostiles among the Chinese. There is even a stockadelike walled outpost moving inexorably toward a Last Stand, a last message sent out through what might in another movie be sent out by the sally port. It is also an intriguing combination of Women's and War. Women here find strength in the very absence of men, the power of their courage put to the test by their own absence from battle. Away from war they face instead certain violence and (always implied) rape when bandits, as they must, overrun the compound. Their fears compound many fears without a face: their future, what will happen when the bandits come, what will happen if the bandits decide to leave, the destruction of their missions and the hard-won victories they represent, culture shock, whether their world can ever be the same again. The movie might be Costume but for its obvious effort to keep itself timeless by means of no-time costuming: the bandits look like Genghis Khan, the women are dressed in something between Twenties and Forties. There is a distinct pastness to the bandits' horses and how they ride them (especially Woody Strode). And as this is a Ford Movie, *Seven Women* also turns on aging, loss, love, and duty.

These are mixed signals. New women arrive; we are given the idea of refugeeing; Dr. D. R. Cartwright (Anne Bancroft) searches for the last remaining drug—serum search is a genre unit of the Costume Film (see *Butch and Sundance: The Early Days, Only Angels Have Wings*). Yellow Peril makes itself felt intermittently as one or another character makes a comparison of Chinese and Western cultures, the American new people versus the thousands-of-years-old Chinese. The variant cultures place variant values on what is at hand; new is not always valued more highly than old, or a Westerner more than a native. It seems pretty clear that the bandits are bad, amoral, violent, and inhumane (at least according to the Western values the missionaries have brought out to China with them). *Seven Women* has Yellow Peril but stops short of Fu Manchu, even though the head honcho, Mike Mazurki, rather resembles Fu Manchu in makeup and getup. When Cartwright at the end comes to make her sacrificial gesture, offering herself up as the tender morsel of white womanhood Yellow Peril villains are said to thrive on, we are struck with how strange a garb this is for so tough a female doctor to choose for her ultimate sacrifice.[3]

Women's Picture crashes through, and it is Women's that finally dominates. The impending delivery of a baby—this movie has not just a weakened new mother, but a weak expec-

WOMEN'S PICTURES: Anne Bancroft changing into something more comfortable, and more uncharacteristic: John Ford's *Seven Women*, 1966

tant father (who finally proves heroic); the older/younger woman interest in Agatha Andrews (Margaret Leighton) for Emma Clark (Sue Lyon); the friendships between Caucasian and Chinese women; the function of missions (women's work) and the ideals that come with them. Small Women's issues —that is, not the issues a putatively Feminist film might choose in the Eighties, or even in the Sixties. Once Dr. D. R. Cartwright is on the scene—that pragmatic and apparently agnostic medical missionary-with-a-past—her arrival displaces the movie's center, takes the movie away from the compound, and makes Cartwright's concerns and her point of view ours. Her astonishing sacrifice not only makes the strongest pitch for thinking this is a Women's Picture, but it also ends up standing on its ear our initial conclusions about female hero-ism and our empathy with her aims and ends. Ford seems, in other words, to be using any old tool from whatever genre comes to hand to see him through Terra Incognita. *Seven Women* may be closer than any other of Ford's pictures to *The Fugitive* in its hermetic enclosure of setting and movement, and of meaning. Why should Ford want to touch so many bases, to cover so much generic ground? Recall the women standing atop the building in the stockade, watching the troop ride off in *Fort Apache*: what if Ford were to take just such an odd lot and give them more than a pageant function, show them as fully formed characters? There's just not enough time left. It's like Verdi at eighty, overflowing with melody, not sure he can get it all in, the old pro showing how much turf he can tear up here at the end—Ford showing off. And there's more and more pressure the older he gets for him to show he's not old. The central aim in *Seven Women* is to astonish us with very narrow means—to make a grand impression with minimal movement, mighty business in a little room. And to make a Women's Picture that will give the genre a turn, partly by the force of personal cinema that sustains all that Ford knows, partly by reexamining Women's in 1966 just when everybody was assuming its heyday was past.

What happens to Women's in the the Seventies and Eight-ies? Much of it goes on television: the TV miniseries is a significant resting place for the generic patterns of Women's (*Princess Daisy*) as it is of Costume (*North and South*). Some of these are first-rate (if formless). Lindsay Wagner made a num-ber of TV features which used the format of the Women's Pic-ture (including the TV *I Want to Live!*, a frank remake), appar-ently a venture to show (it succeeded) that Women's was alive and well and could make money still. There have been a number of Women's lately: *Hanover Street* mixed Women's with Costume of World War II; *Body Heat, Masquerade,* mixtures of Film Noir with Women's, which, because they fail so badly to make it as Noirs (Can we have a Film Noir in color?), emerge from the mix as Women's.

The strongest I think is George Cukor's *Rich and Famous,* a remake of *Old Acquaintance.* The Bette Davis and Miriam Hopkins parts go to Candice Bergen and Jacqueline Bisset, and the theme is female friendship through thick and thin in the world of contemporary best-sellers. The women, old roommates, meet again after years. Bisset, who remained single, has become a woman of letters, Susan Sontag-like in the respect she commands among intellectuals. The other, married to a doctor and living on Malibu, has just tried her hand at constructing a best-seller and insists on reading it aloud to her old friend. Unfortunately for Bisset's peace of mind (she quickly has to admit) it's really very good, and just exactly what Bisset herself could never write. So she can have an affair with Bergen's husband, help out Bergen's daughter when Bergen herself cannot, carry on flaming pickups miles high in the restroom of a jet, or in midtown Manhattan, but she can't have Bergen's popular success. It comes down to a contest over the National Book Award: will Bisset (on the committee) give the nod to Bergen? They spat and split, reune in Connecticut and catch up in rapid alternation; Bisset becomes more and more frantic about why Bergen makes her mad; Bergen, more or less oblivious to the rivalry, becomes more and more frantic about wearing the right thing and making the Right Moves. What the movie does beautifully is take old Women's material into new times. The women of the Women's Picture in the old days (*Doctor Monica, The Women, Portrait in Black*) were powerful but did not come from a world of overtly liberated women (which in many cases made them the more remarkable). *Rich and Famous* does not just rehearse familiar formats to see if they can be made serviceable, it's about women of our time. *Black Widow* is more retro, but there's a new flavor in the woman-against-woman picture at its core, and a new sort of wicked woman. Perhaps because of competition with television the Rich Bitch has taken a turn for the Epic.

Women's Pictures are built reflexively: women see old Women's Pictures and react by making new ones. New ones are built like the old (movies come from movies) but are built by women now (everything changes); the women (and men) are now, for the most part, much more unconscious that there is such a thing as a Women's Picture than their counterparts in the Thirties, Forties, and Fifties: we assume a congruity of interests in a newly (supposedly) integrated world. But they can respond to its patterns and to what is New that has been added. Thus scenarios for our time are made.

For some reason somebody is buying.

# 11. PUBLIC ENEMIES
## Space Slime, Yellow Peril, and Crime

---

*"Look, Dave. I can see you're really upset about this. I honestly think you should sit down calmly, take a stress pill, and think things over."*

—Hal in *2001: A Space Odyssey*

*"Would you add a slice of chocolate cake to your lunch tomorrow? . . . And would you keep an eye open for a handpainted cockroach?"*

—Charles Grodin in *11 Harrowhouse*

Yellow Peril Movies made around the time of World War II (*Black Dragon*, *Purple Heart*) have been much discussed as racialist excess directed against the Japanese, but Yellow Peril has not been defined: it extended much farther back in time, even before Griffith's *Broken Blossoms*. Yellow Peril translates the Asian threat (or rather, the threat imagined by White Americans to be posed by Orientals) into racial stereotype: Yellows conspire to rule Whites. Where does it come from? Certainly from xenophobia: we're not Yellow, they are (or in the case of Space Slime, green, six-eyed, slimy). Back to the old days when we had tales of Indians told by their captives and they ran to extremes—weird pagan rites. Once the Frontier is gone we're afraid we will be trapped inside the perimeter with Aliens, or too many Chinese, or with militant

Blacks. After World War II, accelerating mutation brought on by radiation made a variety of Blobs, all a part of some collective guilt (that we had dropped the Bomb) and resultant paranoia (because it turned out to be true: we had). In every case what we fear is not fear itself but the darker side of ourselves.

The origins of Yellow Peril (this is different from where it came from) are probably literary. It might be categorized as an interesting but minor subgenre of the Crime group had it not spread its influence so wide. It asserts its independence so strongly I must conclude it is an important and apparently perdurable minor genre format. It features race conflict, internecine warfare pursued by families or Tongs (*Hatchet Man, The Mask of Fu Manchu*), strange methods of torture and killing, cult ritual, opium dens and drugged stupor (*Once Upon a Time in America, The Big Sleep*) as an avenue to sexual pliancy, political and criminal conspiracy (*Year of the Dragon, Five Gates to Hell, Big Trouble in Little China*), dark and wet streets leading to dim, smoky, threatening interiors, leading in turn to sensuous and silken secret inner chambers of sexual captivity and bondage (*Broken Blossoms, The Bitter Tea of General Yen*).

Like Westerns, Yellow Perils are geographical: for we go West and (oversimplifying) we have Western; we return and it ceases—geography is definitive.[1] Not so for Women's Pictures; they take place wherever women are—on polar ice caps, in airplanes, in offices—not just in the home. Yellow Peril doesn't necessarily have to go to the Orient: China is anywhere the threat exists; it tends to hang out in the Orient, or in lands occupied by invading Asians, or Chinatown (*Torchy Blane in Chinatown, Big Trouble in Little China, Year of the Dragon*). Sometimes even a Chinese restaurant (*Blind Date*), Chinese chef (*S.O.B.*—he uses a hatchet, his cook's cleaver, on an offending foreign car), or an attack-trained Japanese houseboy (*The Pink Panther*) will do.

Yellow Peril Movies are even more racialist than antebellum South Pictures (*Mandingo, Band of Angels, Raintree County, The*

YELLOW PERIL: Yellow Peril architecture, revenge, and weaponry: Edward G. Robinson in William Wellman's *Hatchet Man*, 1932

*Foxes of Harrow*) because Yellow Peril Movies assign greater criminality and amorality to the Yellow race than those ever did to the Black. Southern Pictures are trapped by boundaries of decorum the genre places on racialist behavior, and Hollywood was very nervous about blacks with guns (see a rare exception in Ford's *The Prisoner of Shark Island*). The moviemakers feel they can get away with it with Asians because they are a "safe" target, less controversial, more securely in the minority than Blacks. Like Bulgarian agents, or Libyan terrorists. In *Back to the Future* I suppose the moviemakers thought they were inflating a safely harmless enemy when they thought up the pursuit by that truckload of mad Libyans: we had not yet decided to bomb Khaddafi's tent and his children (if indeed we *did* bomb them: he's almost as good at scenarios as Hollywood is). The point is not that this movie erred about Libyans, but that racial stereotypes are so useful to fictions even in a time which prides itself on ridding language of them. As stereotypes, Asians were sometimes, of course, stand-ins for Blacks in an odd panracialism: implying something awful about Asians would feed the audience's consciousness of imagined Black atrocities. (Ian Fleming perhaps realized the ideal instrument for this transference when he invented in *Dr. No* the Chigro, trade name for a blended threat devised for his evil purposes by Dr. No, himself stand-in for the Insidious Doctor Fu Manchu.) We now forget, I think, the presumed inflammatory qualities of anything overtly *about* race in movies. Fritz Lang claimed that when he showed a white being lynched in *Fury* he was suggesting a subtle transference to a black victim by showing through a window blacks in a neighboring apartment. The Studio wouldn't permit him to have a black lynched because that would have been inflammatory (and probably because Tracy was a star). Asian/Black transference has an odd stylistic result: the very "safety" of Asians makes the rhetoric of Yellow Peril more extreme (We can get away with Yellow? then let's make them *absolutely* evil); this in turn influences design in some strange ways. New ways of imagining subtle and kinky evil made Yellow Peril a set-fancier's and an image-lover's delight. Madame Goddam, Madame Gin-Sling, the Dragon Lady. And since there are so many Yellow Perils, once Griffith and Josef von Sternberg made Yellow Peril Movies, it became a director's challenge match.

How many such movies do we have? Not as many as we do Westerns, and far more than we do High School Pictures. Why do we have Yellow Peril Pictures at all? Sax Rohmer, the inventor of the Insidious Doctor Fu Manchu, was responding to two incentives: a need to have a safe and permanent archvillain to capitalize upon persistent stereotype. And dressing sets and henchmen with elegance. And sex. The suggestion of Yellow Peril is that "exotics" were capable of giving (as one bad novel put it) "unendurable pleasure indefinitely prolonged."[2] Had something to do with the exquisite way Asians were supposed to have tortured their prisoners.

Yellow Peril provides an excuse for beautiful images, and serves some audience need. Because the racial myth in Yellow Peril becomes fairyland fantasy, a Griffith wet dream of sexual pliancy, dominance, kink (in *Broken Blossoms* and *The Cheat*, at least, imprisonment and threat seem to be more of a turn-on than sexual activity). A more remote answer to why we have Yellow Peril is, as I have said, political: political fear makes a need for racialist alienation. The idea is obvious: in order properly to combat an enemy (and this is true both of Yellow Peril and Space Slime) it is useful first to make that enemy outlandish, heathen, a different color, subject to exotic and probably depraved tastes (it has designs on our fairest women, as if to contrast with its own yellow/slimy/black/green/scaly skin).

Perhaps not so obvious is why Yellow Peril is so similar to Space Slime. They are a vehicle for xenophobia; both groove along generic lines. To appeal to racialism is to invoke recognizable ground rules and categories. And, of course, to become like Hitler. "Take me to your leader" is not just a sentence memorized on the long trip from outer space: it is also a message from Fu Manchu. First we talk, then we set about obliterating from the earth everything that seems to be that particular color. What we do with Space Slime and Yellow Peril is similar: the ideological tools for either are similar: they work the same turf.

How can we be sure that we got them all? is a question that unites epidemiology and genocide, depending upon which organic unit threatens us at the moment (see Elia Kazan's *Panic in the Streets*, about pneumonic plague, riffraff, and crime). I think this parallel has been obvious since the early Fifties when newspaper wags started equating Senator McCarthy's sense of impending Communism with whatever was the latest movie alien or bloodrust threatening whichever American (or, perhaps not so oddly, Japanese) City. The Yellow Peril never really was a peril to whites, but a convenient hook on which to hang economic failure, disquiet, and suspicion of conspiracy. Check this week's newspaper for stories about the way that Chinese organized crime is replacing the Mafia on our great cities' streets. We haven't become less racialist, just more adept at hiding it. The fine print (how these new criminals differ from our Mafia favorites) contains prose which is a near-equivalent of *LIFE*'s famous World War II guide to the differences between Chinese and Japanese.

*The Magazine of Fantasy and Science Fiction* at one point published a simple flowchart on which to track out the simple-minded science-fiction threats to all we hold dear. Essentially it runs, If you do this and this we just might be able to stop this Thing. Then when this and this fail the monster dies of an unaccustomed earth virus. Or melts when it eats a Big Mac. Or If you don't do this and this, then we can't stop it. Sometimes (as with the first *The Thing*) there is a hint of that pity we feel for Frankenstein's Monster, for this carrotlike creature brought unwilling from the deep freeze into a world he never made. Sometimes (*Aliens*) there is just sweet revenge to gratify us: the woman in the technological armor (making her a monster to match the monster she meets) indulges in guilt-free ethical murder and mayhem. The Monster Must Be Destroyed: she lays eggs.

Science Fiction Pictures are cautionary tales. What happens to bad little girls and boys here can become what happens to foolhardy or incautious or prodigal cultures. The broader target area is clear from the immediate (and rather unconsidered) way the scientists of these movies (sometimes themselves responsible for the release of the germ/bloodrust/monster) call in the military (just like out West). The first *Invasion of the Body*

*Snatchers* puts the choice on an individual basis: if one chooses to be wakeful and vigilant, one might be able to keep one's very own podperson surrogate from replacing one. Kevin McCarthy is both wakeful and vigilant (and in the end very nervous), but ends up on the thruway, shouting in vain at cars racing past, apparently driven by (a) the unvigilant, (b) podpeople. Much was made at the time of this movie's political allegory, as if we didn't know, and as if the allegory was necessary to validate the movie: the apolitical image is chilling enough without imbuing it with remote or interpreted significance. In the second *Invasion of the Body Snatchers* vigilance apparently won't do the trick: there are aggressive informers. The ending of this movie is subsequently less powerful.

More appalling enemies from within are found in *Fiend Without a Face* and *Alien*. In the first of these the brain worms move by sudden leaps on the victim's back (a perfect device to cover for rather indifferent special effects: actors playing the victims can grasp them by the head and wiggle them back and forth) and go for the base of the skull to do the job. As I recall the first time I saw the movie, both the sudden leap and the quick work were terrifying. A killer disease, and probably (1958) a direct allegory for the Communist threat.

*Alien* is more of a tease, and more surely parallel to a disease. John Hurt on a reconnaissance mission on a distant planet catches it from an egg case—becomes its host. Back on the ship the doctors find a crablike creature stuck to his face and attempt to remove it, only to find the creature has taken another form, and another route through the host: it pops out of his chest like a toothed phallus, sprays the operating room with chicken parts, and creates a general impression of awful (Science Fiction meets Horror). Placed so early in the movie this seems to come too soon for such a shock, but it serves the movie well; surrounding such gross detail with operating-room calm makes the shock the greater. Just by suggesting it is about to begin a similar sequence, the movie can collect similar shock without similar gross details. It works in an order opposite to what we expect: shocks decrease after that first sequence; by the end of *Alien* we have Sigourney Weaver alone with the kitty in the space ship in which the alien has hidden, pure threat and almost pure silence. *Dark Star*, John Carpenter's space send-up, gets some of the same profits out of an alien that resembles nothing more than a basketball (because the part is played by a basketball) and similar trappings of minimum menace.

   *2001: A Space Odyssey* is I suppose a version of this menace, in a much more intellectualized form. Hal the Computer is responsible for navigation and life support on a long space voyage. He turns lethal, flips space-walkers out into the dark night, never to return. Hal is not organic. He bores from within; he is most menacing because he is a part of the system —indeed, he *is* the system; if he betrays us, not only can we not safely talk and plot against him, but even if we manage this it will do no good. Everything we do, breathe, or eat is determined by him. Hal is the ultimate nightmare of the committed intellectual about the man in the white coat, and thus both ultimate mechanism (Comedy) and ultimate Mad Doctor (Horror). The only weapon against him is mechanical: his power rests in memory boards. (In this, *2001* has become a better movie since its release because so many of us have found ourselves removing a memory or extension board from our personal computers, and seeing it become—more or less —capable only of singing "Daisy, Daisy" or reciting "Mary had a little lamb.") To disable Hal's circuits, though, Bowman (Keir Dullea) must commit himself to losing his way, take a leap of faith into uncontrolled space travel, jump toward the unknown. This provides the movie with its psychedelic (and to enthusiasts of narrative, rather disappointing) light-show climax. *Forbidden Planet* is a version of Shakespeare's *Tempest* complete with Walter Pidgeon's Scientist/Prospero, Anne Francis's innocent Miranda, robot for Ariel, and id-monster for Caliban (gaseous and invisible, this movie's Space Slime). It has something of the enemy-within shape, but little of its menace.

From these movies we know better that our enemy is within our hearts, that social action is of less use than individual nerve when we come to combat one of these things, that the most significant warfare is a result of arming the will to combat. These are, I guess, moral fables rather than political allegories, more fairy story—dragons with a hundred forms—than modern fiction of consciousness. Their scenarios probably influence us most profoundly when something we see on the news demonstrates that responsibility we have delegated to our machines is getting a bit out of hand (air-traffic controllers, armaments production, combating corruption). As with the Mad Doctor, we judge the mild excess of our world by his (or its) lunatic and roughshod ride Beyond the Bounds. The monsters, like their counterparts in Horror, are combated by laughter and derision more frequently than by real fear. But what the movies remind us of in the here and now has a power over us all too real and all too pertinent.

---

Crime Movies are a different matter, but the same subject: social enemies, not only just like us, but sometimes better, cleverer, quicker, more on the make than we are. We're still talking collective (or induced or imagined) paranoia, the Enemy Within, as the F.B.I. likes to say. Yet these movies coopt our sympathies with sociopaths, one of the strange miracles of American film.

I have written of one segment of the Crime group, Prison and Escape, in chapter 6. (I think Crime is really an area, as Horror is, made up of discrete subgenres.) Other subgenres of this group have protagonists cast in a rhetoric different from Yellow Peril and Space Slime: the dominant strategy is to make these enemies resemble us, then cultivate our empathy with them, to make them like members of our family. The strategy works so well that one begins to wonder if a Crime Picture

CRIME/PRISON: Guessing games at home in the cell: James Cagney and Edmond O'Brien in Raoul Walsh's *White Heat*, 1949

which really repelled us from the crime or its criminal *could* work. Such movies, of course, exist. One of the purest and least attractive is *Ten Rillington Place*, a British film in which Richard Attenborough gives us his loathsome impression of Crippen. Or Richard Brooks's *In Cold Blood*. And some near-docudramas—*The Boston Strangler*, *No Way to Treat a Lady*, something like Charlie Starkwether in *Badlands*—work on real fears of real psychopaths. But the dominant stream of American Crime Movies could never have shaped itself this way. It turned toward crook-empathy in the Silents (*Intolerance*), then manifested itself most characteristically in William Wellman's

*The Public Enemy*. Cagney becomes the man we love to hate: he's an immigrant, punished by the system (see also Robert De Niro's Don Corleone in *Godfather II*) who decides to be top dog. He is a clear by-product of the Depression (as is a similar criminal, Cagney in *Roaring Twenties*). In *The Public Enemy* his do-good brother, clearly a wimp, keeps his safe job on the trolleys as Cagney moves up fast in a world of bootleg suds, murder, mayhem, and cute dames. It's only natural that as Americans we'd like to move with him: it's our kind of scenario. Without this bond of empathy, I think the Hollywood movie could not have made the powerful mark it did on the world's consciousness (cops-&-robbers is almost as significant as cowboys-&-Indians). Without it it would never have become so powerful an American scenario.

For violence is, as they say, as American as apple pie. The machine guns of Capone's gang and his enemies brought to our streets (or at any rate the streets of our mind) violent and sudden getting-even that seemed better even than shoot-'em-ups or Westerns because they were more focused and more personal. Anyone could see *he* was our enemy: look at what he just did, just now. Take that! Part of this was the American love affair with lawlessness and the parallels between the criminal's value system and the freedoms necessary for democracy (see the commercials for the National Rifle Association). Both were chords common to Crime and the Western. The form of our fantasy vibrated between these two, depending on the ways this cowboy or outlaw or killer resembled the private roles of our fantasies (see *The Secret Life of Walter Mitty* or *Singin' in the Rain* or *The Seven-Year Itch*) so as to feed our inner selves. By them we worked out adult Dreams of Glory: (some of our sympathy with criminals is built with Little Man (subclass: immigrant) and Melting Pot (subclass: legitimate business) images. This basic group of Public Enemies traces biography and makes it into a classic Rise-and-Fall (*Dillinger*, *Scarface*, *Little Caesar*). The Fall's not a patch on the Rise: the eventual wages of sin are as nothing compared to the pleasures and empathetic fantasy delights of getting there.

Another shape in the Crime group is more general. One or another ambiance becomes obsessive as one thing becomes another (friend becomes enemy in *Godfather II*, nice kid becomes mad-dog killer in *They Live by Night*, mother becomes best girl in *White Heat*, *Bloody Mama*). Or one thing can change everything (one rotten apple spoils the barrel in *Detective Story* or the spoiled barrel spoils any new apple in *Prince of the City*); crisscross crimes, and innocent becomes guilty, guilty innocent (*Strangers on a Train*, *The Wrong Man*, and other Alfred Hitchcocks *passim*); shifting sands cover familiar landmarks (*The Gauntlet*, *Bullitt*), and we are cast adrift in a reordered world to which former rules no longer apply. This is a nightmare counterpart to the Dreams of Glory found in Rise-and-Fall.

Compared to these the Caper or Heist Picture is clear as glass. A very influential Heist Picture that provided the format for *Mission Impossible* on television was *Topkapi*. To rob the Topkapi Museum in Istanbul an ill-assorted gang forms and assigns to its members roles that are never made clear until the time comes for committing the burglary, when all our questions are answered and all omissions of the skillfully timed and carefully elided script are filled in. It's a strong narrative shape that finds its highest generic development in the Heist. We not only know what we didn't know before, as we see the heist proceed, but we can anticipate troubles coming up (Was this dolt meant to accomplish *this*?) and know (by generic signal) just how he is going to fail. *Thunderbolt and Lightfoot*, *11 Harrowhouse*, *The Brink's Job*, *A Fish Called Wanda* work variations on this outline, and there is a parallel to it in some plotty murder schemes (*Dial M for Murder*). The *Topkapi* format also comes in handy for other genres: Comedy (*Unfaithfully Yours*, *The Producers*, *The Court Jester*), Western (*Rio Lobo*), Women's (*Sudden Fear*, *Whatever Happened to Baby Jane?*), Conspiracy (*Twilight's Last Gleaming*).

Another Crime shape comes from literature, a spiritual geography—the detective's journey to the underworld dominates Private Eye Pictures but, unfortunately, is only occasionally featured in Whodunits, the weakest of the Crime group. Some Whodunits have Private Eyes (the Thin Man Series), but Private Eye Pictures generally move toward Film Noir, Whodunits toward the world of creaky dramaturgical device. In Private Eye Pictures what is most important is the journey Sam Spade or Philip Marlowe begins when the first element shows up on his doorstep (something comes through the mail, there's a dame in tears, or a phone call for help); he gets ever more deeply involved as he follows a trail of breadcrumbs leading farther and farther out of the world of normal men and women and into a place of inverted morality, destroyed character, and continual testing. The operative is always being asked to compromise just one more principle to earn the next clue. I call it a journey to the underworld not as an appellative for the underworld of crime, but to invoke literary parallels (Orpheus, Hansel and Gretel, *The Faerie Queene*, Browning's *Childe Roland*). The op's disgust (like Childe Roland's) mounts as it becomes clear that the quest is not at all what he thought it was going to be when he set out, because the rules have changed with the geography. *Murder, My Sweet*, is a proper Noir version of this, *Farewell, My Lovely* a latter-day fake-Noir imitation. Humphrey Bogart (*The Big Sleep, The Maltese Falcon*), knowing as he is, doesn't get a firm sense of how much things have changed until quite a while after it's perfectly clear to us. By the Seventies Elliot Gould (the Philip Marlowe of *The Long Goodbye*) seems to know it's all just different down here, and he expects it (even as he thinks he knows how to fool his cat into eating cheaper cat food). He isn't really touched by the corruption until near the end when he discovers that it's his old buddy the ball player who has betrayed him, and that just proves too much, so he has to blow him away.

A recent transference is found in Terrorist Pictures (*Black Sun-*

*day*, *Sorcerer*, *Juggernaut*, and *The Taking of Pelham One, Two, Three*). These started to come on strong after the Kennedy Assassination: *The Domino Principle*, *The Parallax View*, *Winter Kills*, *Scorpio*. *The Manchurian Candidate*, prophetic in 1962, led the pack. Terrorist has become almost as customary to the movies as Nazis once were in films of the Forties, and they are built on some of the same foundations used for Nazis: they frequently look Aryan and speak German (*Die Hard*, but these guys don't even turn out to be terrorists, they just have to look like terrorists so they can bring off their heist), and may seem nice enough until they undergo the Change and reveal their true colors. As I say, Mideast Terrorists are the greatest gift to movies since the Nazis.

Which brings us to the Spy/Espionage/Secret Mission arm of the Crime Group. This uses many of the same devices as Crime/Heist. "Then one of us must be the Traitor." And as they depend on special effects, so they are frequently also near-cousins to Science Fiction in Weapons and mobile hideouts. Ian Fleming used Yellow Peril to form his villains—in Baron Samedi he had the nerve to give us a black master criminal and Hollywood has only recently (*Colors*) been taking that up. And Action/Adventure, far-flung global wish fulfillment, personal (*Indiana Jones*) and national gratification (*Firefox*, Colonel Oliver North), derring-do and contemporary swashbuckler at once.

What scenarios do these support? The scenarios Yellow Peril and Space Slime feed seem all too clear, and the wish fulfillment of Action/Adventure. Of Crime I suppose we all want to pull the perfect heist, get away with it, and escape to the Islands (where we will Go to Pieces in the Tropics). Cagney's Cody Jarrett and *The Boston Strangler* are tougher nuts, though. It's clear that if we acknowledge the criminal and follow him as closely as these movies expect us to, we must very shortly assimilate them: There but for the Will of God Go I. So maybe it's a device of commerce to sell tickets by making Bonnie and

Clyde cute or Ma Barker funny, or *Scarface* (I and II) sexy. Our need is the reason the pictures get made: to wreak the violence, to be outside the law, so we can sit there and dream on. But that still doesn't explain the reason these unlikely heroes get so thoroughly assimilated for empathy. I suppose that must be our American need to be outlaws (see Slotkin)[3] or our need to impersonate them (cf. one million stand-up comics who do Cagney). Crime, Heist, Conspiracy, and face it, the rise and fall of Legs Diamond are among America's most powerful and pervasive contributions to world culture. Traveling in Europe one often wishes that Emily Dickinson or Charles Ives could have caught on as readily as T-shirts or blue jeans. Not all scenarios, as I keep saying, are to the good, and almost none are deliberately designed to be scenarios. We follow what appeals, sometimes to the worst part of our nature.

# 12. THE BIG TIME
## Epic, Empire, and Westerns

*Rio Bravo was made because I didn't like a picture called High Noon. I saw High Noon . . . and we were talking about western pictures, and they asked me if I liked it, and I said, "Not particularly." I didn't think a good sheriff was going to go running around town like a chicken with his head off asking for help, and finally his Quaker wife had to save him. That isn't my idea of a good western sheriff. I said that a good sheriff would turn around and say, "How good are you? are you good enough to take the best man they've got?" The fellow would probably say no, and he'd say, "Well, then I'd just have to take care of you." And that scene was in Rio Bravo. . . . While we were doing all this, they said, "Why don't you make a picture the other way?" and I said, "OK," and we made Rio Bravo the exact opposite from High Noon.*

—*Hawks on Hawks*

Musical and Comedy offered scenarios made to order for a child and a budding democrat, War and Women for a citizen of that bygone unified society and a potential adult. Crime and Slime and Yellow Peril tried to make us (along with everybody else) into xenophobes and national paranoiacs. But movies are by their essence big, yearning to be bigger, and so America is, was, has been. So Epic, Empire, and Western touch a deeper spring, the yearning to Manifest Destiny in each of us, to match the national each to our own individual destiny, to claim Americanness for our own.

One definition of Epic carries the Costume Picture to its logical extreme (and beyond) what the studio head had in mind: starting as a measured attempt to spend as many zibbledy million bucks as he thinks it will take to bring in zibbledy million more, a production (*Cleopatra*, *Heaven's Gate*, *Apocalypse Now*) gets out of hand and spends money the way the government does. Spending more (it figures in that logical way) must be doing *something* right. But Epics aren't just movies that go over budget: if that were true *Annie* would be Epic. No. The best Epics seem to have been made by the strongest *auteur* directors.

So how can they be defined: Matthew Arnold's definition of epic would be contradicted right off by Epic Film, by its words alone—it tends to be verbose. Great Subject then and a hero perhaps—most movie Epics have a hero. And serious national import. This last is probably less central to movie Epics than written ones, although touting America has surely been one of their strong secondary aims. Epics all share a narrative ordering that leads up to a big or significant climax: this happened, then this, and *that* has made all the difference. Something about this *that* is big, and that's certainly Epic. Of course we don't all agree that what happened in it was of the earthshaking importance an Epic Movie makes it out to have been.

Start over, using movie measurement this time.

1. Epic is a big movie with a broad reach. This might seem too obvious for film: movies by their nature are big and strive to be bigger. Critical training, however, leads us to seek severity, spareness, economy—to feel that quantity is a false god. Form-and-content arguments particularly devalue size. We'd prefer it if we had to admire movies no bigger than *Stagecoach*: economic simplicity restricted by a formal complexity: form meets content. With Epic we keep finding ourselves forced to join the Philistines: Gee, this is really big; gee, this is over-scored; gee, they spent all that money on *me*. There is a mar-

EPIC: Assembled for the homage of the legions: James Mason, Alec Guinness, and Stephen Boyd in Anthony Mann's *The Fall of the Roman Empire*, 1963

velous effulgence in the air when Epic is around. So one problem is that Epic calls upon us to praise what we might feel under most circumstances to be critically regrettable. But we never come to a movie and say, I'm not going to watch because it doesn't have three acts. If we have to adjust dramatic standards to discuss movies, when we discuss Epic Movies we must adjust them even more: in order to value *El Cid* properly we must alter our moral expectations.

2. Big, as I have said, implies overreaching. There's a convincing argument that Anthony Mann's Epics (*The Fall of the Roman Empire*, *El Cid*) were the logical conclusion to a career

that left him nowhere else to go.[1] This too has a measure of *more*. Some of the Epics of the Fifties were so big they employed the Yugoslavian or Egyptian Army: that's Epic overreaching in the manner of the Roman Empire. (Rome is the perfect subject for Epic Movies, mega-big, an Empire's Empire: when in Rome do as the Romans, but do it better, do it more.) Overdoing in this league becomes definitive, of the essence; it becomes the point. In what other kind of movie would we be happy to see the number of people that we see on the screen in Stanley Kubrick's *Spartacus*? Reaching for too much, piling it up on the plate, is at least one of the things Griffith had in mind when he built that mile-long Babylonian set for *Intolerance*. After it was done, the set just sat there for years more, testifying to Griffith the overreacher, the impossibility of anybody's ever going quite that far again to be bigger than everybody else. To do it (big decision), to say you're doing it (big hype), to make it look even bigger on screen (big film), to have people remember you did it and come back to it again and again largely because it was that big and that impossible is Epic. And to have your memory hang around for years, like Griffith's big, empty set.

3. Epic doesn't have to be historical or factual or Costume. So many of these movies use myth that mythic becomes to Epic second nature. As myth Epic can probably be based in any genre. Horror Epic isn't likely, or High School Epic, but who knows? Epics can be lean (witness Jean Renoir's *La Marseillaise*; *El Cid* in a way is lean in its inevitable narrative: compare it to *King of Kings*). Too much can still be small in scale. In *War and Peace* Vidor takes the epic luxury of having us sit there and stare at Audrey Hepburn. He and we know, the camera knows, *she* is epic and this amount of staring is even more epic. *Duel in the Sun* is an Epic. So is *Barry Lyndon*. *Godfather II* is probably an Epic, *Godfather I* probably not. *White Heat* comes close. *They Were Expendable* and *In Harm's Way* are Epics in this sense. One could say that *Duel in the Sun* is a Western

that gets pumped up until it's an Epic. In part this is true: it is an Epic because Selznick expected it to be one. Let there be Epic: he expected Epic so Epic was. But this denies the very real sense in which *Duel in the Sun* is just the Western Vidor wanted to make, the movie that would embody everything Vidor knew about Western, so it came out Epic. *Tora! Tora! Tora!* and *The Longest Day* are Epic without being very good. *Gone With the Wind* probably doesn't have the scope, the leisure, or the grace to be epic, but it has Epic moments (in spite of its worst intentions). Everything about *Intolerance* is Epic, including the Modern Story. *Empire of the Sun* for all its failings, maybe because of some of them, is Epic.

4. Epic is the final stage of something, what comes after everything else has been tried. As genres evolve there comes a stage of self-imitation and decay. That sometimes involves an Epic phase of that genre. *Around the World in 80 Days*, was more destructive of genre than constructive; it was still Epic. This movie's place in film history was as the first in a wave of bad days ahead, when international productions featured narrative and production schedule ruled by personal contract, stars in the same scene who never met each other. But Epic, yes.

5. Movies always wanted to be big and get bigger; like their need to have a chase (because movies could show a chase better than anything), movies had a Manifest Destiny to be big *because* they could. The need to be a movie was a need to be big; but big has an almost organic drive behind it. Without auteurs, movies wouldn't have been able to be big in any good way—without genius, showing something big would have involved nothing more than bigger and bigger stage sets projected on the same size of screen. In a sense, that almost biological urge in movies to make themselves ever bigger was vital to the development of film.

6. We come to *Heaven's Gate* and its zibbledy millions. By its nature Epic invites the director or the producer or the studio

to get into trouble: to make the movie too expensive or too long or too hard or too personal or too overblown. In *El Cid* Mann can't simply have Charlton Heston prop up a church door: he must do it with a crucifix complete with a figure of Christ. In the same picture, the royal family quarrels in front of the huge fresco of the family tree. This is not too much, but Epic. In *The Ten Commandments* DeMille must underline *everything*. In *Intolerance* Griffith's sentimentality underlines some things, but not all: some are done with epic underlining—the razors poised above the strings. *Intolerance* is too long, but the statement is an absurdity. Too long for what? for us? It's better than us, in addition to being bigger, so we can't be its measure. Too long for what it says? Do we really know what it says? To say it is too long is like saying Hitler is funny (or not funny). Who to? and so what's funny? If to be too big is gorgeous then too long cannot be anything but; the *too* is misplaced.

Posing the question What is an Epic? sets an exercise in defining something, but the exercise at best yields only a better description of what that thing is, perhaps what it's good for, not whether it's any good. And, as I've suggested, whether it's any good may not be the aim and end of genre study.

I think, though, that Epics are good or else so many good directors—Griffith, von Stroheim, Ford, Hawks, DeMille, Mann, Ray, Vidor, Kubrick—would never have taken them up. More: Epics are hopelessly American. It's not so much that we align our culture with that of the Romans or that Bible Epics please the Bible Belt, but that this is the Land of Big—aims, needs, desires, ambitions, the Land of Barnum and Buffalo Bill Cody, both of whom found ways, in the comparatively intermediate technology of "show," to express the American Epic sensibility: Barnum toured Grizzly Adams (he knew Epic didn't have to have a huge cast); Buffalo Bill made his shows reflect, regular as clockwork, America's current foreign adventure

—Boxer Rebellion, Philippine Insurrection—whatever. Big *and* American. International adventure is a show.[2]

I have discussed some of the characteristic excesses of Epics under Costume in chapter 1. Why we need Epics is related to these excesses. The first reason we need them is like the dumb answer to "Why climb the mountain?": "Because it is there" is no better an answer for mountains than it is for jumping in the ocean or going under the polar ice cap. But as I have tried to suggest above (point 5) "Because movies can do it" is in some ways an answer sufficient to our need for Epics. Movies do Epic better than the theater or novels or (in the participatory sense) even than Homer. They put huge actions before us—a lot of people, broad scope, ants on the anthill. Epic movies cannot manage to make what they do *mean* what it does when Homer does it, but in them we can have a better sense of cavalry, of uniforms, of the scope of battle. Movies can also better move us about—keep us mobile. A seat in a movie house is infinitely, subjectively movable.

I think we need Epics in order to parallel what we do now to what was done in another time. Any Costume Picture does this (Polish relief of World War II is paralleled in Chopin's concert tour in *A Song to Remember*, his noble host compared to a Quisling, his guest the foreign dignitary compared to a Nazi; see chapter 1). Epic does it with a grander gesture even than Costume. This necessity to compare sometimes gives us a contemporary framing device by which to enter the Epic's world of the past. This seems to have been very important to DeMille and Griffith. DeMille knew he could find more excuse for sex, orgies, and nudity in the past, that the past could be an excuse for double-dealing the censors. Fair enough, but DeMille did all this as well before the Motion Picture Production Code was in force. I think rather that paralleling corresponded to a function he thought very significant for movies, to take us out of ourselves, or rather (because he was nothing if not imperious), a way for DeMille to educate us out of ourselves. Griffith thought that the addition of the modern made ancient stories do better at the box office. And he was a moralist: if one time-level was good, two were better. Epics provide the grandest sort of escapism, by sweep and numbers and costumes, by strange pagan custom and ritual and rite. They pull us out of ourselves and out of our culture; through them we can pretend to be other than what we are. So this makes Epic—the general idea of Epic and what use it has for our times—the ultimate scenario.

Critics have for some time had a lot of laughs describing the Americanization of pagan Rome and Bible lands by DeMille and others, and surely this is one form of the American scenario Epics make available. But it's not silly. When in *The Fall of the Roman Empire* Christopher Plummer succeeds his father Alec Guinness (Marcus Aurelius) and becomes a bad emperor, in our American way we address ourselves to familiar politics made pagan: Guinness's Marcus Aurelius is farther removed from our sense of ruler or statesman than Plummer because he is less like anyone we've seen in power in our own time. We know Plummer: he's a demagogue. The comparison is ready to hand even when it's not explicit (as it is in *A Song to Remember*).

Comparison is one measure of Epic; it's why *2001* is Epic as well as Science Fiction—if it's still our culture sending up spaceships in 2001, this is what they're liable to be like. But *2001* is Epic, *Outland* and *Alien* are not. Paralleling is what Griffith attempts in *The Birth of a Nation*. It is sufficient as Costume Picture or South Picture, but better aligned with Epic. Griffith wants us to take a comparison home with us: blacks in his time are like this because they were like this at the time of the Civil War (good sense of rhythm, bright clothes), but they behave like animals, either like simple house pets or ravening beasts. It's well enough to say *The Birth of a Nation* is a great picture—by virtue of formal qualities and ground-breaking precedents it surely is—but we should get nervous about asserting this (as we do about Leni Riefenstahl's propaganda picture for Hitler, *Triumph of the Will*) because it is also a bad movie, an evil movie. Partly because it is so well done. Formally lovely, but this formal force serves an evil end, and the point is better served because the formal quality makes it possible for it to draw its parallels almost subliminally. We think we are safe at an Epic. Because all are so big and some are so very skillful I think it may be that we seldom are.

Epic asserts its *movie*ness so well that it is *echt* movie, more movie than movie, movie squared. This is, of course, one of its chief pleasures. The national bands tootling out a peaceful world war as they compete at sunrise with national anthems in *55 Days at Peking*, or the commando raid against the Boxer forces played out in conflicting fireworks, such things delight. The parade of the legions in *The Fall of the Roman Empire* or even the queen's entry into Rome in the Elizabeth Taylor *Cleopatra*, the apparently endless passage of the spaceship near the beginning of *2001* to the familiar "Blue Danube"—each is a different sort of spectacle evoking similar responses of pleasure in us: we wish each to go on longer, even, than their Epic extension permits.

Desperate reviewers have sometimes wished Epics less, wished that they might harness bigness by imposing some sort of human scale in dialogue or character so as to reduce the sense they give us of overblown, hyperbolic movies. "Without for one moment neglecting the tempting opportunities for thundering scenes of massive movement and mob excitement that are abundantly contained in the famous novel of Gen. Lew Wallace, upon which this picture is based, Mr. Wyler and his money-free producers have smartly and effectively laid stress on the powerful and meaningful personal conflicts that are strong in this old heroic tale. As a consequence, their mammoth color movie . . . is by far the most stirring and respectable of the Bible-fiction movies ever made."[3] I think (even in

*Ben Hur*, although Canby's word "respectable" does linger in the mind) that such attempts are probably misguided. Anthony Mann's *El Cid* takes large figures and moves them through huge interiors and vast exteriors, epicizing what is already epic. Sophia Loren speaks as she does in *El Cid* because Mann's framing and sequencing has made her earn this movie's presumptive design: she is a creature of that huge world because she takes (as Miles Gloriosus says of himself in *A Funny Thing Happened on the Way to the Forum*) large steps.[4] Every scene of the movie—the meeting of the lovers, the spooky funerallike wedding, rejection on the wedding night, the greeting of the reunited couple by the children in the countryside ("And you must be the beautiful Chimene") builds a context sufficient to her character's formal immensity, sufficient to Loren's epic star-acting. We may have the intimacy of her in close-up, but the intimacy Canby talked about would have been wrong here. If Epic escapes its epic destiny it fails.

Leaving aside such descriptions as "epic destiny" or "movieness" or bigness, definition of Epic is impossible. It is a matter of test cases. Is *2001* an Epic? It seems to me it is. Is *American Graffiti*? Certainly not. *The Deer Hunter*? I don't think so. *Heaven's Gate* and *The Last Emperor*? Of course. Why? Because they seem to share with the big Bible, Greek, and Roman Pictures the sort of grandeur of conception and breadth of scope that remove them from other genres epics might not ordinarily share (Science Fiction, High School, War, Western).

---

Empire Pictures are on clearer ground, perhaps because they come from so clearly defined a literary type, Boys' Book. Even if Ford did not invent the Empire Picture (and I think he did in *The Black Watch* and *Wee Willie Winkie*), it is certain that the genre is dominated by American films: *Beau Geste*, *Lives of a Bengal Lancer*, *Gunga Din*, *The Charge of the Light Brigade*, *The Sun Never Sets*, *Clive of India*. The characteristics are: Boys' Book simplicity (sometimes featuring children acting as adults, as in

*Kim* and *Wee Willie Winkie*), heroic and cowardly military action, patriotism, male bonding, sacrificial death, foreign climes, and condescension toward the natives. We get some elemental underpinnings and some important transferable narrative units from Empire. The map with the animated dotted line perhaps originates here (it is certainly featured); it comes in handy for World War II in turn, in Combat and non-Combat Pictures alike. The buried-youth segments (*Beau Geste*), in which we return to see the children our adult stars once were, already in their infancy acting out various of the stories the adult counterparts will give us later, are another particularly engaging genre unit here and in other applications (*Kings Row*).

The stiff upper lip of these films is not limited to the British Empire—*Beau Geste* and *March or Die* are both French Foreign Legion. But most are British and most are unredeemably racialist. Exceptions are John Huston's *The Man Who Would Be King*, and *Zulu*, made late enough to take into account something of the contemporary feelings about these bloody times. Empire is terribly influential, not just on other genres, but I'm afraid the scenarios it forms persuade us to nationalist foreign adventures.

---

Westerns maybe ought to put us off now as much as revisited Empire Pictures do. They can be racialist, brutal, and filled with outdated Manifest Destiny. And surely the whites' societal campaign against the Red Man and something of the lawless force of the robber baron's greed keep Westerns from having a major revival in the Eighties. But they don't put us off. Indeed, Westerns are the ultimate test case of my argument: they are the most American movie—more so even than Americana. They show us at our best (Pioneer Woman) and our worst (Gunfighter) and so provide an ideal at the same time that they give us the perverse mythicization of the sociopath. They provide the basic scenario. It may be that the Western successfully abstracted itself from historical issues of the

Frontier. Once after I had shown *Stagecoach* a member of the audience said he didn't see why I was waxing rhapsodic: he thought it was a good Western, but nothing much more. The reason Westerns command such automatic acknowledgment (and such a corresponding dismissal) is that they are the *echt* film genre, the first, the best, the most, the genre we take in without even thinking. Even people who have never seen a good Western (and there are surprisingly many of them), or never admired them, are eager to admit that John Wayne in a Western is *The* American, or that watching Westerns they have learned how to be American or that seeing a Western can make them know America in a new way—the landscape, its openness, violent action, the suddenness of the Western's twists, revenge—they may say, with a wave of the hand. Everybody feels they know what they're like: more false genre units and fragments are used to parody Westerns than there are units even *known* for some of the other genres. It is also because out here in the open, issues are at their purest: good and bad, ugly and beautiful, disguised and self-knowing. Here we confront and shoot it out with whomever we must oppose. Both decisive moments and the roots such actions have in the deep past meet in the Western. Quite frequently revenge is given a particularly nationalist turn when a Western shows the source to be something that goes back to an incident of the Civil War (*Rio Lobo*) or the Mexican War (*The Eagle and the Hawk*).

A Western is wonderfully open in reference and meaning. That is, its meaning is less frequently nailed down by the audience as what its moviemaker intended than the meaning of, say, a Costume or even a Horror Film. So the scenarios Westerns provide for us do not become just permanent forms or armatures, but rather something like moments in our experience. The first time we see *Red River* or *Ulzana's Raid* or *She Wore a Yellow Ribbon* is less a note in our viewing history than it is a passage of autobiography. These are epiphanies for life.

I don't go along with Stanley Cavell's principle of companionship at the movies (that we will remember with whom we watched a movie important to us), but I know where I was and what I was thinking the first time I saw each of these movies. So I have their scenarios, actions, frameworks, and characters in which I have later couched something of my individual development, made into figments of experience the empathy with that moment in that Western, my phony memory of its significant decision. If I were to map my sense of geography in terms of roles I have taken (or assigned to others) in my life, the map would have as many movie sets, spaces, and locations as it does rooms in our grandmothers' houses, yards we knew as children, sandboxes of infancy. And many would be Westerns: the cave of *The Searchers*, the jail of *Rio Bravo*, the church of *Rio Grande*, the wagon circle in *Red River*.

If we care for them, movies imprint us anew, make us theirs, convert our accustomed imaginary landscapes to their soundstage streets, make of our enemies their heavies, shift our loves into their dream visions. Our life in them is a powerful parallel to the life we live, eat, and breathe. Their new geography is peopled with stars and bit players, some here, some there, mixing it up on this new imaginary field of vision. Of course it is not (as I've been trying to say here) all Western. For this situation I need a scenario from the Inventor Picture, for that, one from *Dark Victory*; here I go through the change Larry Talbot knows in *The Wolf Man*, there through the transformation Bette Davis wreaks upon herself as she turns from the spinster of the early parts of *Now, Voyager* into the glamorous if somewhat older woman, but still, ah yes, independent of her domineering mother. Here I have Peter Lawford and June Allyson in *Good News* as my automatic friends who support my every wish to back me up and with whom I work my schemes (the Best Things in Life Are Free); there I find myself marked like Peter Lorre in *M* for a crime too awful to tell. Here I know what James Stewart knows in *Two Rode Together*, how impossible are the expectations of the people in the wagon train and how inevitably they will be disappointed, but there I know what only Shirley Jones in that movie knows as she turns away from the lynching of her brother holding in her hands the broken music box. One role for one instance, and a geography to match; another for another, the plenitude of movie memory as our storeroom, the wonder of the stars by which we cast ourselves and our fortunes.

Western offers the greatest purity of shape and substance for this. But it would be an absurd exaggeration to suggest that we go to a Western to learn a role, or that they teach roles, or even that we would necessarily learn what they teach. John Ford's *Fort Apache* is a good (if thorny) example of how a Western finds its way into American scenario.[5]

The message of *Fort Apache* is, I suppose, that authority and the discipline that supports it are bad but that, nevertheless, we've got to have it. (This is as good a movie as any to show how inadequate "message" is to meaning.) The movie's Last Stand demonstrates that authority is bad. York's musing memories of Thursday for the benefit of the reporters (delivered in an unforgettable Ford image, complete with the reflected image of the departing cavalry troop superimposed on John Wayne's face) suggest that we've got to have authority. But to state this baldly, as if message were a sufficient paraphrase of the movie, undercuts the subtlety and grace and ambiguity of what Ford's movie shows us. We have no trouble paraphrasing its precepts (let the Commandant's daughter run his house, she knows better than he does; don't let her visit the scene of a massacre, she won't like it). These are surely there and surely taught, but the truths of the movie lie beyond such precepts and are rather more obscure for this difficult film. The part of the movie that is *not* what it teaches is its most important part. That York is protopacifist (but only that) and Thursday protofascist is only the beginning of a complex scenario that begins to emerge when we think about the movie. Take a wordless

WESTERN: The Grand March at the Noncommissioned Officers Ball: Victor McLaglen, Anna Lee, Henry Fonda, Irene Rich, George O'Brien, Shirley Temple, Ward Bond in John Ford's *Fort Apache*, 1948

sequence as the troop marches out of the stockade and the frieze of women that waits in tableau, watching them go. One of those who march (Collingwood, played by George O'Brien) had orders for new duty and didn't have to go. His wife stands with the women and we all know by generic signal that this condemns him to death as surely as that little pair of red shoes Harry Carey, Jr., buys for his best girl in *Red River* condemns him to death. We know we are to follow the movie by generic hint and nudge, not to grasp a message—or the director's or the studio's (or even the nation's) intended meaning for it. In the first place, it isn't real American to take a message as it comes hot and steaming fresh from anything—pitchman, ad, politician, book, movie. Generic recognition is part of an ideally American and characteristically skeptical autodidacticism. It's American to know better, to figure it out on our own, to know *because* we've been there before and have been through this kind of thing.

This need to *be* better is connected with know-how, the mind's equivalent, I suppose, of the Big Stick—in any event, a blunt instrument. Know-how (as in "he sure does know his stuff") is to be sought only if it never touches the books: book learning is wrong (or must be denied) because it's effete and not practical. We have to acquire know-how ourselves, street smarts instead of book learning. The Virginian "had been equal to the situation. That is the only kind of equality which I recognize."[6]

The value of the American scenario is stronger for Americans than others. A friend who is a native of the People's Republic of China misread *The Last of the Mohicans* by missing the clues James Fenimore Cooper planted about Magua: he missed the villainy because he took the earnestness and strength of purpose more seriously than Cooper's clues (as clear as Dickens gave us for Uriah Heep as we who are Americans know how to read them). We would almost certainly have done the same in his position. American scenarios turn on the overwhelming power of the clue, the unit, the code of hints genre knows and can convey to us without trying. We are Americans and are already clued in by that to much that it says.

We know when It's quiet, *too* quiet. (The ultimate version of this is not what we see in *The Hurricane* just before the storm, but that in *Red River*, the three-hundred-and-sixty-degree stare Hawks gives us of the cattle at rest just before the cattle drive begins.) We know from the dog in *Ulzana's Raid* (and his master's appalling confidence) that Horror is not far away.

*Fort Apache* is a Ford movie in which he nailed down the movie's meaning: we won't get out of this movie without concluding that Thursday is a martinet. Mind you, this is accomplished by subtle hint and gesture. But contrast to it *The Fugitive*, a movie so *un*nailed down that Ford admitted he didn't really watch it a lot (partly because he knew it was a failure), but liked to think of himself watching it (partly because he knew it was a failure). In it we do not know what he has made (or what we are to make) of the vagrant whiskey priest (Henry Fonda) torn between hiding out in the constant jeopardy of anticlerical revolutionary Mexico, and escaping just by not saying Mass or not baptizing infants. In short, the priest lives by slow death of his function, gradually ceasing to be what he is. What we watch is compounded of the character Graham Greene has written (which Ford might not have understood in literary terms, but whom he made more of a human than Greene did), set in Ford's images, the big spaces in the movie. These are not just spaces of the West but spaces for interpretation: nothing is settled. Compare *The Man Who Shot Liberty Valance* in which the particular Fordian moment is similar to *Fort Apache*, the opposite of *The Fugitive*: the meaning is going to be nailed down.[7] There is a great deal of *Liberty Valance*, of course, that defies nailing down—about love (Hallie's attitude now toward Ranse as she visits Tom's grave), about power (is Ranse cursed by his phony reputation as gunfighter?), about the West (is there a dime's worth of difference between Ranse and Liberty Valance?). But as with *Fort Apache*, many of these are *directed* meanings: there is a strong hand to indicate to us that powerful meanings are available.

Both these movies make me wonder about them and about movies, and my conclusion has always been that it's better to make *Seven Women*, with its meaning *undirected*, than to make *Fort Apache* or *The Man Who Shot Liberty Valance*. *Seven Women* gives us a multitude of meanings bound up in an enigmatic package. Ford knows what those meanings are, has certainly put many of them there. But he's not in the business of hawking meaning any more than Westerns are. He's master of the subtle hint, the open-ended meaning (*The Searchers, Two Rode Together, The Horse Soldiers*). Wouldn't Ford prefer to make *Seven Women* to *Fort Apache*? I think I can now see what Ford's answer would be: Not necessarily. And I think this is one of the lessons of genre study. I've said (perhaps once too often) that we deserve the scenarios we get, but this is not what I mean here. Genre study suggests that although much can be known and recognized from passing many times in similar ways over familiar ground, the revelation of familiarities does not necessarily remove mystery. If I am right that Ford's subtlest and most difficult truths are unconventional wisdom revealed by conventional means, then it might be expected that he would think nailed-down meaning, a conventional mode, was better in one movie, free-floating open-ended meaning in another.

And if anyone knew it, he knew that Westerns were sublime: sublimely their own, sublimely indifferent, sublimely open and sublimely free. If the Epic is as big as we Americans can be, the Western is as wonderfully self-sufficient. Its conventions are units with disclaimers and exceptions already built into them, its characters are people too good to meet and people as bad as we see every day. And its places are as empty as those plains and buttes and arroyos, as trackless as when Timothy O'Sullivan and William Henry Jackson first came upon them and fixed them in our imaginations forever.

# 13. HAPPY INDOORS

---

*"The audience don't know somebody sits down and writes a picture; they think the actors just make it up as they go along."*

—William Holden in *Sunset Boulevard*

*". . . And all those wonderful people out there in the dark."*

—Gloria Swanson, ibid.

We recognize things in movies because we love them so, go again and again and seek to be a part of their action. Why else would film nuts wax ecstatic over this or that vanity table in this or that obscure Thirties mobster programmer? The things we watch as film nuts (and it's always better to admit one *is* a nut) may carry a clue to a few final troublesome questions of genre remaining. Thorny problems. What of auteur genre, studio genre, star genre? These are, after all, weighty and central matters: Auteur is at one with American Art, the American Imagination; Studio is American Commerce, Moby Dick; Star is at one with our most fevered dreams, the American Myth.

I've already touched on auteur genre as it applies to John Ford (chapters 10, 12) and Alfred Hitchcock (chapter 5); I didn't say what strong links auteurism has to genre. Auteurism is another way of saying that masters of the art have distinctive style; the more powerful the master, the more certain the style. This makes Auteur Genre because in this instance style has content. A director's work becomes like a genre to an auteurist critic because it is by summing up the director's personal habits of style, lighting, angle, rhythm, formal conjunction and juxtaposition that a critic isolates and defines style. A genre critic becomes an enthusiast of repetition in much the same way: if a kind of movie does something again and again it must be characteristic; if it is characteristic, it is generic. Just so with auteurists: the second film with the same thing is strong evidence, the third is proof. Both genre critic and auteurist move through films with the zeal of newly initiated converts. The difference is that an auteurist must see all the films by good directors, the genre critic must see all the films: consequently the auteurist (he feels) can judge absolute quality, the genre critic can judge genre.

There's a high-flown school of film criticism that holds that what it calls "staring at the screen" is a bad thing, that movie criticism has to be more than knowing what's going on in movies. That is, it says we must get away from "just" staring at the screen if we want to be grown-up about movies. Genre study would not be quite the thing for these folks because for one thing genre rests (as auteurist criticism does not) on a lifetime of staring at the screen. You have to look at a great many odd lots of movies to find out what's going on in genre. For another thing, you must never lose the sense that there's a game going on here. Genre isn't very highbrow. And as I have said, no respecter or judge of quality: genre study takes it as it comes. When it comes down to *House of Women* or *Class of 1984* or *The Cheat*, genre study howls because it knows it has struck the Mother Lode, but it never has to claim that it has come upon a masterpiece. Any of these is just perfect of that kind, but not necessarily better than any other movie.

Is Auteur Genre truly generic? Auteurism is reserved for a few directors whose work seems to thrive by its discussion (or whose work has earned it auteurist criticism); it is then more elitist than generic criticism. Genre applies to the total output of movies: the generic outline of some is clearer than that of others; some movies are mixed up and cannot be clearly labeled, but all movies are generic. As I have said in the Introduction, only Film Noir is restricted by quality, because its measure of composition and formal rigor assures that a Film Noir may range from first-rate to pretty good, but never be a bummer: there's no bottom of the barrel. A Western can be a movie of any quality and turn out to be a Western, even if it's been made by pupils in an elementary school project. Not so Film Noir. So perhaps Auteurist Film is a genre like Film Noir: marked by examples ranging from pretty good to superb. Minimal style is a necessary generic attribute of Auteur Genre.

The elitism of Auteur Film makes another proviso: every film by that director will be marked by the similar definition, even as auteurist criticism refines his style. This doesn't carry over to generic criticism: not every film the director makes can be designated by the generic label Auteur Film (Fordian, Hawksian, Hitchcockian). An auteurist might segregate some films from the director's best work as "contract work," and for these, conventional genre labels will be more significant in designating what genre the picture falls into. *Wee Willie Winkie* is pretty good Empire, pretty lame Ford; *Waltzes from Vienna* is O.K. Costume, pretty fair Musical, but not on the map for Hitchcockian. *Seven Women* is good Women's, O.K. Yellow Peril, great Ford.

What good does it do us to have Auteur Genre? It is most helpful for mixed-genre films with an auteur director. John Ford's *The Fugitive* makes little sense as a Western, but great sense as a Fordian film; *Wings of Eagles* is a first-rate Film-Bio, but the best explanation for why it is better than most is that

Ford consistently frustrates the usual course of Film-Bio. Every time *Wings of Eagles* becomes solemn or conventional, Ford heads it off at the pass.

Howard Hawks's Westerns are another nice case. *Rio Bravo*, *El Dorado*, and *Rio Lobo*, all powerfully Hawksian, give us—one to the next, in their consistency and evolution—a primer of directorial style, theme, and variation. We could conclude from these three Westerns that they are most significant as a comment upon the use of space in ordinary Westerns. These three, contrary, turn inward, go indoors, frustrate the wide open spaces we suspect still lie all around them—in situation, character, and dialogue. They alternate between giving us the sense that *El Dorado* and *Rio Lobo* contain no words we haven't already heard in *Rio Bravo* (inside the besieged jail), and at the same time the sense that each was completely different from the others (the Civil War sequence that opens *Rio Lobo*). Every bit of complexity in each makes sense as hallmarks of a superb Western; but they are also first-rate evidence for defining Auteur Genre.

Is every auteur movie that falls into Auteur Genre dominated by that label? No. Does every auteur produce similiarly well defined Auteur Genre? No more than every one of them produces an equally consistent body of work: some are more than others. Is Auteur Genre as important as Star Vehicle? Not to genre criticism. Do we need it? Perhaps not. But it is possible that generic criticism can better serve the next generation of auteur critics: the exclusionist quality of auteurism might otherwise stifle its sense that there is life beyond that criticism's deliberately elitist walls.

---

Can a studio be a genre? Was input sufficiently organized and consistent to amount to a generic coherence? Is MGM, for example, a generic label? I guess I could argue that studio look, theme, specialty, character are all things we can recognize, so it must be generic. But once I've said that, I cease to believe it.

Some management decisions (Warners jumping into sound), some studio "looks" (RKO's crispness and finish, Warners' dim fog), some atmospherics (MGM's opulence and finish) were clearly cultivated by management and augmented by everyone working there, from studio head on down. Studio consistency also responded to the test of commerce, which tended to make it generic. But I think all this comes better at another point in the recipe: What happens to a cake (or a Horror Picture) when it's been baked at too high an altitude (at MGM)? We get the Spencer Tracy *Dr. Jekyll and Mr. Hyde*.[1] This is not a bad thing, but it's turned out this way because of that—studio.

Studios (see Disney, for instance) were aces at giving the public what it wanted, and at finding a way to do this within the confines of the money available (see Republic, generally B-Picture to its eyeballs, but still the studio of Nicholas Ray's *Johnny Guitar*, and if there is such a thing as studio genre, Republic has left its mark on this movie). Frequently I find myself wishing a particular movie had come out of a different studio, though. Much of what poured from the studios in the Thirties and Forties gives a sense of how inappropriate this or that factory was to the products it produced. This is I think antigeneric, as it runs against the nature of fitness, of recognizable characteristics, of the skill it takes to combine interchangeable parts. Maybe Studio is better left out of the genre recipe. But not stars. Stars belong to genre: created by them, thriving in them, part of them.

---

Yet Stars occupy an odd position in film study. They have to be included even though most everybody is still nervous about them: scholars feel stars have been too central (maybe because they resent that the stars thought they were the whole show). They have too much glitz and film is an art; their skills are haphazard; they aren't much more than products of a system, not workers in the vineyard. All this has always been a bit of an embarrassment. The result is we know less about John

Wayne and Joan Crawford than we should: the biographies cannot be depended on, innuendo passes for knowledge. Even more than the study of an auteur director, the study of actor-as-auteur cries out for a lot more (and a lot more dependable) knowledge than we have: of John Wayne's influence over Howard Hawks, over John Ford; of Joan Crawford's freedom in the Forties to influence the pictures she was given to do; of the Marx Brothers' share in directing.

Of course the public demands more Yellow Peril Movies, or more Space Slime, or the public wants a Betty Hutton. All this is generic. William Holden, the writer in *Sunset Boulevard*, gets Fred Clark, the producer, into one of the most thoroughgoing discussions of film genre on film (because it was written by professionals who knew what they were talking about). We hear a very serious genre question: "Do you see it as a Betty Hutton?" This seems funny, but to them it seems no sillier than a lot of other questions they are asking each other (Is it a Baseball Picture? Not a dumb question, given the realities of studio production and balance sheets. And, I would have to add, given the realities of genre.)

Where does Star Vehicle belong? I suppose most would say Joan Crawford Picture is not a genre, even if they admitted that the problem of what a Joan Crawford movie *is* is pretty much generic: Joan Crawford is . . . hard to make a rule for. John Wayne belongs in Western and War and is also hard to make a rule for. Yet everyone admits that stars more frequently are the reason a movie is made than all the genres put together: more frequently stars determine script, studio pressure on the production, a director's freedom. The shape and feel of a movie and some of its subtler clues and signals come from this. And star was around from the beginning—almost as soon as genre was.

Stars came about because audiences cried out for another picture featuring them, and when they got them asked for more of him or them or new ones. So moviemakers granted their wish. With bigger stars the moviemakers discovered one thing early: star implied a context. In order to bring in the best returns and arrange the best hype, a setting must be devised for this jewel. Setting and context, even if at first it seemed to be no more than a story that would best let the star go on being what had made her/him popular, very soon turned into a complex of elements, more generic than narrative. The "kind of thing" that was good for a Joan Crawford was definitive of a certain kind of Women's Picture. Maybe Star Genre is less a genre in itself than a signal that for the length of this picture all systems will be subjugated to a peculiar kind of generic overdrive: as long as this project is going on, everything will serve stardom.

Rita Hayworth was a product: if you need convincing, look up *Dante's Inferno* and see what she looked like before they raised her hairline and changed her style from sultry Latin to brimming Colleen. Star Vehicle in her case was not so much a matter of building a display box to contain, promote, exploit her as it was the mold that would be her making. The lesson of this star, though, is that everything she is cannot be accounted for by what Harry Cohn and the rest of her Pygmalions made of her: something of her always surprises. My favorite is *Cover Girl* and if I wrote at any length about it I would likely lapse into pubescent worship of the way she dances along a sidewalk or sits down on a counter stool, or just lies there posing for that picture in the chiffon dress. No need to apologize: this is the general level of criticism extant on this picture, and it's a better movie than this kind of slobbering implies. She was never lovelier than in this picture because she's always better than the dumb things the picture has her do (such as play her own grandmother). She dances, she sings, she's in repose. The camera loves her and everybody in the picture matches this love. It is a hymn to the mindless worship of a dame.

In *Only Angels Have Wings*, an earlier movie, not much more acting is evident, but Hayworth has greater depths. Judy has been around: she used to know Jeff (Cary Grant), evidently as a woman who hung around aerodromes after the war. She's married to Bat (Richard Barthelmess); she drinks a little; she likes smart clothes; and it looks as if she is in the state that any jolt could trigger a major emotional jag. She is so very young, and looks it—too young for Bat, too young to have been around as much as she says she has. Hayworth's vulnerability rests on a dislocation between what she expects and what she gets. Experience has not hardened her, but the threat of getting hardened is never very far away: even something that took place in the distant past she brings on screen with a look, a pause, a sideways comment. So the star is built of bits and hints—all generic: winks and hesitancies, compromises suggested and hard times rendered in shorthand. Drinking a little is different with her (see Susan Hayward, Claire Trevor, Elizabeth Taylor, Jane Fonda), but the same in generic gesture. What we see we get before we go on to see that Hayworth is wreaking a change on the Old Familiar. Just so does star interact with genre.

Part of this was nothing much more than casting by type—taking what Hayworth had done and having her do it again, but a little different this time (Garbo Laughs!). Part of it can never be touched by anything so mechanical: when Judy comes up for air after Jeff dumps the pitcher of water on her; when she first enters the picture, coming down the stairway. Some of this, as with Marlene Dietrich, was the product of sensational lighting, stunning hairstyle, good clothes. But not all. Some of it was Hayworth, or we should have had others as good as Hayworth was. Nobody even came close to what it was she could do. So the molds that made her new were also the boxes that attempted to contain that old prime force she'd had from the start. She was perhaps the only woman of whom it could be said that Love Goddess was poor hype—not quite up to the mark.[2]

Welles married her and made her a blonde for *Lady from Shanghai*. But he also understood profoundly the elemental forces in the face and body and being. In *Lady from Shanghai* we are not given just a Film Noir version of *Only Angels Have Wings*'s Judy. There's deliberate and helplessly applied evil here: she knows she can't stop or help herself but she certainly isn't going to warn the poor bastard. She believes in her myth; this time it'll turn out okay—she may even turn out to be good. Fat chance.

The genres of these three movies are Musical, Action/Adventure, Film Noir. Of them only *Cover Girl* would be termed a Rita Hayworth Picture by most people, but her role in defining genre for each picture is decisive. I cannot think of a more definitive Noir temptress of this sort than she is in *Lady from Shanghai*. For *Cover Girl* another woman could have played the part, but without her, even with that wonderful score, it's hard to think we would still call up that movie so frequently to play in our minds. An elemental force finds its proper valence in a Star Vehicle.

And *Gilda*. Noir again, but Noir as *Mildred Pierce* is Noir: a movie that stands as exemplum of genre thought of as Rita Hayworth because it is as impossible to think of it without her as it is impossible to think of *Mildred Pierce* without Crawford. That's another thing that's wrong with the term Love Goddess: it implies that this is the only thing Rita Hayworth is worth, all she's good for. These movies imply otherwise; each implies something different from the next. She could not (witness several of her weaker movies) play any role, but she could play many and be memorable in almost all. And she could command our tongue-tied failure to come up with a sufficient equivalent, metaphor, or epithet.

This corresponds to one of the powers of genre: never to be satisfied with formula but always to exceed whatever that combination of elements looked capable of producing, looked as if it was about to produce. The wonder is not that Rita Hayworth moved through several genres (Musical, Noir, Women's, Adventure, Western, Costume) but that she made each of them seem something new once it was hers.

Because of the way his career timed out in relationship to the decaying studio system Clint Eastwood was able to take control of his fortunes as star early on and become his own director (and producer). Of the two other significant directors he worked with most, Don Siegel has praised his work, called it collaboration; Sergio Leone compared Eastwood to a lump of stone. Eastwood's own direction has proved Siegel right, Leone wrong; lumps don't direct *The Gauntlet*.

Eastwood has made films in a great many genres: Westerns (*A Fistful of Dollars, Hang 'em High, For a Few Dollars More, High Plains Drifter, The Outlaw Josey Wales, Pale Rider*), Costume (*The Beguiled*), Mountain (*The Eiger Sanction*), Comedy (*Bronco Billy, Any Which Way but Loose, Every Which Way You Can*), Crime (*Dirty Harry, The Enforcer, Magnum Force, The Gauntlet, City Heat, Tightrope, The Dead Pool*), Espionage (*Where Eagles Dare, Firefox*), Prison and Escape (*Escape from Alcatraz*), Psychological Thriller (*Play Misty for Me*), Musical (*Paint Your Wagon*), War (*Heartbreak Ridge*), and some mixtures which are rather tough to define: Women's (*Breezy*), Caper or Road Picture (*Thunderbolt and Lightfoot*), Americana (*Honkytonk Man*).

He sought out many of these projects deliberately to vary, broaden, diversify his company's chief asset, Clint. He is an artist of genre, not its creature or willing subject, willing to take on an unsavory image (a philandering rat in *The Beguiled*, drunks in *The Gauntlet* and *Honkytonk Man*) in order to give Clint his chance. And he had realized if he was going to do this Clint had to be exploitable in more ways than he was when he started out—a cold and rather alienated Western hero—not so much to stretch himself as an actor, the usual excuse, as to be able to keep on making movies, make a lot of them, get the most bucks for the bang. This is probably the most astonish-

ing thing about Eastwood: very early on—like Joan Crawford
—he knew his product had to evolve (although his evolved
much differently from Crawford's). Eastwood managed to fit
Clint into a broader spectrum of genres even than Crawford.
The cliché of Dirty Harry or the cold and silent Western hero
that usually passes in the popular media as representing him
ignores this versatility, the career's variety, the repertory power
of his change from one movie to the next.

Has this asset-exploitation improved the genres? Spaghetti-
Western hero broke no new ground in the Western, but how
this hero was related to us as audience was, I think, new. And
perhaps even calling this character a hero was new to the
world, if not to the world of movies (see chapter 11, and the
assimilation of the criminal). Something similar is happening
in the evolution between Western killer types that John Ireland
and James Arness (in *Wagonmaster*) played and Eastwood's Spa-
ghetti gunfighter. The world has turned just a bit and we are
now ready to accept an emphathetic monster as hero.

I think Dirty Harry, too, is a major twist on a familiar type in
the Crime Picture: the cop who has had to adapt ethics to
situation in order to serve the dirty world he works (*Detective
Story* and many Film Noirs). Harry is something else, makes
life on this brutal edge into bravura performance, dances the
borders of the law, somewhere between inside and outside.
Lonely, he forms alliances that turn out to be temporary: an
ally will die or he has to kill him when he turns bad. One of
Dirty Harry's most winning (and most original) characteristics
is his interest in talking to thugs. Conversation brings out the
best in Harry (and Clint).

These innovations are familiar within generic outlines compared to the way Eastwood varies the types to become a new
Eastwood, play against type, bring us another Clint, and another, and another. The happiest and most unexpected is
*Bronco Billy*. The movie is very funny, but we could have pro-

jected this from what we saw in the Westerns and Dirty Harry Pictures. Eastwood does comedy so well because the character undercuts not just his Western hero and Harry Callahan, but the originals they were busy undercutting. The result is very American: a man who, like Buffalo Bill, wants to take the house for all it's good for, but then believes his own hype and cannot stop being the hero he knows he invented, determined never to let down the "little buckaroos" of his audience even when he can't pay his troupe. A charitable con artist, a small-town carnival version of the big-time phony showman, commanding respect not just of little buckaroos but of everybody in his company.

The advance of *The Gauntlet* over *Dirty Harry* is similar to that of *Bronco Billy* over *Hang 'em High*. Ben Shockley in *The Gauntlet* gets the job of transporting Gus Mally, mob canary, to testify in court. Presumably (he is a drinking plainclothes cop) he knows the world is corrupt. But he still believes in the police: he is not prepared to have a tract house he's in blown away under him by one police force, or to have his armored bus turned into a shooting-gallery target by another. His buddy Pat Hingle tips him off to corruption on a national scale, complete with a gratifyingly unctuous Mr. Big (William Prince). Once he gets the idea, Shockley is no more surprised than Dirty Harry, but better prepared to finish his job anyway with éclat and pep. Shockley is a hero for terrorist times, a warrior against not just police corruption, but whatever has turned law and order on its ear. Self-defense resorts to tank warfare nowadays.

Some of this resilience is evident in the d.j. of *Play Misty for Me*, a cool man forced to go on the defensive against his will because he has been sought out by an unlikely nemesis, a fan (Jessica Walter), a woman not so much intent on smothering him as on obliterating him. His coolness is station hype combined with a device of professional broadcasting, distant intimacy. This gets him in trouble and brings Clint to a more vulnerable defensiveness than he has permitted himself since, another measure (in his first directing job) of how determined he is to vary the type.

What does this make of genre? First that genre is no less an issue in the Seventies and Eighties than in the Thirties and Forties—for Eastwood perhaps more so. And that Star Vehicle is no less an issue—probably more so. Neither as actor nor director is Eastwood content to take genre as he finds it, or take genre to be rulebook or formula. He knows that unless a change takes place before our eyes, genre cannot be fulfilled, even if it's only some adjustment in type, or genre unit or subgenre—necessary to legitimize the tradition: movie comes from movie comes from movie.

Perhaps the oddest example in this varied career is Siegel's *The Beguiled*, with Eastwood as an unsavory aggressive male victim of his several female quarries. They discover that he is two-, three-, and four-timing them, and instead of fighting each other, seek solidarity (or near-solidarity, one remains true to love instead) in amputating his leg, then poisoning him with mushrooms. The themes of the movie are true to the shapes of Costume and of Southern Picture. Geraldine Page is carrying a torch for her dead brother (as always, incest rears its head),[3] Clint goes for the nymphet, the plot turns on an odd mixture of embroidery class and amputation, race warfare and clean nightshirts. The mixture is not only powerful but generically inventive, an evolutionary stage for Costume and Southern Picture.

What Eastwood does (and his career, I hope, is still far from over) is going to change the nature of whatever genre his pictures touch because his work as a director and an actor is enormously intelligent—about film, audience, star, and especially about genre. It's perfectly possible, as I have said more than once in these pages, to accomplish something in genre without being very smart or even very deliberate. This is not the case with Eastwood. To the aficionado of genre, smart and careful and respectful work even better.

Is Star Vehicle a genre? Good cooks always know something nobody else knows. Genre is a recipe; Star Vehicle is a wild ingredient added to the genre "recipe" as the extra egg. Or extra Pepsi-Cola, if we were required to add Pepsi-Cola as an extra ingredient to every recipe we were whipping up. Fred Clark tells William Holden, We love your script but we can't do it unless it's a Betty Hutton. Wild ingredient of Pepsi-Cola is the wrong term because more frequently the star was the bran muffin a recipe was trying to produce: the Western or Horror or Women's or Costume Western with Music was the Pepsi-Cola added to produce that bran muffin (that Betty Hutton).

Genre came into being because movies weren't sure what they knew how to do—or rather they weren't sure they could do anything as well as the theater could. So the movie pioneers churned it out, what worked last time. A few familiar shapes worked consistently, so they found they knew better and better how to do these even though by now they were less and less sure just what it was they knew how to do. Probably more a failure of confidence than of knowledge because the moviemakers knew how to make a Western but (jumping to the wrong conclusion) they thought this was no great thing. Western they knew and made, and Costume they knew and made again and again, and New York Movie and train ride and after a while Pirate Movie and Joan Crawford Movie. They found how to do Writer and New York and Desert and Cockroach Race and Lincoln Picture. And they never forgot *anything*: they added on. And they did all this so clearly, or maybe so habitually, that once we saw it, we could recognize Writer or Cockroach or the others again and again, they summon up the rest of the sequence from the clue we'd been given.

A more difficult question is, as movies make things up out of spare parts, how can we always end up with a different movie? Or in the terms of the metaphor I have suggested, that genre works like a language, why, 999 times out of 1000, do I speak a sentence I have never heard myself speak? Part, of course, is the moviemakers' desire not to be sued: wanting to use something to which they own a clear title so they can get all the bucks—the heart of the profit motive, owning the store. But out of these mechanisms for conformity, there results such variety. This is genre's great gift.

Genre never withers because it is always so useful without anybody's having to be real sure of what it is. That confusion or lack of confidence early on in what they were doing enabled genre to become perhaps the only *lingua franca* that unites studio head, producer, star, director, technical staff, exhibitor, and audience. Every one of them can say Western and more or less know what that is. And they're all likely to think it's the same thing, even if they all mean something different. Thinking in this simultaneously confident and aberrant way ("You don't know what a Western is!" "I do too!") makes genre a wonderful game of indeterminacy, makes film-genre exchanges a path to sure-fire, zesty, yeasty recipes. Producer, Exhibitor, and Audience—input, retailer, and target—come together and are liable to agree they all mean the same thing. They mean nothing of the sort. The Producer sees genre as a shape, an item on a balance sheet or, worse (like Selznick—see *Memo from David O. Selznick*), on his own balance sheet of life achievement as the movie's supreme artist; the Studio Head sees his as items on his personal balance sheet (see *Indecent Exposure*), which rationalizes a literal balance sheet of the studio for money the movies brought in or lost. The Director thinks genres are something he can use to fool the Studio Head (see Ford's tale of Carl Laemmle's visit to his set, or Raoul Walsh's tales of Jack Warner). The Star sees a new genre as a way to try on a hat different from what he wore in the last one and do something unexpected for his image. The Audience just wants to feel as good as it did the last time it saw one of these things it liked, or feel at least the same. Or even feel bad in a way they can understand, feel bad in a recognizable way.

I think alliance of interests outweighs dialectics. For instance, commerce unites the Studio Head with us in the Audience—the more of us who want to go to his picture, the happier he is; if more of us go to Western, then Western it will be. If we like Westerns we're happy too. A Star's image unites Star and Audience: when a star comes up with an image that pleases us we go to that movie. A generic type or a subgenre or a story unites us of the Audience with the Director and Writer in an imaginary compact. If we like this variation, they'll make more variations not that much different from what's gone before. *Almost* the same. And we all *almost* mean the same thing. Mean *almost* the same thing. The conservative force of genre won't permit fixing it if it isn't broken. This is also the key to genre's variety, its variations, its finagle factor.

Recognition is the name of the game. Our ability to handle the *lingua franca*, our out-here-in-the-dark generic knowledge that gives us the ability to recognize obscure or arcane generic signals, convert what we see into what we know, the unfamiliar into the familiar, is what counts. Recognition rests on repetition. It could be said Hollywood had no new idea under the sun only as long as critics rejected repetition. Once they stopped seeing it as lack of originality (rather than seeing it as the essence of movies) we had a film heritage. Repetition was the surest sort of populism, the way movies pressed the flesh. Movies needed to handle us and we needed to feel comfortable that they were doing it, to vote for them with our fifty-cent pieces and five-bucks-at-a-time. They gave us what we didn't know how to ask for as long as we didn't know what we really wanted; once we did we asked for more than they at first thought they could come up with. Our ability to handle generic shorthand was skillful and subtly discriminating. Great abstraction was possible because movies were made of such down-home substance: the second time around genre gave us back something at once familiar and abstract, permitting even more abstraction and condensation next time around.

Some of these signals were distinctly American. How do we know so well what a Baby Brother is like? from the movies and then from the comics. And how do we know that, as Americans, we are Europe's Baby Brother? Because we know how to behave as Americans from that wonderful mirror always reeling off its images before us on the screen. How do we know to expect Happy Endings? More important, how do we know that neither the happy endings nor the sudden swift punishment meted out by the Production Code can be depended on in our own lives? By comparison of movie signals and what we see in our lives. Scenarios are, after all, only scenarios, not lesson plans.

In *The General* Buster Keaton, trying to clear the track of a railroad tie (dropped by the spies) which will surely wreck his locomotive, manages to get it loose in the nick of time, but its weight pins him to the cowcatcher. The train pulls slowly toward a second railroad tie. Buster tosses the one he holds to dislodge the next one. We know what he's doing but we have never seen it before. The essence of visual shorthand. But without down-home cues of girlfriend, bear, little boys, generals, spies, lost shoe—all shorthand—even *The General* couldn't bring us to this bit of sophisticated abstraction.

This dazzling immediacy leads us to comfortable recognitions, but also to false generalizations of genre. When we start to summarize what we have seen, try to reduce what has happened to the simple cues the movie used to get us there instead of trying to understand the subtle abstractions they have enabled, we mistake genre for narrative. And we remember (falsely) that all Westerns have chases. This can become an argument that the chase is endemic to the Western or that the oxygen tent is endemic to the Women's Picture, the swamp to the Southern Picture. Generalization turns against detailed knowledge, bringing us to remember things we have not seen.

This is both characteristic of film's great power and of bad film scholarship. In the grip of the power of genre our eagerness to generalize from familiar individual instance into universal cliché leads us to misstate, and so we lose what makes genre tick: repetition of its many little pieces.

There are worse sins against genre, of course. When a pompous director presumes he can make an honest woman of genre, raise its sights by making a movie a little bit more like theater or novel or work of art, genre digs in its heels and resists. If he would just shut up and use it, genre would hang in there and help in more ways than he knew it had. Genre is generous. Even when he doesn't know he's dialing a number he gets the party. Genre gives directors more than they have the wit to ask.

Genre is a working stiff, not an aesthete. It does its job, tips us off, helps a director define meaning, frees a star, or enables a writer, gives a studio a name for doing this or that simple kind of thing. Of course, in that it's a working stiff, it gets no pay. Who would think of praising the American Film for the emotional clarity of its Women's Pictures, instead of thinking them a joke or a cruel necessity of commerce? Of course Women's Pictures *are* economic necessity. If we are to look at American movies we must acknowledge this, but we also have to acknowledge that the Women's Picture gives American film its heart. Any genre deserves serious (and that generally means complex) critical examination. We have to juggle genre, portable units, transferable generic fragments, mixed genre, genre exchange and transference, if we are to come up with how in practice all this works. Genre is the study of the practical as clearly as politics is the art of the practical.

---

Plato's Cave is a movie house and we who love movies will never get out past the fire and into the sun to see the truth: we like it better in the dark because we prefer glancing and dart-ing images on the screen to whatever might be between us and the light-projecting fire, much less the sun outside the cave. We are happy indoors. But finally when we do go out and return to our lives, we find we have adopted attitudes and speak in lines we have ripped off from the movies. It helps us handle the exigencies of life. Probably we'd rather *stay* at the movies but when we get out of the cave we walk taller, judge more quickly, jump farther, hang on longer, play it cool, because of what we have seen there. Costume Pictures show us that even Liszt was once unknown, Inventor Pictures that Eureka comes with a joke attached, Film-Bio that the blessing will come unexpected, just about the time we had decided we were standing in the wrong line to be blessed. Horror gives us the awful possibility that our friends *are* reading it right, that we really are suffering the Change; Place Genre, I suppose, that even in Oz there's still No Place Like Home. Prison Pictures get us ready for getting caught and surviving; High School shows us a perfect world for us as we were, without us as we are now. The Cockroach Race gives us a time out of sequence, a time of true escape, a time out of time, a time with all narrative stilled.

Why is Shepler's Catalogue able to sell all that Western gear (to say nothing of Frederick's of Hollywood all that embarrassing lingerie)? Why did *Flashdance* pervade the minds of the young so that children even now, long after the movie's heyday, still rip a sweatshirt to expose one shoulder? Because not all American scenarios are complete. The President says "Make my Day," and according to some ran both terms of his office using only (but never exhausting) the lines from his old movies. I have a friend who is a senator who in the Navy showed *Top Hat* on his ship so many times (because he knew he'd never have this chance again) that the crew rose as one and put it on the screen upside down, and another, a distinguished professor, who admits to twitching an imaginary cape on the land-ing of the grand staircase at the Loew's Poli in New Haven. Happy indoors, but still, in a sense, indoors even when we get up and leave the cave.

The study of genre is the proper study of movies for this kind of moviegoer. Instead of regretting the lack of remote meaning, we would prefer to describe properly what's on the screen, what's here right now, all of it—stinkers together with landmark films.

Genre enables not just moneymaking and the rise and fall of stars (just as genres rise and fall in that mysterious cosmic dance, maybe the most difficult thing to understand about genre), but it enables narrative, not only by means of the expansion of our psychic universe all fiction works, but by the miraculous expansion of a wonderful movie—expansion not just through space but through time, an expansion of experience and memory and mind. By genre and its changes we can see how our times evolve, even as the fact that Garbo can still stare at us, unchanged, is corroboration that we have changed utterly. Here, happy indoors, out here in the dark.

**NOTES**
**BIBLIOGRAPHY**
**FILM INDEX**
**INDEX**

# NOTES

## Introduction

1. See Richard S. Slotkin, *Regeneration Through Violence*, introduction.
2. Edmund Wilson, *Patriotic Gore*, "Abraham Lincoln," p. 99.
3. See Chapter 5.
4. Jeanine Basinger, *The World War II Combat Film*, pp. 15ff.
5. See Todd McCarthy and Charles Flynn, eds., *Kings of the Bs*, pp. 317–20.

## Chapter 1. Writing with a Feather

1. Siegfried Kracauer, *A Theory of Film*, introduction and chapter 5, pp. 3–23, 77–92.
2. In regard to Napoleons, see Basinger, *Combat Film*, pp. 190–91. Roland Barthes writes: "In *The Guermantes Way*, Proust writes: 'We see . . . in a gazetteer of the works of Balzac, where the most illustrious personages figure only according to their connexion with the *Comédie humaine*, Napoleon occupy a space considerably less than that allotted to Rastignac, and occupy that space solely because he once spoke to the young ladies of Cinq-Cygne.' It is precisely this minor importance which gives the historical character its *exact* weight of reality: this *minor* is the measure of authenticity: Diderot, Mme de Pompadour, later Sophie Arnould, Rousseau, d'Holbach, are introduced into the fiction laterally, obliquely, *in passing*, painted on the scenery, not represented on the stage; for if the historical character were to assume its real importance, the discourse would be forced to yield it a role which would, paradoxically, make it less real (thus the characters in Balzac's *Catherine de Médicis*, Alexandre Dumas's novels, or Sacha Guitry's plays: absurdly improbable): they would give themselves away. Yet if they are merely mixed in with their fictional neighbors, mentioned as having simply been present at some social gathering, their modesty, like a lock between two levels of water, equalizes novel and history: they reinstate the novel as a family, and like ancestors who are contradictorily famous and absurd, they give the novel the glow of reality, not of glory: they are superlative effects of the real" (Barthes, *S-Z*, 101–2). I am grateful to Jon Barlow for pointing this out to me. The point is that of the familiarizing power of the familiar. If

Doctor Johnson passes by in the street in a Costume Picture, few of us will be sure it is he; if he is introduced on screen, those of us who know Johnson may scoff at the representation, but if we are also Costume Picture fiends, we cannot but admire the power of the genre: get in, get on with it, get it over with, and get out is a telling rule for the Costume Picture, and a part of our joy when we see the directness and bluntness of its hale efficiency.

3. Many swear that Hitchcock's *Stage Fright* is in color because the closeup of the bloody doll makes such a powerful visual impression that they colorize the blood in their head; others see the lady from the restaurant in *Cat People* return in the lobby of the women's hotel.

4. Adam Leff, commenting on *The Sea Hawk*.

5. Here I acknowledge Andrew Sarris's sense of the different viewing selves at subsequent viewings in *The Primal Screen*.

6. Grand space is sometimes thought to be an essential characteristic of the Costume Picture. I think it is of the Epic, but some Costumes (like some Westerns) can, by using our expectation of grand space, make an intimate Costume very exciting: see *Hangover Square* (Costume/Horror) or Renoir's *La Marseillaise*. The mixture of Epic and intimate seems to improve either extreme.

7. Some of this is surely the simple desperation of screenwriters. A made-for-television movie, *The Pat Neal Story*, becomes a Costume Picture when someone remarks on the sales of her husband's *Charlie and the Chocolate Factory*, not so much because it's trying to place us in any particular time (we are more likely to be able to assign a date to Pat Neal's stroke than we are to *Charlie and the Chocolate Factory*), but that it is the kind of thing that such pictures feel they have to do. The awkward ending of Billy Wilder's *The Private Life of Sherlock Holmes* falters on an overzealous New Thing with Queen Victoria and the submarine: the idea is a proper New Thing and the attitudes taken toward it are appropriate, but cuteness conquers high seriousness. This is fatal, for Costume Pictures must always hold on to high seriousness for their lives. Sometimes it is all they have.

8. For a thorough discussion of the complexity of mixture, see Basinger's essay on *Frenchman's Creek* in *The Women's Picture*, forthcoming.

9. See Jeanine Basinger, *The World War II Combat Film*, pp. 15ff.

## Chapter 2. A Better Mousetrap

1. James Watson and Donald Crick, *The Double Helix*.

2. See chapter 5 on the professions and their role in genre.

3. A good gauge for this was the "Jack Benny Show" or Sid Caesar's "Show of Shows." Both generally took for parody only very recognizable generic elements of very popular movies. I can recall at least two parodies of Inventor Movies on the Benny show.

## Chapter 3. As Good as Real Life

1. There are no prints of *Hellzapoppin'* available to check this quotation with, at least not known to me. This demonstrates something the film scholar knows only too well: the grim reaper has wiped out films in a completely erratic way that has little to do with contemporary popularity or relative age of the film.

2. Curtiz gets little credit as *auteur*, but it seems rather facile to assume he is a hack when one tots up the good pictures he is responsible for and remembers how frequently we find ourselves giving credit for Michael Curtiz's films to others (to Flynn or Korngold for *The Adventures of Robin Hood*, to Bergman or Bogart, the Epstein Twins, or even Lorre or Greenstreet for *Casablanca*). He is not just efficient: he is some kind of artist. See chapter 10.

## Chapter 4. Faust and His Disease

1. Horror's rules make it possible for the monster to rise, for the disease to reveal itself, and are again invoked when the movie decides it is time to get rid of the monster or cure the disease. Costume's rules are invoked less for the good of what's on the screen than to cover, to protect itself from the age-old question, Who'd want to watch a movie where guys write with feathers?

2. Lon Chaney, Jr., was not, like Walter Brennan, playing old-age pensioners in his twenties, but he never looked quite comfortable as young anything. The onus of being junior.

3. Fear of concussion is an almost forgotten fear of the period between World Wars I and II which turns up in an Empire Picture: *The Sun Never Sets*. There was a similar early emphasis on the blast force of atomic explosions which for a time in the late Forties preyed far more upon the imagination than radiation did.

4. Chopin's sister (played by Nina Foch) gives him a little bag of Polish earth as he leaves his native land. She later shows up in Paris to use the same dirt to humble him and try to get him to take up a concert tour for Polish relief. The shape is the same, the application different. George Sand seems to regard Chopin's Polish side as distinctly aberrant.

5. The significance of the Academy in these pictures is very interesting (see especially *The Fly* II). It seems rather strange that movies, ordinarily so distant from the concerns of intellectuals, should so insist on the approval of scholarly projects by the commonalty of the guild. This, like breathing through a reed, is a specialty somehow too special to learn from a movie.

6. It may be hard to think of any of these subgenres as capable of having a sound center, since they all involve some kind of certifiable behavior. But I think sound center in the case of Horror rests on its strict ground

rules, its more or less invariable sequencing, its strict subgeneric distinctions. Mad Doctor slides around too much to be as strong as Wolfman, firmly rooted in that psychological threat to each of us it represents.

7. Patricide and suicide meet in the Cronenberg version of *The Fly*: Brundle must obliterate himself in his Frankenstein's Monster in order to prove a point completely. Compare the doctor in *The Citadel*, a medical picture with elements of Inventor and Mad Doctor.

8. Bette Davis plays her own twin sister frequently; once (*Dead Ringer*) she was an evil *and* an evil sister.

9. Horror Pictures tend to European, especially Central European settings, except for many Possession Pictures (*The Exorcist*). Leslie Fiedler might be right and we want our evil (*and* our innocence) prepubescent. Maybe this is now changed and American Horror is O.K. (see *An American Werewolf in London, Prince of Darkness, Halloween, The Fog*).

## Chapter 5. Jobs, Geography, and Ritual

1. See Reed, *Three American Originals*, pp. 111, 113.

2. This somewhat inverts origins: movies set after the war are likely to be Westerns because it became convenient for Westerns to turn on a grudge buried somewhere in that war, to refer to what has now, in any of these movies, become a lost past.

3. First through Europe, aided by foreign currency debts and now throughout this Great Land of Ours, aided by regional film boards to encourage local expenditure of Hollywood's hard currency.

4. A fleeting romantic enthusiasm of the fictional American scenario: see James Jones's novel *Some Came Running*.

## Chapter 6. Breathing Through a Reed

1. François Truffaut, *Hitchcock*.

2. Good one-liners are a hallmark of Raoul Walsh's films, so one begins to suspect the auteur writes.

3. Reed, *Faulkner's Narrative*, chapter 2.

4. The best POW fiction of the past decade is *Tenko*, a British miniseries made for television and filmed in Australia. It was about an all-woman prison camp, a triumph of character design and fine scripting. Unlike most POW films, its popularity continued it beyond their liberation, through their rehabilitation, and finally (in another special) into a reunion years later.

## Chapter 7. Let's Burn the School

1. Joseph W. Reed, *Faulkner's Narrative*, pp. 34–41, 43–46.

2. Jeanine Basinger, *The World War II Combat Film*, chapter 3, "Evolution," pp. 121–219.

3. For *Americana*, see chapter 9.

4. Servants? Part of the affectionate fancy of the Depression, along with black glass floors, white tie and tails, and being in the money. *A Family Affair* has a domestic crisis, part of the denouement of *Craig's Wife* turns on the resignation of a housekeeper. This is what makes watching Thirties movies so much fun, this and the discovery that mothers then wanted to look older, and that spinster (or grass-widow) sisters of the male head of the household were better taken care of then.

5. Not really a genre, but a convenient bin in which to put serious exploitation pictures, that is, pictures seriously exploitative of serious crime. Most of the movies are so deadening and tiresome that I do not address them directly. In a sense *The Public Enemy* and *I Am a Fugitive from a Chain Gang* are Problem Pictures by virtue of their title-card headnotes, but fortunately they are something else as well. *On the Waterfront* and *Man with a Golden Arm* may be, for want of a better bin to put them in. *Pinky* set out to be a Problem Picture but ended up Women's: it's a deliberately chosen genre, but it doesn't always work out for its director that a Problem stays a Problem.

6. Strangely, Navy movies with marriages specialize in domestic unrest: the Air Force wife worries about *him*; the Navy wife worries about *them*: see *Wings of Eagles* and chapter 3, *Air Force, Strategic Air Command, In Harm's Way, Back to Bataan, Submarine D-1*). Ford borrows it for his *Rio Grande* as well.

7. Compare *Dawn of the Dead*. Considering how much time we spend in malls, how little films have utilized these characteristic spaces. Compare, for instance, what film has done with sidewalk cafés.

8. Nerds study too much, don't make out, fall down, wear glasses, invent things, get their revenge. They have been around a long time, long before the High School Picture. They used to be fiancés and unsuccessful suitors, even first husbands. The female counterpart (although High School Pictures have shown us female nerds) was the blind date who was a dog (*On the Town*), even as the earlier version of the Male Virginity Picture was the inexperienced sailor (*Anchors Aweigh*) in search of his first date who drinks milk (*They Were Expendable*).

9. There is one appalling Military School Picture, a comedy with the signal distinction of making literal the old saying "As unwelcome as the turd in the punchbowl." The presence of a British genre of public school movies and the absence there of a considerable body of films about state secondary schools suggests a difference between our national psyche and theirs, if such a difference needs to be noted.

10. The assistant is generalized Horror, most frequently seen in Frankenstein and Mad Doctor Movies—but see Robert Walker in *Madame Curie* and Henry Fonda in *Alexander Graham Bell* (chapter 2).

11. "Carrie is an elegant box lunch that got dropped. The wine is all over the rolls. Caviar is embedded in the turkey, and there is lettuce in the

mousse. It is a mess with bits of salvage floating usefully around in it" (Richard Eder in *The New York Times*).

12. Brian de Palma perhaps wants too much to be taken for an auteur to make this an easy question. He is certainly not consistent, but his excess is, and sometimes, as in *Carrie*, he can use it for memorable results. And he has a magisterial hand with genre at some other times. But it's a tough one to call.

## Chapter 8. The Cockroach Race

1. See *Hell Below*. These movies started out mixed and stayed that way. A mixture of World War I Combat (out of *Journey's End* and the photoplay-centered trench movies) with something out of College Movies, moved into prophecy of the World War II Combat Film (see Jeanine Basinger, *The World War II Combat Film*) mixed with Men-at-Work Movies (*High Tension, They Drive by Night*).

2. *Beau Geste, Unconquered*, one of my favorite genre units. But see the beautiful shift on it in *El Cid* as the Cid rides out dead to lead the living. It matches, in the same movie, the barrage of bread which is shot into the besieged fortress by catapult.

## Chapter 9. All Singing, All Dancing, a Million Laffs

1. I now feel I was rather hard on St. Petersburg, Florida, but I never felt it at the time. I wanted out, desperately. But for moviegoing, it was a very heaven: a first-run house designed by the Mizener Brothers with a mighty Wurlitzer and an orchestra pit; another with wicker chairs, that showed first-run Warner Brothers movies exclusively; a second-run house with double features and a plaza sweeping up to the entrance, and now and again, a rat; a (sometimes) roadshow house one entered from the street by coming in *under the screen*; a fourteenth-run house with wonderful double features that had been released a decade earlier. And another house with a Western double bill plus a serial on Saturday afternoon. Just after World War II a movie house which had fallen into desuetude was reopened to show only British films. And most of it for nine cents (then thirty or fifty cents) a pop. And two drive-ins.

2. There should be a genre unit noted of difficult recording devices: in *Sudden Fear* Joan Crawford the playwright hears her husband plotting with his girlfriend their murder of her; Claude Rains in *The Unsuspected* plans with a recording device not wisely, but too well. Trapping people by maneuvering them into blurting it all out over live radio had a decided vogue for a time, too (*Margin for Error, Hitler's Children*).

3. Daniel Moews, *Keaton*, pp. 128–55.

## Chapter 10. Women's, War, and the Way We Were

1. Joan Mellen, *Women and their Sexuality in the New Film,* for instance. For more capable readings of women in film, see Molly Haskell, *From Reverence to Rape.*
2. He worked from 8 A.M. to 5 P.M. on *The Cheat,* took a nap, and started in on *The Golden Chance* at 8 P.M. Both were finished on time (*Autobiography,* pp. 149–150).
3. Joseph W. Reed, *Three American Originals,* p. 95–9.

## Chapter 11. Public Enemies

1. See Jeanine Basinger's exception, *The World War II Combat Film,* p. 277.
2. From a novel called *My First Two Thousand Years,* but I doubt it was original there.
3. Richard S. Slotkin is currently working on this chapter of his American continued story in *Gunfighter Nation,* the third volume that began with *Regeneration Through Violence* and continued with *The Fatal Environment.*

## Chapter 12. The Big Time

1. The standard discussion of this film, indeed of everything about its director as well, is found in Jeanine Basinger, *Anthony Mann,* 159–76.
2. Richard S. Slotkin, "The Wild West," in *Buffalo Bill and the Wild West* (New York: Brooklyn Museum, 1981), pp. 27–44.
3. Vincent Canby, *New York Times,* 19 November 1959, 50:2.
4. Basinger, *Anthony Mann.*
5. Lieutenant Colonel Thursday (Henry Fonda), who runs his military career by the book, takes command of this Western outpost, bringing Philadelphia (Shirley Temple), his daughter, as mistress of his household. She is attracted to Lieutenant Michael O'Rourke (John Agar), son of the sergeant major and his wife (Ward Bond and Irene Rich). Captain York (John Wayne) has been negotiating peace with Cochise of the Comanches (Miguel Inclan). In the middle of the noncommissioned officers' ball, Thursday receives news of the Indians and commands the post into battle against them, a doomed cavalry charge conducted by the book. He refuses to be rescued by York and dies in a Last Stand. The movie ends on a press conference as York, now in command, recalls Colonel Thursday for a group of reporters as the cavalry troop passes across his face in reflection.
6. Joseph W. Reed, *Three American Originals,* pp. 4–5.
7. Senator Ransom Stoddard and Hallie, his wife (James Stewart, Vera Miles) return to Shinbone for the funeral of Tom Doniphon (John Wayne). The senator tells reporters a story that is to be the movie's major action. He came West to practice law and his stage is held up as it

approaches Shinbone. He is beaten up by an outlaw, Liberty Valance (Lee Marvin). Doniphon finds him and takes him to be doctored by Hallie, Doniphon's girl; he stays on as dishwasher at the restaurant, then starts a school. Doniphon again protects him from Valance. He publishes with the assistance of Dutton Peabody (Edmond O'Brien) a story about Valance and his dirty deeds for the cattle interests. Peabody is beaten up and Liberty spreads the word he will get Ranse. Ranse goes out to meet him, is shot, and with his left hand fires at Valance, who falls dead. Hallie grabs Ranse, and Tom, watching, takes this to show that she loves Ranse. Tom gets drunk and burns down the house he has been building for her. Ranse is elected governor (then senator) after momentary misgivings: he fears he is riding a gunfighter's victory to political power, but Tom tells him the truth, that Tom killed Valance. Back once again in the present the editor decides not to print this, the true story, because "the legend has become fact."

## Chapter 13. Happy Indoors

1. Successive remakes tend to be identified by the name of the star, which may be yet another way of identifying Star Genre: that's the reason multiple remakes (except for Disaster Films and recent Teen Splatters) tend to get made. For *Jekyll and Hyde* there were (in addition to Silents in 1908, 1910, 1911, and two versions in 1913) 1920 John Barrymore (John S. Robertson, Paramount), and 1920 Sheldon Lewis (MGM); 1932 Fredric March (Rouben Mamoulian, Paramount); 1941 Spencer Tracy (Victor Fleming, MGM). Later we have 1953 *Abbott and Costello Meet Dr. Jekyll and Mr. Hyde*, 1970 Peter Cushing, and a Jack Palance made-for-television version, to say nothing of *Dr. Jekyll and Sister Hyde, The Son of Dr. Jekyll, Daughter of Dr. Jekyll*.

2. It is not known who first came up with the term, but it was probably not *Life* magazine where it found its maximum penetration.

3. Particularly generic is Page's role of headmistress, hung up on a clearly incestuous (and as clearly Southern-Picture) attachment to her brother, revealed in a paired portrait and a nightmarish erotic dream.

# BIBLIOGRAPHY

Barthes, Roland. *S-Z*. New York: Hill & Wang, 1974.

Basinger, Jeanine. *Anthony Mann*. Boston: Twayne, 1979.

———. *Shirley Temple*. New York: Pyramid Publications, 1975.

———. *The World War II Combat Film: Anatomy of a Genre*. New York: Columbia University Press, 1986.

Bogdanovich, Peter. *John Ford*. London: Secker & Warburg in association with the British Film Institute (Cinema One), 1967; revised, Berkeley: University of California Press, 1978.

Capra, Frank. *The Name above the Title: An Autobiography*. New York: The Macmillan Company, 1971.

Cavell, Stanley. *Pursuits of Happiness*. Cambridge: Harvard University Press, 1971.

———. *The World Viewed*. New York: The Viking Press, 1971.

Ciment, Michel. *Kazan on Kazan*. New York: The Viking Press (Cinema One), 1974.

DeMille, Cecil B. *The Autobiography*, ed. Donald Hayne. Englewood Cliffs, N.J.: Prentice-Hall, 1959.

Derry, Charles. *Dark Dreams: The Horror Film from Psycho to Jaws*. New York: A. S. Barnes and Co., 1977.

Everson, William K. *Classics of the Horror Film from the Days of the Silent Film*. Secaucus, N.J.: The Citadel Press, 1974.

*The Film Daily Year Book of Motion Pictures*, ed. Jack Alicoate et al. Los Angeles: The Film Daily, 1930–63.

Gifford, Dennis. *A Pictorial History of Horror Movies*. London: Hamlyn, 1973.

Harvey, James. *Romantic Comedy from Lubitsch to Sturges*. New York: Knopf, 1987.

Haskell, Molly. *From Reverence to Rape: The Treatment of Women in the Movies*. New York: Holt, Rinehart and Winston, 1973, 1974.

Kracauer, Siegfried. *A Theory of Film: The Redemption of Physical Reality*. New York: Oxford University Press, 1960.

McBride, Joseph. *Hawks on Hawks*. Berkeley: University of California Press, 1982.

McCarthy, Todd, and Flynn, Charles, eds. *Kings of the Bs: Working within the Hollywood System*. New York: E. P. Dutton & Co., Inc., 1975.

Madsen, Axel. *Billy Wilder*. London: Secker & Warburg in association with the British Film Institute (Cinema One), [1968].

Moews, Daniel. *Keaton: The Silent Features Close Up*. Berkeley: University of California Press, 1977.

*The New York Times Directory of the Film*. New York: Arno, 1971.

Reed, Joseph W. *Faulkner's Narrative*. New Haven: Yale University Press, 1974.

———. *Three American Originals*. Middletown, CT: Wesleyan University Press, 1984.

Robinson, David. *Buster Keaton*. London: Secker & Warburg in association with the British Film Institute (Cinema One), [1969].

Sarris, Andrew. *The Primal Screen*. New York: Simon and Schuster, 1973.

Selznick, David O. *Memo from David O. Selznick*, ed. Rudy Behlmer. New York: The Viking Press, 1972.

Slotkin, Richard S. *The Fatal Environment*. New York: Atheneum, 1987.

———. *Gunfighter Nation*, forthcoming.

———. *Regeneration Through Violence*. Middletown, CT: Wesleyan University Press, 1973.

Solomon, Stanley J. *Beyond Formula: American Film Genres*. New York: Harcourt Brace Jovanovich, Inc., 1976.

Truffaut, François. *Hitchcock*. London: Secker & Warburg, 1966.

Watson, James, and Crick, Donald. *The Double Helix*. New York: Atheneum, 1968.

Wilson, Edmund. *Patriotic Gore*, "Abraham Lincoln." New York: Oxford University Press, 1962.

Wood, Robin. *Howard Hawks*. London: Secker & Warburg in association with the British Film Institute. (Cinema One), 1968.

———. *Hollywood from Vietnam to Reagan*. New York: Columbia University Press, 1986.

# FILM INDEX

Following are brief credits for films mentioned in the text; numbers at the end of entry comprise the title index.

## Abbreviations

| | |
|---|---|
| *d* | directed by |
| *p* | produced by |
| *d&p* | directed and produced by |

## Studios

| | | | |
|---|---|---|---|
| 1stN | First National | Par | Paramount |
| AA | Allied Artists | Rep | Republic |
| AmIn | American International | 20th | 20th Century-Fox |
| AvEm | Avco Embassy | UnIn | Universal-International |
| Col | Columbia | Univ | Universal |
| Fox | Fox Studios | UA | United Artists |
| MGM | Metro-Goldwyn-Mayer | WB | Warner Brothers |
| NGen | National General | | |

*The Abominable Dr. Phibes,* 1971: AmIn (UK); *d* Robert Fuest; *p* Louis M. Heyward; Ronald S. Dunas; Vincent Price, Joseph Cotten, Hugh Griffith.

*Ace in the Hole,* see *The Big Carnival.*

*Across the Pacific,* 1942: WB; *d* John Huston; Humphrey Bogart, Mary Astor, Sydney Greenstreet.

*Adam's Rib,* 1949: MGM; *d* George Cukor; *p* Lawrence Weingarten; Spencer Tracy, Katharine Hepburn, Judy Holliday.

*The Adventures of Buckaroo Banzai Across the Eighth Dimension,* 1984: 20th; *d* W. D. Richter; *p* Neil Cantor, W. D. Richter; Peter Weller, John Lithgow, Ellen Barkin. (Also known as *Buckaroo Banzai.*)

———, 1986: 20th; *d* David Cronenberg; *p* Stuart Cornfeld; Jeff Goldblum, Geena Davis, John Getz, 88–9, 109

*The Fog*, 1980: AvEm; *d* John Carpenter; *p* Debra Hill; Janet Leigh, Adrienne Barbeau, Hal Holbrook.

*Footlight Parade*, 1933: WB; *d* Lloyd Bacon; James Cagney, Joan Blondell, Ruby Keeler.

*Footloose*, 1984: Par; *d* Herbert Ross; *p* L. J. Rachmil, C. Zadan; Kevin Bacon, Lori Singer, John Lithgow.

*For Me and My Gal*, 1942: MGM; *d* Busby Berkeley; Judy Garland, Gene Kelly, George Murphy, 42, 64

*The Forbidden Alliance*, see *The Barretts of Wimpole Street*.

*Forbidden Paradise*, see *Hurricane*.

*Forbidden Planet*, 1956: MGM; *d* Fred McLeod Wilcox; *p* Nicholas Nayfack; Walter Pidgeon, Anne Francis, Leslie Nielsen, 237

*Foreign Correspondent*, 1940: UA; *d* Alfred Hitchcock; *p* Walter Wanger; Joel McCrea, Laraine Day, Herbert Marshall, 102

*Forever Amber*, 1947: 20th; *d* Otto Preminger; *p* William Perlberg; Linda Darnell, Cornel Wilde, George Sanders, 23, 28, 31, 107

*Fort Apache*, 1948: RKO; *d* John Ford; *p* John Ford, Merian C. Cooper; Henry Fonda, Shirley Temple, Ward Bond, 227, 258, 259, 260–61

*The Fountainhead*, 1949: WB; *d* King Vidor; *p* Henry Blanke; Gary Cooper, Patricia Neal, Raymond Massey, 107

*Four Feathers*, 1939: UA (UK); *d* Zoltan Korda; *p* Alexander Korda; Ralph Richardson, John Neville, June Duprez (another version in 1977), 96

*The Four Musketeers*, 1975: *d* Richard Lester; Oliver Reed, Michael York, Raquel Welch, 27, 42

*The Foxes of Harrow*, 1947: 20th; *d* John M. Stahl; *p* William A. Baker; Rex Harrison, Maureen O'Hara, Patricia Medina, 231–2

*Frankenstein*, 1931: Univ; *d* James Whale; *p* Carl Laemmle, Jr.; Boris Karloff, Colin Clive, Mae Clarke, 15, 90, 219

*The French Connection*, 1971: 20th; *d* William Friedkin; *p* Philip D'Antoni; Gene Hackman, Roy Scheider, Fernando Rey, 100–1, 104

*Frenchman's Creek*, 1944: Par; *d* Mitchell Leisen; *p* B. G. DeSylva; Joan Fontaine, Arturo de Cordova, Basil Rathbone.

*Frenzy*, 1972: Univ (UK); *d&p* Alfred Hitchcock; Jon Finch, Barry Foster, Barbara Leigh-Hunt, 102

*Friday the 13th*, 1980: Par; *d&p* Sean S. Cunningham; Betsy Palmer, Adrienne King, Harry Crosby, 81, 92, 155

*From Here to Eternity*, 1953: Col; *d* Fred Zinnemann; *p* Buddy Adler; Burt Lancaster, Deborah Kerr, Montgomery Clift, 210–12

*The Front Page*, see *His Girl Friday*.

*They Drive By Night*, 1940: WB; *d* Raoul Walsh; *p* Hal B. Wallis; Humphrey Bogart, George Raft, Ann Sheridan.

*They Live by Night*, 1949: RKO; *d* Nicholas Ray; Farley Granger, Howard da Silva, Jay C. Flippen (Remade in 1974 by Robert Altman as *Thieves Like Us*, the title of the novel from which it was adapted), 241

*They Were Expendable*, 1945: MGM; *d* John Ford; *p* Cliff Reid, assoc.; John Wayne, Robert Montgomery, Donna Reed, 208

*The Thin Man*, 1934: MGM; *d* W. S. Van Dyke II; William Powell, Myrna Loy, Maureen O'Sullivan.

*The Thing (From Another World)*, 1951: RKO; *d* Christian Nyby; *p* Howard Hawks; Kenneth Tobey, Margaret Sheridan, Robert Cornthwaite.

*The Thing*, 1982: *d* John Carpenter; *p* David Foster, Lawrence Turman; Kurt Russell, A. Wilford Brimley, Richard Dysart, 235

*Things to Come*, 1935: London Films (UK); *d* William Cameron Menzies; *p* Alexander Korda; Raymond Massey, Ralph Richardson, Cedric Hardwicke, 105

*The Third Man*, 1949: (UK); *d* Carol Reed; Orson Welles, Joseph Cotten, (Alida) Valli, 99

*13 Rue Madeleine*, 1946: 20th; *d* Henry Hathaway; *p* Louis de Rochemont; James Cagney, Annabella, Richard Conte, 210

*The 39 Steps*, 1935: British Gaumont (UK); *d&p* Alfred Hitchcock; Robert Donat, Madeleine Carroll, Lucie Mannheim. (Another version in 1959 and 1978), 102

*This Is the Army*, 1943: WB; *d* Michael Curtiz; George Murphy, Ronald Reagan, Joan Leslie, 182

*Three Godfathers*, 1948: WB; *d* John Ford; *p* Merian C. Cooper; John Wayne, Pedro Armendariz, Harry Carey, Jr. (Other films under this title in 1916, 1936, and for TV.)

*The Three Musketeers*, 1935: RKO; *d* Rowland V. Lee; *p* Cliff Reid; Walter Abel, Paul Lukas, Ian Keith.

———, 1939: Fox; *d* Allan Dwan; *p* Raymond Griffith, assoc.; Don Ameche, Ritz Brothers, Lionel Atwill.

———, 1948: MGM; *d* George Sidney; *p* Pandro S. Berman; Gene Kelly, Lana Turner, June Allyson, 27

———, 1974: (UK); *d* Richard Lester; Charlton Heston, Oliver Reed, Raquel Welch, 27, 42, 44 (An earlier version from UA in 1921, and see also *The Four Musketeers*, filmed simultaneously with the 1974 *Three*)

*Thunderbolt and Lightfoot*, 1974: Malpaso; *d* Michael Cimino; *p* Robert Daley; Clint Eastwood, Jeff Bridges, George Kennedy, 241, 272

*Tightrope*, 1984: *d* Richard Tuggle; Clint Eastwood, Genevieve Bujold, Alison Eastwood, 272

## Also Playing

Films in this list are mentioned briefly or in passing:

# INDEX